elementary

C000133023

coursebook
Innovations
a course in natural English

Hugh Dellar and Andrew Walkley

THOMSON

United Kingdom • United States • Australia • Canada • Mexico • Singapore • Spain

Innovations Elementary Coursebook
Dellar/Walkley

Publisher: *Christopher Wenger*
Series Editor: *Jimmie Hill*
Director of Development: *Anita Raducanu*
Director of Marketing: *Amy Mabley*
Editorial Manager: *Howard Middle/HM ELT Services*
International Marketing Manager: *Eric Bredenberg*
Editor: *Liz Driscoll*
Production Development: *Oxford Designers & Illustrators*

Sr. Print Buyer: *Mary Beth Hennebury*
Associate Marketing Manager: *Laura Needham*
Illustrator: *David Mostyn*
Photo Researcher: *Suzanne Williams*
Cover/Text Designer: *Studio Image & Photographic Art*
(www.studio-image.com)
Printer: *Canale*

Cover Images: Kandinsky: © 2003 Artists Rights Society (ARS), New York/ADAGP, Paris; Da Vinci: © Bettmann/CORBIS; Guggenheim Museum: *Tim Hursley/SuperStock*

Copyright © 2005 by Thomson ELT, a part of the Thomson Corporation. Thomson ELT and the Thomson logo are trademarks used herein under license.

All rights reserved. No part of this work covered by the copyright hereon may be reproduced or used in any form or by any means—graphic, electronic, or mechanical, including photocopying, recording, taping, Web distribution or information storage and retrieval systems—without the written permission of the publisher.

Printed in U.S.A.
4 5 6 09 08 07 06

For more information, contact Thomson Learning, High Holborn House, 50/51 Bedford Row, London WC1R 4LR United Kingdom or Thomson ELT, 25 Thomson Place, Boston, Massachusetts 02210 USA. You can visit our Web site at http://www.elt.thomson.com

For permission to use material from this text or product, submit a request online at:
www.thomsonrights.com
Any additional questions about permissions can be submitted by email to: thomsonrights@thomson.com

ISBN: 1-4130-1268-X
(Coursebook)

Illustrations
Mark Duffin: pp 80, 90, 109, 118, 158, 160; David Mostyn pp 52, 62, 68, 76, 104

Photo credits

The publishers would like to thank the following sources for permission to reproduce their copyright protected photographs:
Alamy: pp 12 (Robert Harding World Imagery), 13/D (Iain Masterton), 13/F (Roger Bamber), 20/B (Brad Mitchell), 20/D (Janine Wiedel), 20/E (Jacky Chapman), 20/G (The Photolibrary Wales), 22 (Justin Kase), 23clt (Travel-Shots), 23bl (Peter Scholey/Robert Harding Picture Library), 25t (John Morrison/LGPL), 26tr (Guy Spangenberg), 27tl (Peter Adams), 31tr (David Stares), 31br (Janine Wiedel), 36l (Gabe Palmer), 36br (Janine Wiedel), 37 (Gabe Palmer), 38r (Popperfoto), 43t (Tim Hill), 43b (Dominic Burke), 44tl (Mark Dyball), 44tr (Crispin Hughes), 45tl (David Sanger), 45br (Plainpicture/TatjaB.), 49 (Sylvain Grandadam/Robert Harding Picture Library Ltd), 50t (Magnus Hjorleifsson/Nordicphotos), 50b (Steve Allen), 51 (Brian Lawrence/ImageState), 55b (Travel-Shots), 58b (Mark Pedley Photography), 65 (Bob Thomas), 66c (Justin Kase), 70 (David Hoffman), 71 (Janine Wiedel), 78l (Alex Segre), 78r (MacDonald), 79 (Sami Sarkis), 86 (Alex Segre), 93 (National Motor Museum), 94 (Hemera Technologies), 96b (Janine Wiedel), 101t (Elmtree Images), 101b (Pawel Libera), 103r (Brian Harris), 110/A (Chris Ballentine), 110/C (Lucinda Marland), 110/D (Tim Street-Porter), 113lb (Dennis MacDonald), 114 (apply pictures); **Corbis:** pp 13/B (Paul Hutley), 13/C (David Sailors), 14tl (Roman Soumar), 15r (Bob Krist), 16/C (Bob Krist), 16/D (Dave Bartruff), 18b (Gerhard Steiner), 20/A (Peter M. Fisher), 23tl (Carlos Dominguez), 23cr (Chris Parker), 23br (Dave G. Houser), 25b (Adam Woolfitt), 26br (Volker Möhrke), 30b (Rob Lewine), 30ct (Chris Carroll), 30c (Jose Luis Pelaez, Inc), 36tr (Joe Bator), 41tr (© Reuters/Corbis), 42b (Kevin Fleming), 43c (Keren Su), 45bl (Dave G. Houser), 46t (Pablo Corral Vega), 58t (Adam Woolfitt), 66b (Charles Gupton), 73r (Marco Cristofori), 74 (Tim Hawkins), 83r (Laurence Fordyce), 83l (Richard Hamilton Smith), 96tr (Aaron Horowitz), 106l (Tim Graham), 106c (Selwyn Tait), 112

(Brooklyn Production), 115 (Raymond Reuter); **Ruth Corney:** pp 8bl, 10bl, 144-145; **Getty Images:** pp 9t (Philip Lee Harvey), 10tr (James Darell), 10bc (Charles Gupton), 10br (Simon Watson), 11tr (Ron Chapple), 14cl (Robert Harding World Imagery/Ruth Tomlinson), 14bl (Toyohiro Yamada), 15l (Walter Bibikow), 16/A (Burke/Triolo Productions), 16/E (Nick Dolding), 18t (Catherine Ledner), 18c (Steve Mercer), 19 (Guido Bertram), 20/C (Xavier Bonghi), 27bl (Jean Louis Batt), 41bl (AFP), 41rc (Benjamin F Fink Jr), 41bl (WidgetStudio), 42t (Peter Beavis), 44br (Bruno De Hogues), 46ct (Leslie Williamson), 46b (Chabruken), 48l (Ellen Rooney), 50c (Robert Daly), 59 (Ghislain & Marie David de Lossy), 72l (Sarma Ozols), 72r (Andrea Pistolesi), 73l (Chris Clinton), 82 (Timothy Shonnard), 95 (Yellow Dog Productions), 96c (Mike Hewitt), 99 (GDT), 106r (NicoCasamassima/AFP), 107r (David Sacks); **Ian Lees:** pp 11tl, 11b, 13/A, 20/F, 20/H, 45tr, 55c; **ODI:** p 29; **Punchstock:** pp 8tl & 9b (Photodisc Red), 10tl (Photodisc Blue), 13/E (RoyaltyFree/Corbis), 16/B (Mark Andersen/Rubberball Productions), 23clb (Photodisc Green/C Squared Studios), 26l (Comstock Images), 27r & 28 (Digital Vision), 30t (Photodisc), 30cb (Ron Chapple/Thinkstock), 31l (Mark Thornton/Brand X Pictures), 38l (Stockbyte), 46cb (Image Source), 48r (Photodisc), 53 (RoyaltyFree/Corbis), 56l (Mel Curtis), 56r (BananaStock), 57 (PhotoDisc Ryan McVay), 66t (RubberBall), 92 (Robert Koene), 96tl (Royalty-Free/Corbis), 110/B (Rob Melnychuk), 113lt (Comstock Images), 113r (Image Source); **Rex Features:** pp 23tr (Andy Drysdale), 44bl (Philippe Hays), 87 (Alex Segre), 103l (Alisdair Macdonald), 107l (Everett Collection); **Still Pictures:** p 14br (Jorgan Schytte); **Thomson:** p 8tr, 39

To the student

This book is written to help you feel comfortable with normal everyday spoken English.
It starts from the natural conversations people have – and then teaches you the language you need to have conversations like this in English!

To make this process interesting for you, the **Innovations** series:

- has lots of examples of how grammar and vocabulary are really used. You can learn a lot of useful vocabulary from good grammar exercises – and good vocabulary exercises will also help you practise the grammar of English.
- gives you the chance to practise English in useful ways. This will help you get ready to use your English outside of the classroom.
- has interesting reading texts. They will give you lots of things to talk about – and think about.
- Has Review units to help you remember what you studied in class.

We hope you enjoy using **Innovations** – and we hope it helps your English to get better!

Acknowledgements

Hugh Dellar has taught EFL, ESP and EAP in Indonesia and Britain, where he is now a teacher and teacher-trainer at the University of Westminster, London. He trains both native-speaker and non-native speaker teachers. He also gives papers and teacher development workshops all over the world.

Hugh would like to thank the following people: Lisa – for putting up with him; his mum and dad – for inadvertently setting him on the right track; Julian Savage, Cherry Gough, Ivor Timmis, Andrew Walkley, Andrew Fairhurst, Darryl Hocking, Scott Thornbury and Sally Dalzell – for their support and help over the years.

He would also like to thank the genuis of Arsene Wenger, Thierry Henry and all at Highbury, London N5, as well as Tony Joe White, Nigel Slater, Ronnie Lane, Lee Perry, Jonathon Safron Foer and Shane Meadows for inspiration and joy!

Andrew Walkley has taught mainly in Spain and Britain, where he is now a teacher and teacher-trainer at the University of Westminster, London. He trains both native-speaker and non-native speaker teachers. He also gives papers and teacher development workshops all over the world.

Andrew would like to thank Macu, Rebecca and Santiago for their love and for putting up with his bad moods and travel.

He would also like to thank the following for their friendship, and many interesting and helpful conversations about teaching: Richard Falvey, Hugh Dellar, Rebecca Sewell, Zeynep Ürkün and Paul Meehan.

Hugh and Andrew would both like to thank:
Jimmie Hill, Chris Wenger, Howard Middle, Stuart Tipping, Stephanie Walters, Liz Driscoll, Nick Broom, Nick Barrett, Ian Martin and all at Thomson ELT for their support and belief in us. We would also like to thank Ken Paterson at the University of Westminster for his continued support.

Finally, we'd like to say a big hello to all our former CELTA trainees and students (we learnt it all from you!); the fine people we've met on our travels round the world and the good people at The Social. This book wouldn't have happened without you!

Contents

Hi. What's your name? • Is that your surname or your first name? • Do you have a middle name? • Whe[re] are you from? • I'm from Swansea in Wales. • Nice to meet you. • This is Rebecca. She works with me[.] What's your father's name? • Hiya. • My name's Kenneth, but people usually call me Ken. • I live with [my] gran and granddad. • I don't see my dad very often. • I live quite near the capital. • People hardly ev[er] use my middle name. • Where were y[ou] born? • Have you got any kids?

1 What's your name?

Conversation

1 | Hello

🎧 **Look at the photo. Listen and practise the conversation with a partner.**

Hello, I'm Dan. What's your name?

Rebecca. Hi.

Now have conversations with some other students. Use your own names.

A: Hello. I'm ... . What's your name?

B: ... . Hi.

2 | Names

Read the sentences about one of the writers of this book. Then make sentences about yourself.

- My full name's Hugh Sebastian Dellar.
- My surname's (or My family name's) Dellar.
- My first name's Hugh.
- My middle name's Sebastian.

Ask and answer questions with a partner. For example:

A: What's your surname?

B: Hill.

A: Do you have a middle name?

B: No, I don't.

3 | Using vocabulary: countries

Match the flags with the countries in the box.

Brazil	Japan	Poland	Spain
Italy	Mexico	South Africa	Switzerland

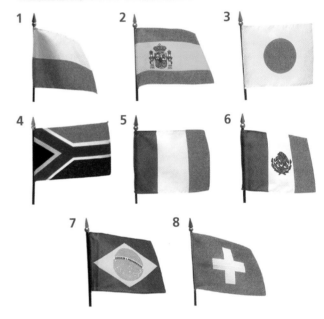

1
2
3
4
5
6
7
8

🎧 **Listen and check your answers.**

Practise the conversation below with a partner. Use the names of the countries above.

A: Where are you from?

B: ... . What about you?

A: ... .

Do you know the names of any other countries in English?

4 | Listening: *Do you know my sister?*

🎧 **Listen to three conversations. Complete the sentences with the names and countries you hear.**

Conversation 1

- I'm Peter. I'm from ....
- I'm .... I'm from Japan.

Conversation 2

- I'm Maria. I'm from ....
- I'm Franco. I'm from ....

Conversation 3

- I'm Hiro. I'm from ....
- I'm .... I live in Hull.

5 | Listen again

Listen to Conversation 3 between Hiro, Brenda and Leanne again. Complete the conversation with the words in the box.

how	nice	think	what
live	sorry	too	works
my sister	the weekend		

H: Hello!

B: Hi, (1) .... are you?

H: Fine. And you?

B: OK. So (2) .... are you doing here?

H: I'm doing some shopping.

B: Yes, we are (3) .... Do you know
(4) .... Leanne?

H: No, I don't (5) .... so. Hiya, I'm Hiro.

B: Hiro (6) .... with me.

L: Oh really. Well, it's (7) .... to meet you.
Where are you from, Hiro?

H: Japan. I'm (8) .... , how do you say your
name?

L: Leanne.

H: Oh, OK. Leanne. Right. So Leanne, do you
(9) .... here?

L: No, I'm just visiting Brenda for
(10) .... I live in Hull.

6 | Useful expressions

Look at these expressions from the conversations. Translate them into your language.

1. How are you?
2. We are too.
3. Do you know my sister?
4. No, I don't think so.
5. This is my friend Hiro.
6. He works with me.
7. Nice to meet you.
8. Do you live here?

Practise reading Conversation 3 with a partner.

Real English: hiya

There are several ways of saying 'hello' in English.
People often say hi or hiya.

7 | Let me introduce you.

Make sure that you understand the words in red. Complete the sentences with the names of people you know.

1. This is my friend ... .
2. This is my brother ... .
3. This is my sister ... .
4. This is my flatmate ... .
5. This is my boyfriend / girlfriend ... .
6. This is my husband / wife ... .
7. This is my cousin ... .
8. This is my teacher ... .
9. This is ... . He / She works with me.
10. This is ... . He / She studies English with me.

Spend two minutes memorising the words in red. Then close your book. Your partner will ask you questions like these:

A: What's your friend's name?
B: This is Teresa. She works with me.

A: What's your brother's name?
B: I haven't got a brother.

▷ For more information on using possessive s ('s), see G1.

Reading

1 | Using grammar: *always ... never*

Translate the words in red into your language.

always usually often sometimes hardly ever never
100% ·· 0%

Read the sentences about one of the writers of this book. Choose the words you think he uses to complete the sentences.

1. My full name is Andrew John Walkley. When I meet someone for the first time, I never / usually just say my first name.

2. People sometimes / hardly ever call me Andy, but my old friends from school usually / sometimes call me Andrew.

3. My doctor always / often calls me by my surname. He calls me Mr Walkley.

4. In English, we sometimes / always use Mr or Mrs with a surname. We never / sometimes say Mr Andrew or Mrs Maria.

5. People often / hardly ever say my middle name, but my mum sometimes / hardly ever calls me Andrew John.

6. My wife usually / sometimes calls me Andrew, but she usually / sometimes calls me 'my love'.

7. My children always / usually call me Dad or Daddy, but they sometimes / often call me by my first name, Andrew.

∩ **Listen and check your answers.**

What do different people call you? Tell some other students.

> For more information on using words like *always* and *never*, see G2.

Real English: mum / dad

In normal spoken English, most people say mum and dad instead of 'mother' and 'father'. Lots of people also say gran and granddad instead of 'grandmother' and 'grandfather'.

---

2 | Meeting people

Look at the photos. Do you do these things when you say hello? Who to? Tell a partner. Use always / usually / sometimes, etc. For example:

- I usually kiss my friends when I say hello.
- I hardly ever kiss new friends. I usually just shake hands.

shake hands

kiss each other on the cheek(s)

bow to each other

hug each other

3 | Using grammar: *be*

Be **is a very common verb. It is also an irregular verb. Complete the sentences with the correct form of *be*: am, are or is.**

1. My surname .... Higashi.

2. I .... English. I .... from a small town near Liverpool.

3. How .... you?

4. How .... your parents? .... they OK?

5. My brother's middle name .... Peter.

6. My mum's middle names .... Rachel and Antoinette.

7. This .... my friend Tony.

8. What .... your dad's name?

> For more information on using the verb *be*, see G3.

4 | While you read

∩ **Read the text on the opposite page. Match three of the descriptions with the photos.**

People I Know

1 This is me with my family. My name's Gerry and I'm from Scotland. I live in Edinburgh, which is the capital. I live with my wife and my two kids, Lily and Larry. Lily's four and Larry's six months. We live in a small house three kilometres from the city centre.

2 This is my wife Jodie. She's from South Africa. She works at Edinburgh University. I work there too. That's how we met.

3 This is my younger brother Jonathan. He's 23. I don't see him very often because he lives in Mexico. He's a teacher. I usually e-mail him every day and I sometimes phone him as well – maybe once a month. I want to go and visit him next year.

4 This is my neighbour Phil. Phil lives in the house next to us. He lives with his son and their dog Tigger. Phil is very nice. He always smiles and says hello when he sees us. I sometimes go to his house for a coffee or a beer.

5 This is my gran. She's 88. She lives in Edinburgh too. My granddad died in 1998, so she lives on her own now. She always does everything herself. She walks to the shops, and she does the cooking and cleaning in her house. My mum tries to help her sometimes, but my gran doesn't like it.

6 This is my friend Ruben. He's Scottish. He was born here, but his mum is from Spain and his father is from India. I know him from school. I don't see him very often because he works in London. I see him maybe twice a year when he comes back to Edinburgh to see his parents. I sometimes speak to him on the phone.

Real English: kids

In spoken English, we often say kids instead of 'children'.

A: Have you got any kids?
B: Yes. We've got two – a boy and a girl.

5 | Word check

The missing words in these sentences are all in the text. Complete the sentences without looking at the text.

1. Edinburgh is the .... of Scotland.

2. My house is five kilometres .... the city centre.

3. I .... my wife at the university here in Edinburgh.

4. Give me your phone number and I'll .... you.

5. He usually smiles and .... hello.

6. Do you want to go .... a coffee?

7. I live on my ....

8. I was .... in Birmingham.

Now look at the text and check your answers.

6 | Speaking

Discuss these questions with a partner. Use the words in red to help you.

A: Where were you born?
B: I was born in ... .
A: Have you got family or friends in different countries or cities?
B: Yes, my ... lives in ... .
A: Do you know anyone who lives on their own?
B: Yes, my ... lives on his / her own.
A: How old are the people in your family?
B: My ... is ... .

Where are you from? • Oh really? Whereabouts? • You probably don't know it. • It's in the north. • that the capital? • No, it's the second city. • It's in the south. • Is it far from the city centre? • It's ab an hour by train. • It's only three or four minutes on foot. • It's about a quarter of an hour by und ground. • It's a lovely place to live. • It's very quiet. • It's by the sea. • It's got good public transport. • got great nightlife. • It's a nice pl to walk around. • It's very pollut

2 Where are you from?

Conversation

1 Using vocabulary: countries and cities

Match the countries with the cities.

1. England		a. Paris
2. France		b. São Paulo
3. South Africa		c. Milan
4. Brazil		d. Barcelona
5. Peru		e. Birmingham
6. Italy		f. Hiroshima
7. Spain		g. Cape Town
8. Japan		h. Lima

2 Whereabouts?

Complete these conversations with the names of places in Activity 1. Don't look – try to remember the places!

1. A: Where are you from?
   B: ....
   A: Oh really? Whereabouts?
   B: Paris, the capital.

2. A: Where are you from?
   B: Italy.
   A: Oh really? Whereabouts?
   B: .... – in the north.

3. A: Where are you from?
   B: ....
   A: Oh really? Whereabouts?
   B: Hiroshima – in the south.

4. A: Where are you from?
   B: England.
   A: Oh really? Whereabouts?
   B: .... – the second city.

∩ **Listen and check your answers.**

Listen again. Then practise reading the conversations with a partner.

Have similar conversations with some other students. Use other countries and cities in Activity 1.

3 Listening: *Whereabouts? Is it far?*

∩ **Listen to three short conversations. Which countries are the people from?**

Can you remember anything else about the speakers? Compare what you remember with a partner.

4 Listen again

Listen to Conversation 3 again. June and Artur are talking in London. Complete the conversation with the words in the box.

by bus	it's	the capital
from here	really	whereabouts

J: So where are you from, Artur?

A: Poland.

J: Oh (1) .... ? Whereabouts?

A: I'm from Warsaw, (2) .... What about you? Where are you from?

J: I'm from London, actually.

A: Oh really? (3) .... ?

J: Bow. In east London.

A: Oh wow! Is it far (4) .... ?

J: No, not really. (5) .... twenty minutes by underground and maybe half an hour (6) ....

A: Oh, that's great.

Practise reading the conversation with a partner.

5 | Using vocabulary: ways of travelling

Match the ways of travelling with the photos.

1. by bus
2. by train
3. by plane
4. by car
5. by underground
6. on foot

6 | Is it far from here?

Here are ten answers to the question above. Complete the answers with Yes or No, not really. The first one has been done for you.

1. _No, not really_ . It's ten minutes by train.
2. .... It's about four hours by train.
3. .... It's twenty minutes by car.
4. .... It's two and a half hours by car.
5. .... It's five or six minutes on foot.
6. .... It's about three hours by plane.
7. .... It's about an hour and a quarter by underground.
8. .... It's about a quarter of an hour by underground.
9. .... It's about forty-five minutes by bus.
10. .... It's about ten minutes by bus.

Ask some other students Is your house far from here? Use answers like those above.

7 | Pronunciation: stressed sounds

All words have one stressed – strong – sound. Say these countries.

bra ZIL	MEX i co
ENG land	PO land
I ta ly	south AF ri ca
ja PAN	SWI tzer land

∩ **Listen and check your pronunciation**

∩ **Listen to these nationalities. Where are the stressed sounds?**

Brazilian	Mexican
English	Polish
Italian	South African
Japanese	Swiss

Ask and answer these questions with a partner. Use the words above.

1. Do you know any ... people?
2. What language do they speak in ... ?
3. Do you speak ... ?

Reading

1 | Describing places

🎧 Match the descriptions with the photos.

Which of the places sound nice to you? Compare your ideas with a partner.

A

B

C

D

My home town

1 I'm from Austria – from the capital city Vienna. It's a very old city and it's a nice place to live. It's on a river – the Danube. It's a nice city to walk around. I love it there.

2 *I'm from Sweden – from Luleå, a small town in the north. It's by the sea. It's very cold in winter. It's got a university, so there are lots of students there. There's a lot to do there – museums, shops, restaurants. It's great.*

3 I'm from Japan – from Osaka, the second city. It's a great place to live. It's quite big – there are five or six million people there. It's a very modern city – it has good public transport, good restaurants, good nightlife. I love it there.

4 *I'm from Nepal – from Pokhara. It's a small town in the mountains. It's a very beautiful place, but there's not a lot to do there. Most people move to the capital Katmandu after they leave school. It takes a long time to get there. It's quite far from Pokhara.*

5 I'm from Egypt – from the capital city Cairo. It's a big city and it's very polluted and very crowded. There are maybe eleven million people living there – and they have maybe eleven million cars! It takes a long time to travel around the city.

6 *I'm from England – from Cowden, a little village in the south. It's very old. Not many people live there – maybe only four or five hundred. It's very quiet. There are only two shops and one pub. It's a nice place to live if you're old, like I am.*

2 | Word check

Complete the sentences with these words from the text.

| nice | town | public transport | crowded | village |

1. There are maybe eight million people living here. It's very .... I don't like it.
2. My home town is by the sea. It's really .... I love it.
3. My grandparents live in a little .... in the north. Only two hundred people live there.
4. We have good .... here – the buses are good, the trains are good, the underground is good.
5. I live in a .... in the east of the country. Maybe sixty or seventy thousand people live there.

Now complete these sentences with more words from the text.

| city | place | north | sea | second |

6. I come from a small town by the ....
7. I live in the capital ....
8. My brother and sister live in the south of the country, but I live in the ....
9. I live in the capital city, but my brother lives in the .... city. It's quite far from here.
10. I love it here. It's a really nice .... to live.

E

3 | Using grammar: questions with *is* and *are*

Complete the questions with is or are.

1. Where .... you from?
2. .... it a nice place to live?
3. .... it a big place?
4. What .... the population?
5. .... it far from the capital?
6. .... it far from the sea?
7. .... the public transport OK?
8. Where .... your parents from?

Ask some other students the questions. Try to use some of the language in Activity 2 when you answer.

> For more information on questions using *is* and *are*, see G4.

4 | Pronunciation: sentence stress

⌒ **When we say sentences, some sounds are stronger than others. Listen and repeat these sentences.**

1. WHERE are you FROM?
2. WhereaBOUTS?
3. Is it FAR from HERE?
4. I LIVE with my FAmily.
5. I LIVE on my OWN.
6. It's the SEcond CIty.
7. It's BY the SEA.
8. It's in the SOUTH of the COUNtry.
9. I LOVE it there.
10. It's an HOur by BUS.

Translate the sentences into your language. Try to learn them this week.

F

15

My mum's a teacher. • She works in a secondary school in Leicester. • My brother's a civil servant. • to Istanbul University. • I work in a sports shop in town. • Do you enjoy it? • The money's good. • I w really long hours. • I love working with children. • My boss is awful. • I'm a housewife. • I work part-ti in a supermarket. • I earn about £10,000 a year. • I work for a big computer company. • I want to w for myself. • He does all the cleaning! • My mu a housewife. • I work for a big law firm.

3 What do you do?

Conversation

1 | Using vocabulary: *What do you do?*

Which of these jobs can you see in the photos?

an accountant	a doctor	a student
a barman	a lawyer	a teacher
a businessman	a shop assistant	a waitress
a civil servant		

⋂ **Listen and repeat the jobs.**

Do you know anyone who does these jobs? Tell a partner. For example:

- My brother is a doctor.
- My friend Jane is a waitress.

2 | Practice

Cover the jobs in Activity 1. Complete the sentences with the jobs.

1. I'm a .... I work in a clinic in my town.
2. I'm a .... I work in a pub in the centre of town.
3. I'm a .... I work in a primary school in São Paolo.
4. I'm a .... I work in a clothes shop in town.
5. I'm a .... I work in a government department.
6. I'm a .... I work in a restaurant in a big hotel.
7. I'm a .... I go to Hull University.
8. I'm a .... I work for an import–export company.
9. I'm a .... I work for a big law firm.
10. I'm an .... I work for a small accounting firm.

3 | Further practice

With a partner, have conversations like this:

A: What do you do?
B: I'm a waitress.
A: Oh right. Where do you work?
B: In a big restaurant in the centre of town.

4 | Using grammar: more questions

Complete these questions with is it, are you or do you.

1. What .... do?
2. Where .... work?
3. .... the boss?
4. .... a good place to work?
5. .... like the people you work with?
6. .... far from your house to where you work?

Work with a partner.
Student A: Choose a job. Imagine this is your job.
Student B: Ask your partner the questions above.

▶ For more information on using questions like these, see G5.

5 | Listening: *What do you do?*

🎧 **Listen to four conversations. Which jobs do the speakers talk about? Where do they work?**

6 | Listen again

Listen to Conversation 4 again. Terry is talking to Lesley at a party. Complete the conversation with the words in the box.

boring	doctor	helping	money	the north
clinic	enjoy	long hours	primary	working

T: What do you do?

L: I'm a (1) ....

T: Oh right. Where do you work?

L: In a (2) .... in a small town in (3) .... of the country.

T: And do you enjoy it?

L: Yes. I work (4) .... and it's quite difficult sometimes, but I like (5) .... people. The money is good too. What do you do?

T: I'm a teacher.

L: Oh right. Where do you do that?

T: In a (6) .... school in Bournemouth – in the south of England.

L: And do you (7) .... it?

T: It's OK. The (8) .... isn't very good and I work really long hours. I like (9) .... with children, but sometimes I do a lot of paperwork too. That's really (10) ....

Practise reading the conversation with a partner.

7 | Do you enjoy it?

Here are ten answers to the question above. Complete the answers with Yes or No, not really.

1. .... The hours are good.
2. .... The money is awful.
3. .... My boss is great.
4. .... It's really boring.
5. .... It's great.
6. .... It's really interesting.
7. .... I work really long hours.
8. .... The money is good.
9. .... It's really difficult.
10. .... My boss is awful.

Do any of the sentences describe YOUR job? Tell a partner. For example:

*   The hours are good, but my boss is awful.

Now have conversations like Conversation 4 with your partner. Use the jobs in Activity 1. Ask each other:

*   So what do you do?
*   Where do you work?
*   Do you enjoy it?

Use answers like those above to answer the last question.

8 | Pronunciation: /ə/

🎧 **Listen and repeat the sound /ə/. Look at the picture on page 144 for help if you need to.**

🎧 **All these sentences have /ə/ in them. It is a weak sound. Listen and mark the stressed sounds in each sentence.**

1. I'm *a* lawyer.
2. I'm *an* accountant.
3. Where *are* you from?
4. Where*a*bouts?
5. It's *about an* hour by car.
6. It's the second city.
7. It's very quiet.
8. You probably don't know it.

Listen again and repeat.

Reading

1 | Before you read

Look at the photos. Which person do you think said each of these sentences? Compare your ideas with a partner.

I'm a barman.	I'm a student.
I'm a housewife.	I was an accountant.
I'm an actor.	I work in an office.

2 | While you read

∩ **Read what the three people in the photos actually say about their jobs. Did you guess correctly?**

Real English: actor

If you are an actor, you work in films or in plays. Some people call a man who does this an actor and a woman who does this an actress, but lots of women prefer to be called actors.

My Job

Ting Ting

Before I got married, I worked for a big company. I was an accountant. Now I'm a housewife. I don't like it when people say, 'Oh, so you don't work' or 'You're really lucky. I'd like to stay at home all day.' They don't understand I'm very busy all day. I get up before my husband to make breakfast for him and the children. Then I take my son Henry to school. I have another son Alex who is three, so I look after him during the day. I do the washing, I do the shopping, I do the cleaning, I do the cooking. It's a very difficult job.

José

I'm a student. I go to Valencia University, where I'm studying medicine. I want to be a doctor. It's a very hard course and I study a lot, but I also need money to live. I'm a barman in a disco in town. I work part-time, three nights a week. I work on Thursdays, Fridays and Saturdays. On Thursdays, I usually get home at three or four o'clock in the morning and then my classes start at nine o'clock, so I'm really tired on Friday mornings.

Frances

I'm an actor, but it's difficult to find work and the money is quite bad. Of course, I want to be a film star and earn lots of money, but it's very difficult. When I don't have any acting work, I do office work. At the moment, I'm working in an office in the centre of town. The people are very nice and the money is good, so I'm quite happy. I started working here two years ago.

3 | Speaking

Discuss these questions with a partner.

1. Do you think it's good to work when you have kids?
2. Do you think it's good to work part-time when you're studying?
3. Do you think working in an office is a good job?
4. Do you think being an actor is a good job?
5. Do you think housewives work hard?
6. Who has the best life – Ting Ting, José or Frances? Why?

4 | Word check

Match these verbs from the text with the words they go – collocate – with.

1. get   a. for a big company
2. work   b. my kids to school
3. take   c. married
4. do   d. the cleaning

Now match these verbs with the words they collocate with.

5. work   e. the cooking
6. study   f. lots of money
7. earn   g. medicine
8. do   h. in an office

Cover the words above. Complete the sentences with some of the words.

1. I .... £25,000 a year.
2. In my house, I .... all the cleaning and all the cooking. My husband does the shopping and the washing.
3. I .... in a bank in the centre of town.
4. I .... English and Spanish at Bristol University.
5. Every Thursday evening, I .... my daughter to her dance class.
6. I'm an accountant. I work .... a big computer company.
7. My boyfriend wants us to get .... , but I think we're too young. I'm 21 and he's only 20.

5 | Your future

Choose the expression in each sentence that is true for you. Cross out the expression that is NOT true.

1. I *want to / don't want to* work for a really big company.
2. I *want to / don't want to* work for myself.
3. I *want to / don't want to* work for the government.
4. I *want to / don't want to* work in a shop.
5. I *want to / don't want to* work in the city centre.
6. I *want to / don't want to* work in lots of different places.
7. I *want to / don't want to* work with children.
8. I *want to / don't want to* work with computers.
9. I *want to / don't want to* get married.
10. I *want to / don't want to* study at university.

Tell a partner your choices.

6 | Pronunciation: stressed sounds

Mark the stressed sound in these words. The first one has been done for you.

awful   centre

thousand   government

accountant   company

paperwork   difficult

department   university

🎧 **Now listen and repeat the words.**

Find sentences from this unit that use these words. Then work with a partner and test each other.
Student A: Say the words.
Student B: Say the sentences. Can you remember all the sentences?

I'm going to watch a DVD. • I'm going to write some letters. • What're you doing this weeker
Nothing much. • Do you want to come with me? • Maybe some other time. • I'm going wi
friend from work. • I'm going to go on my own. • I'm going to meet a friend of mine. • It so
really boring. • It sounds interesting. • I don't really like that kind of thing. • It costs about £10.

4 **What're you doing tonight?**

Conversation

1 | Using vocabulary: activities

Which of these activities can you see in the photos?

go back to the hotel	go for a walk	read my book
go to bed	go home	study
go to the cinema	go shopping	watch TV
go for a meal	play tennis	write an e-mail

🎧 **Listen and repeat the activities.**

Work with a partner.
**Student A: Act or draw the activities.
          DON'T use any words.**
**Student B: With your book closed, say
          the activities. Can you
          remember all the activities?**

Match these verbs with the nouns they collocate with.

1. go to ☐   a. swimming
2. go for ☐   b. some letters
3. go ☐   c. a drink
4. write ☐   d. the supermarket

Now match these verbs with the nouns they collocate with.

5. play ☐   e. a video
6. read ☐   f. my exam
7. watch ☐   g. the newspaper
8. study for ☐   h. basketball

2 | Using vocabulary: time expressions

We often use What are you doing + time expression? to ask about the future.

<u>Underline</u> **the time expressions in these questions.**

1. What are you doing today?
2. What are you doing after the class?
3. What are you doing now?
4. What are you doing tonight?
5. What are you doing at the weekend?

Translate the questions into your language.

3 | Listening: *What're you doing tonight?*

🎧 Listen to five conversations. Which things in Activity 1 do the speakers talk about?

4 | Listen again

Listen to Conversation 5 again. Keith and Nicola are staying in a hostel. Complete the conversation with the words in the box.

a meal	money	nothing	walk
going to	my own	tonight	want to

K: What are you doing (1) .... ?
N: I'm going to go for (2) .... in the town.
K: Are there any good restaurants?
N: I don't know. I'm just going to (3) .... round the town and see what there is. What about you?
K: Oh, I don't know. (4) .... much. I think I'm just (5) .... stay here and read my book.
N: Do you (6) .... come with me? I'm going on (7) ....
K: Thanks, but I don't have much (8) .... I'm going to eat here at the hostel.

Practise reading the conversation with a partner.

5 | Using grammar: *going to* + verb

We often answer the questions in Activity 2 by saying:

• I'm going to + verb
• We're going to + verb

Look at the tapescript for the five conversations at the back of the book and find all the I'm going to + verb expressions. Write them down.

Ask a partner the questions in Activity 2. Use the expressions from the tapescript in your answers.

Real English: I'm going to go / I'm going

Both I'm going to go and I'm going are natural and correct.
I'm going (to go) running later.
I'm going (to go) swimming with a friend of mine tomorrow.
I'm going (to go) to a concert tomorrow night.

➤ For more information on talking about the future, see G6.

6 | Who with?

We often say *who* we are going to do something with. Complete the sentences with the words in the box.

dad	friends	girlfriend	own	work

1. I'm going to go for a meal with some ....
2. I'm going to go on my ....
3. I'm going to go for a walk with my mum and ....
4. I'm going to play golf with a friend from ....
5. I'm going to go shopping with my ....

Write true answers to the five questions in Activity 2. Then ask and answer the questions with some other students.

7 | Pronunciation: /iː/ and /uː/

🎧 Listen and repeat the sounds /iː/ and /uː/. Look at the pictures on page 144 for help if you need to.

🎧 Listen and repeat these words.

teach	you	leave	university
do	e-mail	student	Greece
meet	two	feel	

Where are the /iː/ and /uː/ sounds in this conversation?

A: Where are you from?
B: Greece.
A: What do you do?
B: I'm a teacher.
A: Do you enjoy it?
B: Yes, it's great. What about you? What do you do?

🎧 Listen and check your pronunciation.

Practise the conversation with a partner. Give your own answers and continue the conversation.

Reading

1 | While you read

🎧 **Imagine you are on holiday in Britain. Read the text on the opposite page about six places to visit. Decide which places you want to go to and which places you don't want to go to. Tell a partner about your choices. Use these expressions.**

1. I don't want to go to ... . It sounds boring.
2. I don't want to go to ... . It's too expensive.
3. I don't want to go to ... . I don't really like that kind of thing.
4. I want to go to ... . It sounds interesting.
5. I want to go to ... . It sounds good.
6. I want to go to ... . I really like that kind of thing.

Compare your choices with a partner. Have conversations like this:

A: Do you want to go to Legoland?

B: Yes, it sounds good.

A: I don't want to go to there. It's too expensive.

2 | Vocabulary check

The missing words in these sentences are all in the text. Complete the sentences without looking at the text.

1. It's a museum about the .... of Britain.
2. It's in the .... of London.
3. It's two thousand years ....
4. It's three hours by .... from London.
5. .... is free.
6. A bottle of coke .... about £2.
7. It takes about two hours to .... round the museum.
8. It costs £20. Everything is .... in the price.

Now look at the text and check your answers.

3 | Role play

Look at this example conversation.

A: tonight?

B: the Hard Rock café / you?

A: stay at home / watch TV

B: sounds OK

A: What are you doing tonight?

B: I'm going to go to the Hard Rock café. What about you?

A: I'm going to stay at home and watch TV.

B: Oh, that sounds OK.

Work with a partner. Write conversations using the ideas below.

1. A: tonight?
   B: a walk / the park / you?
   A: go to the cinema / some friends
   B: sounds good

2. A: this afternoon?
   B: go shopping / Bluewater / you?
   A: Tower of London
   B: sounds good

3. A: this weekend?
   B: nothing much / go to the park / Saturday / study / Sunday / you?
   A: York for the weekend
   B: sounds OK

Now read your conversations with your partner.

4 | Pronunciation: /iː/, /ɪ/, /ʊ/ and /uː/

🎧 **Listen and repeat the sounds /iː/, /ɪ/, /ʊ/ and /uː/. Look at the pictures on page 144 for help if you need to.**

🎧 **Listen and repeat these sentences.**

1. It's good.   /ɪts gʊd/
2. It's free.   /ɪts friː/
3. It's two pounds.   /ɪts tuː paʊndz/
4. Everything is included.   /ˈevrɪθɪŋ ɪz ɪnˈkluːdɪd/
5. It's really interesting.   /ɪts ˈrɪəlɪ ˈɪntrəstɪŋ/
6. I need to write an e-mail.   /aɪ niːd tə raɪt ən iːmeɪl/
7. It's a good book.   /ɪts ə gʊd bʊk/
8. Are the tickets expensive?   /aː ðə ˈtɪkɪts ɪkˈspensɪv/
9. Which video do you want?   /wɪtʃ vɪdɪəʊ də jə wɒnt/
10. You choose.   /juː tʃuːz/

Places to visit

The Museum of the Moving Image

This is a museum about films and the cinema. It's really interesting. It has examples of the first cameras and information on old film stars and the history of TV.

Entrance:
Adults £8 Children £4
Children under 5 free

The Tower of London

This is a beautiful old castle in the centre of London, next to the River Thames. The castle is a thousand years old and is full of history. You can also see the Crown Jewels. You can spend all day looking round the castle.

Adults £12

The old town of York

York is a city in the north of England. It's three hours by train from London. The city is over two thousand years old, and you can still walk round the old city walls and the old town. There is also a beautiful cathedral called York Minster and several interesting museums.

Trains from London cost between £25 and £50.
Entrance fees to the museums are between £5 and £10 for adults.

Bluewater

Bluewater is a huge shopping centre near London. It's one of the biggest in Europe. There are over a thousand shops, so you can find everything you want. Take lots of money with you!

The Hard Rock Café

The world-famous Hard Rock Café is in the centre of London. It's a very big bar which is decorated with things from famous rock stars. Entrance is free, but a bottle of beer costs about £5 and a burger with French fries costs about £10.

Legoland

This theme park is in Windsor – near one of the Queen's castles – and about twenty minutes by train from London. You can walk round hundreds of models of famous places which are made out of Lego. There are also lots of fun rides. Entrance is £25 and all rides are included in the price.

5 | Did you have a nice weekend?

Conversation

1 | Using grammar: past simple forms

We form the past simple of most verbs by adding -ed to the basic form of the verb.

listen – listened   stay – stayed
play – played   watch – watched

If a verb ends in a consonant + -y, we remove the -y and add -ied.

study – studied   try – tried

Lots of the most common verbs have irregular past simple forms. You just need to learn them.

am / is – was	give – gave	read – read
are – were	go – went	see – saw
buy – bought	have – had	take – took
do – did	hear – heard	write – wrote
get – got		

> For more information on irregular verbs, see the list on page 142.

∩ **Listen and repeat the basic and past simple verb forms.**

Now work with a partner and test each other.
Student A: Say the basic verb forms.
Student B: With your book closed, say the past simple forms.

Complete the sentences with past simple verb forms.

1. I .... to the cinema on Friday.
2. I .... football on Sunday morning.
3. I .... a good programme on TV last night.
4. I .... shopping on Saturday and I .... some new clothes.
5. I .... a letter to my dad last night.
6. I .... at home and I .... for my exams.
7. I .... the newspaper in the morning and in the afternoon I .... some cleaning.
8. I .... to bed early last night, because I .... really tired.
9. I .... a book all weekend. It .... really good.
10. I .... to work on Saturday morning.

> For more information on using the past simple, see G7.

Real English: newspaper / paper

We often just say paper instead of 'newspaper'. For example:
I'm going to get the paper.
Did you buy the paper today?
Is there anything interesting in the paper?

2 | Practice

Look at the sentences in Activity 1. Did you do any of the things:

* last night?
* yesterday?
* at the weekend?

Tell a partner. For example:

* I read a book last night.
* I played football at the weekend.

3 | Listening: *Did you have a nice weekend?*

∩ **Listen to four conversations. In which conversations do the speakers use these expressions?**

a. 😊   Yes, it was great.

b. 🙂   It was OK.

c. ☹️   No, not really.

Which of these things did the speakers say in each conversation? Listen again if you need to.

Conversation 1
a. I just stayed at home.
b. I watched TV.
c. I read a book.

Conversation 2
a. We went for a walk.
b. It rained.
c. I read the paper.

Conversation 3
a. I saw a good film.
b. I was really ill.
c. I stayed in bed all weekend.

Conversation 4
a. I went on a trip.
b. We went shopping.
c. We went to the pub.

4 | Listen again

**Listen to Conversation 4 between Josh and Helen
again. Complete the conversation with the words
in the box.**

did	nice	on	saw	sounds	together	walked	with

J: Did you have a (1) .... weekend?

H: Yes, it was great.

J: Really? What (2) .... you do?

H: Well, I went to the cinema (3) .... Friday
with my friend Jules. We saw a great film. Then on
Saturday I went on a trip to York (4) ....
some people from my class. It was great. We
(5) .... all round the old town. We
(6) .... the cathedral. It was beautiful.
And then we went to the pub (7) .... in
the evening.

J: It (8) .... great.

H: Yes, it was. We really enjoyed it.

Practise reading the conversation with a partner.

5 | Practice

**Work with a partner. Write conversations like
those in Activity 3. Use the ideas below.**

1. great / went to a party / Saturday / relaxed / Sunday

2. OK / nothing much / went to a friend's house /
Saturday / did some housework / Sunday

3. no, not really / did the cleaning and shopping /
Saturday / studied / Sunday / boring

Now read your conversations with your partner.

**Have conversations like these with some other
students. Ask Did you have a nice weekend? Give
true answers.**

6 | Pronunciation: /iː/, /e/ and /æ/

🎧 **Listen and repeat the sounds /iː/, /e/ and /æ/.
Look at the pictures on page 144 for help if you
need to.**

🎧 **Listen and repeat these words.**

read	feel	meal	week	e-mail
bed	well	went	send	get
bad	that	had	relax	back

Work with a partner.
Student A: Say the words silently.
**Student B: Can you guess which word your
partner is saying?**

**Now practise these conversations with your
partner.**

1. A: What did you do last night?
    B: I went to see a film with a friend and we had a
        meal together.

2. A: What are you doing tonight?
    B: I'm going to read my book.

3. A: What are you doing tonight?
    B: I'm going to go to bed early.

4. A: What are you doing after the class?
    B: I'm going back home to send some e-mails.

🎧 **Listen and check your pronunciation.**

**Close your books and have the four conversations
again. Can you remember all four?**

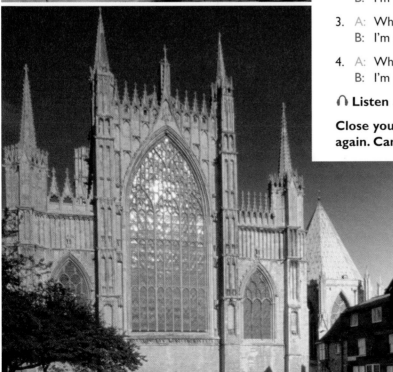

Reading

1 | Using vocabulary: useful verbs

Complete the collocations with the verbs in the box.

asked	gave	opened	said

1. .... no / yes
2. .... the door / the window
3. .... me a question / me to marry him
4. .... me a present / a big bunch of flowers to her

Now complete these collocations with the verbs in the box.

hired	paid	took	was

5. .... sad / cold
6. .... me out for dinner / me to the airport
7. .... for everything / £50 for the flight
8. .... a car / bicycle

All the verbs above are in the past simple. Can you remember the present forms?

2 | Before you read

You are going to read a text about what four people did at the weekend. Look at all the photos. What do you think they did? Use some of the expressions in Activity 1 to help you.

3 | While you read

∩ **Now read the text on the opposite page. Did the four people have a nice weekend? What did they do?**

4 | After you read

Look at the words below. Use them to try and say what happened to each person at the weekend.

Emily	dinner / door / bunch of flowers / car
Paulo	house / weekends / degrees / October
Junko	restaurant / ring / no / angry
Ron	our son / airport / tickets / the night we got married

5 | Speaking

Discuss these questions with a partner. Use the words in red to help you.

A: Are you married?

B: Yes. / No.

A: When did your parents get married?

B: ... years ago.

A: Have your family got two flats / houses?

B: No. / Yes, we have another ... in ... .

A: Do you buy people expensive presents?

B: No never. / Sometimes. I once bought a ... for ... .

– – My weekend – –

Emily

It was my birthday. My boyfriend David came to my house to take me out for dinner. I opened the door, and he had a big bunch of flowers and a Ferrari! He hired the car just to take me out. I was really surprised.

Paulo

I went to our house in the country with my family. It's a small house in a village in the mountains. We often go there at the weekends and we usually go there for a few weeks in the summer. It was really hot when we went this weekend. It was 32 degrees. I was surprised because it's October. It's usually cold.

Junko

I had a really terrible weekend. My boyfriend took me out to this really expensive restaurant. In the middle of our dinner, he gave me a beautiful ring and he asked me to marry him. I was really surprised. I said no. I like him, but I knew I didn't want to marry him. He was quite angry and sad. It was awful.

Ron

I had a great weekend. My wife and I got married 25 years ago. My wife and I were really surprised when our son came to our house on Friday evening. He then took us to the airport and gave us two tickets to go to Paris! He paid for everything: the flight, the hotel, everything. We had a lovely weekend. We remembered the night we got married. It was wonderful.

6 | Role play

With a partner, write a conversation with one of the people in the text. Begin like this:

A: Hello.
B: Hi. How are you? Did you have a nice weekend?

Now read your conversation to another pair.

7 | Pronunciation: /eɪ/, /aɪ/, /aʊ/ and /əʊ/

Try saying these sounds.

/ɪ/   /ʊ/   /e/   /ə/   /æ/

∩ **Now listen and check your pronunciation.**

We can make new vowel sounds using these five sounds. They are:

/eɪ/   /aɪ/   /aʊ/   /əʊ/

∩ **Listen and repeat the vowel sounds.**

Say the words in each line. They all have one of the sounds above. Which sound does each line have?

1. round, town, housework, flowers, out
2. take, stay, paper, great, rain, gave, paid, came, late
3. open, don't, go, cold, October
4. write, nice, hired, bicycle, flight, night, surprised

∩ **Listen and check your answers.**

∩ **Now listen and repeat these sentences.**

a. I hired a bike.
b. Don't go in October. It's cold.
c. My flight is at night.
d. We walked round town.
e. It's a great game to play.
f. They came late.

27

What're you studying? • I'm studying engineering at Nottingham University. • Oh right. • My brot
studied mathematics at Edinburgh University. • What year are you in? • What're you going to do a
university? • I hope you get the job you want. • Have you got a dictionary? • Have you got a piece
paper? • Yes, here you are. • Can I go to the toilet? • What does this word mean? • Underline it. •

6 What are you studying?

going to do a Master
I started three years ago

Conversation

1 Using vocabulary: subjects at university

⌒ **Listen and repeat the subjects. Where's the stress in these words?**

business	geography	literature
economics	history	mathematics
engineering	languages	tourism

Which of these nine subjects do you think are:

*   interesting?
*   boring?
*   difficult?

⌒ **Now listen to this conversation. <u>Underline</u> the stressed sounds in each sentence.**

A: What do you do?
B: I'm a student at university.
A: What are you studying?
B: Geography.

Have conversations with a partner using the subjects above. Can you continue each conversation?

2 Listening: *I'm a student*

⌒ **Listen to four conversations. Take notes and complete the chart.**

	subject	year	like it? (✓ or ✗)
1		final year at school / start university in September	doesn't say
2		first	
3	geography		
4			

3 Listen again

Listen to Conversation 4 again. Carole is talking to Mark. They don't know each other very well. Complete the conversation with the words in the box.

at university	going to	in	travel
difficult	good luck	interesting	want to

C: What do you do?
M: I'm a student (1) ....
C: Oh right. What are you studying?
M: Tourism.
C: Really? What year are you (2) .... ?
M: My third.
C: And do you like it?
M: Yes, it's great. It's quite (3) .... , but it's really (4) ....
C: Well, that's good. What're you (5) .... do after university?
M: I'm going to find a job, I hope. I (6) .... work for a big company and I want to (7) .... more.
C: Well, (8) .... I hope you get the job you want.

Practise reading the conversation with a partner.

4 | Speaking

Work with a partner. Have conversations like Conversation 4 using the subjects in Activity 1. Ask each other:

- What do you do?
- What are you studying?
- What year are you in?
- And do you like it?

5 | Using vocabulary: conversations in class (1)

Match the things with the photos.

1. a pen
2. a rubber
3. a dictionary
4. a tissue
5. a piece of paper
6. a pencil

Work with a partner. Have conversations like these:

A: Have you got ... ?
B: Yes, here you are.
A: Thanks.

A: Have you got ... ?
B: No, sorry. Ask ... . I think he / she 's got one.

6 | Using vocabulary: conversations in class (2)

Decide who says these sentences. Is it a teacher (T) or a student (S)? Compare your ideas with a partner. Do you agree?

1. Match the questions with the answers.
2. Can I go to the toilet?
3. Compare your ideas with a partner.
4. How do you pronounce this word?
5. I'm sorry I'm late.
6. For homework, do Exercise 3 in the workbook.
7. Underline the words that go together.
8. How do you say 'bebek' in English?
9. OK. Let's check the answers.
10. What does 'awful' mean?

Now translate the sentences into your language. Test each other.

Look quickly at the words in white at the top of page 96. Find some words which you don't understand.

Ask some other students What does ... mean? If no-one can help you, ask your teacher.

7 | Pronunciation: the weak form of *are*

🎧 **We often pronounce *are* as /ə/. Listen and repeat these questions.**

1. Where are you from?
2. What are you doing tonight?
3. What are you studying?
4. What year are you in?
5. What are you going to study?
6. Are you OK?
7. Where are you going?

Ask and answer the questions with a partner.

Reading

1   Before you read

Read the sentences. Which sentences are about:

1. the past?
2. the present?
3. the future?

a. I'm going to do a Masters.
b. I left school ten years ago.
c. I work in a primary school.
d. I did economics at university.
e. I teach in a university.

Compare your ideas with a partner. How did you make your decisions?

Now look at the photos. Which person do you think said each of the sentences above? Compare your ideas with a partner.

2   While you read

🎧 **Read what the five people in the photos actually say about their education. Did you guess correctly?**

School and university

Pardeep

I left school ten years ago – when I was only sixteen. When I left, I didn't have a job for three years. It was awful. Then, when I was nineteen, I opened a shop. Some of my family in India make shoes. I buy them and then sell them in England for more money. The business is doing really well at the moment. I'm going to open another shop next year.

Charlotte

I teach in a university. I teach literature to first- and second-year students. I tell them the books I want them to read. Usually, these are books by women writers. We then talk about them. I tell my students about the writers and give them things to write about. I really enjoy it. I'm very lucky.

Clare

I'm going to do a Master's next year. I finished my first degree two months ago and now I want to travel for a few months. The last three years were really difficult, so I need some time to relax. I did art at university. For my Master's, I'm going to do art history. After my Master's degree, I want to work in an art gallery.

Colin

I work in a primary school. I started here fifteen years ago and I really enjoy it. I love teaching children. I get very tired sometimes, but it's great. I really like watching the kids grow up and learn how to do new things. I have two kids – a son and a daughter – but they go to a different school.

Lee

I did economics at university. I really enjoyed it. It was a very interesting subject to study. When I left university, I started my own company. Everything I learned at university was very useful. My company is doing very well now. I have eighteen people working for me.

3 | Word check

The missing words in these sentences are all in the text. Complete the sentences without looking at the text.

1. I .... have a job for two years. I was unemployed.
2. My family has a factory where they .... clothes.
3. Our teacher doesn't .... us much homework or anything to write.
4. I've got a good job and a nice home. I'm very ....
5. I'm going to do a .... in genetics after I finish my degree.
6. I'm really tired. I need to .... tonight and do nothing!
7. I started teaching here fifteen years ....
8. Children really .... up fast these days.
9. I .... my own company five years ago.
10. My company is .... very badly.

Now look at the text and check your answers.

Do you know anyone who has their own company / factory / shop? What do they do / make / sell?

4 | Role play

Imagine you are one of the people in Activity 2. How would you answer these questions?

- What do you do?
- Where do you work?
- Do you enjoy it?

Now have conversations with some other students. Ask and answer the questions.

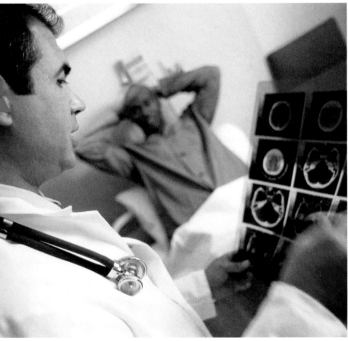

5 | Pronunciation: -ed endings

Regular past simple forms end in -ed. When we say this, we usually say /d/. For example:

played   /pleɪd/

Some verbs are difficult to say with /d/ at the end, so we say /t/ or /ɪd/. For example:

liked   /laɪkt/

wanted   /wɒntɪd/

Make the past simple forms of these verbs by adding /d/. If you can't, try /t/ or /ɪd/. Which feels right to you?

ask	hate	listen	need	phone	visit
call	hire	live	open	rain	wait
decide	learn	love	pay	stay	walk
enjoy	like	move	play	study	want

🎧 **Listen and repeat the past simple forms.**

Use five of the verbs to talk about things you did yesterday – or things that happened yesterday.

Review: Units 1-6

1 | Grammar: past, present and future

Do these sentences talk about the present (PR), the past (PA) or the future (F)? The first one has been done for you.

1. I don't have a job at the moment. (PR)
2. I didn't go to the class.
3. I'm not going to ask her again.
4. I don't go to the cinema very often.
5. I'm not Japanese. I'm Korean.
6. I went to see a film, but I didn't like it very much.
7. Sorry, I didn't hear what you said.
8. I don't remember.
9. I had English lessons before, but I didn't learn much.
10. I'm not going to do anything.

2 | Grammar: negatives

Complete the sentences with the negatives in the box.

'm not	don't	didn't	wasn't

Present: I .... know.
Present: I .... sure.
Past: I .... enjoy it very much.
Past: It .... very nice.
Future: I .... going to see him.

Complete the conversations with don't or didn't.

1. A: Where's the toilet?
   B: I .... know. Ask the waiter.

2. A: Por favor, me puede ayudar?
   B: I'm sorry, I .... speak Spanish. I'm English.

3. A: Did you have a nice weekend?
   B: It was OK. I .... do very much because of the rain.

4. A: Are you going to come for a drink later?
   B: I .... think so. I .... really like going to pubs.

5. A: Did you tell Pablo about the party?
   B: No, I .... see him.

6. A: What did you do in class on Tuesday?
   B: I .... know. I .... go.

3 | Questions and answers

Put the words in order and make questions.

1. are / Where / from / you ?
2. What / you / do / do ?
3. are / What / doing / tonight / you ?
4. weekend / you / nice / have / a / Did ?
5. did / do / you / What ?
6. studying / are / you / What ?

Match the questions with the answers.

1. ☐   2. ☐   3. ☐   4. ☐   5. ☐   6. ☐

a. I'm a teacher.
b. Yes, it was great.
c. I'm going to a friend's house for dinner.
d. I went to see a friend who lives in Sheffield.
e. Australia.
f. Business management.

Ask a partner the questions and find out their answers.

4 | Adjectives

Complete the expressions on the right so that they have the opposite meaning of those on the left.

bad	cold	empty	interesting	near
cheap	easy	great	late	small

1. hot weather   .... weather
2. a good film   a .... film
3. a hard job   an .... job
4. far from here   .... here
5. a boring subject   an .... subject
6. an awful weekend   a .... weekend
7. a big company   a .... company
8. an expensive hotel   a .... hotel
9. go to bed early   go to bed ....
10. a crowded train   an .... train

Use some of the expressions above to tell a partner things that are true for you. For example:

- My brother works for a small company.
- I usually go to bed early.
- The last train I took was almost empty.

5 | Verbs (1)

Complete the common pairs of verbs with the words in the box.

answer finish have dinner learn play

1. start and ....
2. ask and ....
3. listen and ....
4. stay and ....
5. work and ....

Now complete these common pairs of verbs with the words in the box.

feel hate see sell write

6. read and ....
7. buy and ....
8. love and ....
9. go and ....
10. think and ....

Work with a partner.
Student A: Act or draw one of the verbs in each pair. **DON'T** use any words.
Student B: With your book closed, say the pair of verbs. Can you remember all the pairs?

6 | Verbs (2)

Complete the sentences with the words in the box.

do earn studying takes work walk

1. I .... in an office.
2. I don't .... very much money.
3. I'm .... business management at university.
4. I usually .... to work.
5. It .... me 20 minutes to get here by car.
6. I always .... the cleaning in my house.

Now complete these sentences with the words in the box.

go live speak send stay takes

7. I .... in a flat in the city centre.
8. My girlfriend never .... me out for dinner.
9. I don't .... to the cinema very often.
10. I always .... to my mum on the phone every day.
11. I usually .... five or six e-mails every day.
12. I usually .... at home at the weekend.

Are any of the sentences true for you? Can you change them so that they are true?

7 | Look back and check

Work with a partner and do one of these activities again.

a. Role play in Unit 4 on page 22.
b. Role play in Unit 5 on page 27.

8 | What can you remember?

With a partner, write down as much as you can remember about the people you read about in the texts in Unit 3 and Unit 5.

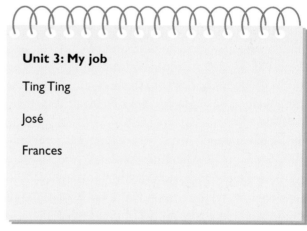

Unit 3: My job

Ting Ting

José

Frances

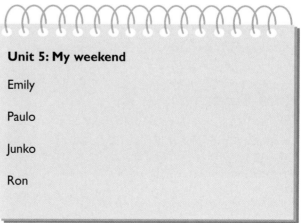

Unit 5: My weekend

Emily

Paulo

Junko

Ron

9 | Vocabulary builder: your house

Put the things in the boxes into the rooms where YOU usually have them or do them.

bed	mirror
bookshelves	sink
cupboard	sofa
dining table	table
drawers	

brushing your teeth
chatting to a friend
checking your e-mail
cooking dinner
doing some gardening
doing some work
having a bath
having a shower
having a sleep
having dinner
listening to music
making some tea
playing
playing video games
reading
reading the paper
shaving
sunbathing
talking to someone on the phone
washing up
watching TV
writing some letters

Compare your ideas with a partner.

Now use your ideas to have conversations like this:

A: Where's Andrew?

B: I think he's in the bathroom, brushing his teeth.

Real English: living room

In Britain, people often call the living room different things. For example, front room, sitting room or lounge.

the living room

your bedroom

the kitchen

the spare room

the bathroom

the garden

10 | Listening: *I'm quite tired*

🎧 Listen to a conversation between Claudio and Margrit. They are talking before their English class. Cover the conversation below. Take notes on everything you understand.

Listen again and complete the conversation. Write ONE word in each space.

C: Hello. How are you?

M: Hi. I'm fine.

C: Can I sit here?

M: Of course. So how are you?

C: Oh OK. I'm quite (1) ....

M: Did you go out last night?

C: Yes, I went out with my brother. It was his birthday.

M: Really? (2) .... old is he?

C: Twenty-three.

M: Right. What does he do?

C: He's a student.

M: What's he (3) .... ?

C: Law.

M: That's the same as you, isn't it?

C: Yes, but he's in his final year.

M: OK. So what (4) .... are you in?

C: My second year.

M: Right. I thought you were older.

C: No, I'm only twenty.

M: Right. So what time (5) .... you go to bed?

C: Four in the morning.

M: I'm not (6) .... you're tired.

C: Actually, I'm going out again after the class.

M: Really?

C: Yes, I'm (7) .... to see a film with a friend.

M: What film?

C: *Monster.* Are you (8) .... anything later? Do you want to come?

M: I'm sorry. I can't. I've got a French class.

C: Oh well. Maybe some other time.

Discuss these questions with a partner.

1. What did you do on your last birthday?
2. What was the last film you saw?

11 | Pronunciation: the letter 'a'

The letter 'a' can be pronounced in lots of different ways. For example:

/ə/	another
/e/	any
/æ/	relax
/ɑː/	far
/ɔː/	talk
/eɪ/	make

🎧 Listen and repeat these sounds and words.

Look at the grid. Try to find a way from START to FINISH which only uses the sound /eɪ/. You can only go →, ← or ↓.

🎧 Now listen and check your answer.

START			
made	past	exams	awful
paid	paper	fast	another
relax	Monday	take	wanted
answer	anything	game	say
ask	all	last	wait
accountant	company	e-mail	played
civil servant	watch	great	August
badly	after	late	sofa
walk	ago	April	came
			FINISH

12 | Collocations

Now find another way from START to FINISH by choosing the correct words to complete the expressions below.

1. I ... a mistake. / I ... the dinner. / I ... some pasta.
2. I ... £500 for it. / I ... for my meal. / He ... for everything.
3. Stay at home and ... . / I just want to ... . / ... for a few minutes.
4. I don't know the ... . / Can you ... the phone? / That's the right ... .
5. Can I ... a question? / ... her. / ... the teacher.
6. I do it ... the time. / We ... went together. / I stayed out ... night.
7. ... week / ... year / ... Sunday / the ... time I went
8. ... here. / ... for me. / I'll ... for you outside.
9. I ... tennis. / I ... video games. / I ... the piano.
10. It's the 1st of ... . / It's ... the 10th. / I'm on holiday in ... .
11. It was ... . / The weather was ... . / It was a ... match.
12. Sorry I'm ... . / I was ... for the class. / It's very ... .
13. It's the 2nd of ... . / It's ... the 23rd. / I went there in ... .
14. I ... here last year. / My friend ... with me. / I ... on my own.

I went to my aerobics class last night. • I went to my first yoga class last night. • My son had a g
lesson yesterday afternoon. • We went skiing last week. • It was great. • That sounds good. • How
do you do that? • Quite often – once or twice a week. • How long've you been doing that? • Qu
long time – about eight or nine years. • I'm a big fan of hers. • I went to church. • I went to the mos

7 What did you do last night?

Conversation

1 | Using vocabulary: free time activities

Make sure that you understand the words in red.
Look up any new words in your dictionary – or ask
your teacher.

go to my aerobics class	have a driving lesson
go to my yoga class	have a piano lesson
go running	play baseball
go skiing	play golf

🎧 **Listen and repeat the activities.**

Which of the activities can you see in the photos?

Work with a partner.
Student A: Act or draw the activities. DON'T use
any words.
Student B: With your book closed, say the
activities. Can you remember all the
activities?

2 | Listening: *So what did you do last night?*

🎧 **Listen to three conversations. Take notes about
what the people did last night.**

3 | Listen again

**Listen to Conversation 3 again. Dean is talking to
Jan at work. Complete the conversation.**

D: Hi, Jan. How're you?

J: Fine, thanks. And you?

D: Oh, (1) .... So what did you
do last night?

J: Well, after work, I met a friend and we played golf
together for a couple of hours.

D: That sounds good. (2) .... do
you do that?

J: Not very often. Once or (3) .... a month,
but I'm better than my friend. I beat her last night.
Anyway, what about you? What did you do last night?

D: I had a piano lesson.

J: Oh really? You're (4) .... !
That's great! (5) .... have you
been doing that?

D: (6) .... Yesterday was only my
second lesson, actually.

J: Really? Well, good luck with it!

Practise reading the conversation with a partner.

4 Using grammar: *How often / How long ... ?*

Match these questions from Conversation 3 with the answers.

1. How often do you do that? ☐ ☐ ☐ ☐
2. How long've you been doing that? ☐ ☐ ☐ ☐

a. Quite a long time – about nine or ten years.
b. Quite often – once or twice a week.
c. Not very often – only about once a month.
d. Not very long – only about three weeks.
e. Not very long – only about a month.
f. Quite a long time – about six or seven months.
g. Not very often – only about two or three times a year.
h. Quite often – nearly every day.

Cover the answers above. Now complete these answers. Use ONE word in each space.

a. Not .... often – about three .... four times a year.
b. Not .... often – .... once or twice a year.
c. Quite often – nearly .... day.
d. Not .... long – only .... a week.
e. Not .... long – .... about a month.
f. Quite a long .... – about .... or ten years.

> For more information on using *How often* and *How long*, see G8.

5 Practice

Work with a partner. Have conversations like Conversation 3. Use the expressions in Activity 1. Begin like this:

A: Hi. How're you?
B: Fine, thanks. And you?
A: Oh, not too bad. So what did you do last night?
B: Oh, I went ... / had ... / played ... .

Make sure that you ask each other the two questions in Activity 4.

6 Further practice

Try to complete the sentences below so that they are true for you. Use the time expressions in the box.

| last night | a few days ago | last week |
| yesterday morning | last weekend | |

1. I went to my ... class ... .
2. I had a ... lesson ... .
3. I played ... .
4. I went ...-ing ... .

Work in pairs.
Student A: Tell your partner what you have written.
Student B: Ask the two questions in Activity 4. Try to continue the conversation.

7 Using vocabulary: free time

Here are five lists of activities. Match the words in the box with the lists of activities.

| art | films | music | religion | travelling |

1. ....
   go to the cinema
   laugh a lot
   cry

2. ....
   go sightseeing
   get a visa
   take photos

3. ....
   go to concerts
   be a big fan
   download songs from the internet

4. ....
   go to exhibitions
   paint
   draw

5. ....
   go to church
   go to the temple
   pray

Work with a partner.
Student A: Act or draw the activities above. DON'T use any words.
Student B: With your book closed, say the activities. Can you remember all the activities?

> **Real English:** a fan
>
> If you are a fan of an actor or a singer or a football club, you really like them. For example:
> A: *Do you like Bob Marley?*
> B: *Yes, I'm a big fan.*
> *I'm a fan of Sevilla football club.*
> Are you a big fan of anyone?

Reading

1 | Speaking

Do you ever do these things?

- go to art exhibitions?
- go to concerts?
- go to the cinema?
- go travelling?
- paint?
- download songs from the internet?

Have conversations like this with a partner:

A: Do you ever go to art exhibitions?

B: Yes, quite a lot. I usually go to one every month. I went to one last week, actually.

or: Yes, sometimes. Maybe once or twice a year.

or: No, never.

2 | While you read (1)

🎧 **You are going to read some adverts by people looking for pen pals – people in different parts of the world that you write to but usually don't meet.**

As you read, decide if you would answer any of these adverts. Why / why not?

Compare your answers with a partner. Use these ideas to explain how you feel.

- I'd write to … . She / He sounds nice.
- I'd write to … . She / He likes the same things as me.
- I wouldn't write to … . She / He sounds strange.
- I wouldn't write to … . I don't really like … .
- I wouldn't write to … . I don't think he / she only wants to write!

Pen Pal Friends International

1 Sara

Language: English   **Age:** 36
E-mail: bottsara@mac.net

I'm an English mum with two kids. I love reading, dancing and making clothes. Write to me. Any country. Any religion. If you're a mother too and share my interests, tell me all about it.

2 Justine

Language: French   **Age:** 16
E-mail: justinf3@yaboo.com

I'm a big fan of Robbie Williams. Write to me if you're a fan too. I had some bad experiences with boy pen pals – so girls only please.

3 Isaac

Language: English   **Age:** 23
E-mail: hayes@fleece.gh.net

I'm looking for a nice English girl 18–25. I like travelling and music. I would like to visit the UK in the summer and want someone who can write me an invitation letter for my visa.

4 Baz

Language: English   **Age:** 15
E-mail: baz_za@nerd.com

I'm looking for girls or computer gamers – or both. E-mail me.

5 Antonio

Language: Spanish   **Age:** 21
E-mail: antoniovargas@shotmail.es.net

I'm a student studying languages. I'm Catholic. I love art, classical music, films and travel. I want to chat to someone who likes these things and improve my English.

6 Jurgen

Language: German   **Age:** 23
E-mail: spacker@spack.de

I'm a medical student. I love sport. I go skiing a lot and I race cars. I'm looking for a friend.

3 | While you read (2)

Read these e-mails. Which adverts are the people replying to?

🎧 Compare your answers with a partner. Then listen and check your answers.

Do you think anyone will reply to Isaac, Baz or Jurgen? Why / why not?

> **Real English:** though
>
> We often use though to mean 'but' in spoken English. The grammar is different. For example:
> *I don't really like classical music, but I like jazz.*
> *I don't really like classical music. I like jazz, though.*

4 | Using grammar: *who* and *what*

In their e-mails, Izzy asks **Who's your favourite actor?** and Sam asks **What's your favourite song?** We use **who** to ask about people and **what** to ask about things.

Complete these questions with **Who's** or **What's**?

1. .... your favourite singer?
2. .... your favourite song?
3. .... your favourite CD?
4. .... your favourite film?
5. .... your favourite actor?
6. .... your favourite writer?
7. .... your favourite director?
8. .... your favourite book?
9. .... your favourite football player?
10. .... your favourite restaurant?

Ask and answer the questions with some other students.

Now write an e-mail to one of the pen pals in the adverts on the opposite page.

5 | Pronunciation: /f/ and /v/

🎧 Listen and repeat the sounds with /f/ and /v/. Look at the pictures on page 145 for help if you need to.

🎧 Listen to ten sentences and write them down. Compare what you wrote with the tapescript at the back of the book. Then practise saying the sentences.

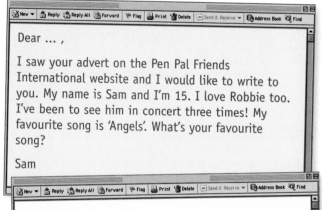

Dear ... ,

I saw your advert on the Pen Pal Friends International website and I would like to write to you. My name is Sam and I'm 15. I love Robbie too. I've been to see him in concert three times! My favourite song is 'Angels'. What's your favourite song?

Sam

Dear ... ,

My name is Gustav. I am an Austrian businessman living in London. I saw your advert on the Pen Pal Friends International website and I would like to write to you. I love ballet and go to the theatre a lot. I also go to salsa classes once a week and I sometimes go to Latin dance clubs, but I don't go very often because I don't have many friends in London. It's difficult to meet people and I work long hours. It would be nice to write to you. You sound nice. I don't have any children – I'm not married – but my sister has two children. I really love them and I usually see them once a month when I go back to Austria or when my sister visits me.

Gustav

Dear ... ,

I saw your advert on the Pen Pal Friends International website and I would like to write to you. My name is Isabella, but most people call me Izzy for short. I'm 19 and I'm studying graphic design at a college in Norwich, which is a city in the east of England. I really love painting and drawing, and I go to exhibitions quite a lot. I went to an exhibition of paintings by Goya last year, which was really good. I've never been to Spain, but I'd love to go one day and visit some of the great galleries there. Whereabouts do you live?

I don't really like classical music. I prefer indie rock music like Badass and the Beatpack. I like going to the cinema, though. My favourite actor is Sean Penn and my favourite film is Carlito's Way. What kind of films do you like? Who's your favourite actor?

Write to me soon.

Izzy

What kind of music do you listen to? • She's my favourite singer. • They're OK. I quite like them. • H
OK, but I prefer Sly Stone. • I enjoy doing it. • I'm not very good at it, though. • I find it really boring. •
too. • I don't really like his books. • Me neither. • He's not very easy to talk to. • It's deliciou
I think Thai food is better than English food. • What do you think of the people here? • I always step
other people's feet. • The way they cook in the no
is very different. • He owns eight TV channels.

8 Do you like ... ?

Conversation

1 | What kind of ... ? / Do you like ... ?

Match the general questions with the follow-up questions.

1. What kind of books do you read?
2. What kind of music do you listen to?
3. What kind of music do you dance to?
4. What kind of films do you watch?
5. What kind of food do you like?

a. Do you like The Kills? They're my favourite band.
b. Do you like ballet?
c. Do you like spicy things?
d. Do you like Janet Cain? She's my favourite writer.
e. Do you like Ben Stiller? I love his films.

2 | Practice

Cover the questions in Activity 1. Complete the conversations.

1. A: What .... of books do you
   .... ?
   B: I really like detective novels.
   A: Me too. .... you like Janet Cain?
   She's my .... writer.
   B: Yes, she's OK. I quite like her books.

2. A: What kind of .... do you listen
   .... ?
   B: I love rock music.
   A: Me too. Do you .... The Stands?
   They're .... favourite
   ....
   B: No, not really. I prefer things like The Heroes.

Write three more conversations using the other questions in Activity 1. Notice that we answer Do you like ...? questions like this:

😃 Yes, it's / she's / they're great.
I love it / her / them.

🙂 Yes, it's / he's / they're OK.
I quite like it / him / them.

🙁 No, not really.

3 | Listening: free time

🎧 **Listen to three conversations about free time. In which conversation do the speakers talk about each of these things?**

About a Boy	dancing	reading	shopping
action movies	Harry Robins	running	tennis
cinema	Paulo Coelho	salsa	Wimbledon

Can you remember who or what was:

- great?
- not very good?
- a bit boring?
- quite funny?
- sad and funny?
- embarrassing?

Listen again if you need to.

4 | Listen again

Listen to Conversation 3 again. Penny and Dennis are talking at work. Complete the conversation with the words in the box.

| been | dancing | great | love | too |
| class | embarrassing | kind | should | very |

P: What are you doing tonight?
D: I'm going to my salsa (1) ....
P: Really? How long have you (2) .... doing that?
D: Not very long. This is my third lesson. Do you like (3) .... ?
P: No, not really. I'm not (4) .... good at it. I always step on other people's feet and I find it really (5) ....
D: So what do you do in your free time?
P: Well, I (6) .... shopping and I go to the cinema a lot.
D: Me too. What (7) .... of films do you like?
P: Action movies and comedies.
D: Me (8) .... Do you like Harry Robbins?
P: Yes. He's great. He's got a new film out.
D: Yes. We (9) .... go and see it together.
P: Yes. That'd be (10) ....

Practise reading the conversation with a partner.

40

5 | Using grammar: *me too / me neither*

We agree with another person by saying me too or me neither.

We use me too to agree with positive statements. For example:

A: I quite like swimming.

B: Yes, me too. (I quite like swimming.)

A: I think football is really boring.

B: Yes, me too. (I think football is really boring.)

We use me neither to agree with negative statements. For example:

A: I don't really like shopping.

B: No, me neither. (I don't really like shopping.)

A: I never read the newspaper.

B: No, me neither. (I never read the newspaper.)

Look at these statements and responses. Both replies are grammatically correct. Choose the response which is true for you.

1. I love dancing.
   a. Yes, me too.
   b. Really? I don't really like it.
2. I watch TV a lot.
   a. Yes, me too.
   b. Really? I don't watch it very often.
3. I quite like spicy food.
   a. Yes, me too.
   b. Really? I don't really like it.
4. I hate Hollywood films.
   a. Yes, me too.
   b. Really? I love them.
5. I don't really like shopping.
   a. No, me neither.
   b. Really? I love it.
6. I never do any sport.
   a. No, me neither.
   b. Really? I do lots.

Memorise your answers. Then work with a partner.
Student A: Read the statements.
Student B: With your book closed, reply.

6 | Practice

Complete these sentences so that they are true for you.

1. I love ... .
2. I quite like ... .
3. I don't really like ... .
4. I hate ... .
5. I never ... .
6. I ... a lot.

Work with a partner.
Student A: Read your sentences.
Student B: Agree or disagree with your partner.
Try to continue the conversation.
Use one or two of these questions:

- How long have you been doing that?
- How often do you do that?
- What kind of ... do you like?
- Do you like ... ?
- What's / who's your favourite ... ?

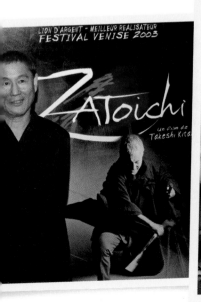

Reading

1 | Using vocabulary: describing

Here are five lists of expressions you can use to describe the things and people in the box. Match the words in the box with the lists of expressions.

| food   people   prime minister   TV   weather |

1. ....
   They're very friendly.
   They're not very easy to talk to.
   They're quiet.

2. ....
   It rains a lot.
   It's quite warm.
   It's very hot.

3. ....
   He's very strong.
   She's weak.
   He's not very intelligent.

4. ....
   There's lots of choice.
   There's not much choice.
   It's awful sometimes.

5. ....
   It's delicious.
   It's good for you.
   It's spicy.

Can you think of one more expression to add to each group? Which expressions would you use to describe your country?

2 | While you read

Read this interview with Robert, a British man living abroad – in another country. As you read, complete each question by adding one of the words from the box in Activity 1.

∩ Listen and check your answers. Which country do you think Robert is living in? Why?

LIVING ABROAD

1 *So Robert, what do you think of the .... here?*

Robert Oh, I love it. It's nicer than in Britain. It's really healthy, really good for you. In Britain, we eat a lot more fried food – chips, burgers, that kind of thing. Another good thing here is that each area still has its own special food. The way they cook in the north of the country is very different from the way they cook in the south. I love that. I also love the wine!

2 *That's nice to know. And what do you think of the .... here?*

Robert It's great. It rains a lot more in England and it's colder. The summers here are hotter and the winters are warmer too. It's lovely.

3 *And what about the .... ? What do you think of them?*

Robert Well, to begin with, I thought they weren't very easy to talk to, but now I realise that that was because I always spoke English – I didn't speak the language very well. Now I think they're friendlier, but in Britain we're friendly too. I think we're very easy to talk to.

4 *Talking of Britain, what do you think of your .... ?*

Robert Oh, that's a really difficult question. I don't know how to answer that. I don't agree with some things he does, but other things he does are good. He's strong, but sometimes he needs to listen to other people more, I think.

5 *And, finally, what do you think of the .... here?*

Robert That's an easy question to answer. I hate it! There's not much choice and a lot of the programmes are really stupid! Lots of programmes in Britain are more interesting and better. There's more choice as well. One problem here is that one person owns lots of channels, so he can decide what to show. I don't think that's very good.

3 | Word check

The missing words in these sentences are all in the text. Complete the sentences without looking at the text.

1. The food here is good for you, really ....

2. The .... they cook in the west is different from the .... they cook in the east.

3. To begin .... , I thought the people weren't very friendly, but now I have lots of friends.

4. That's a really .... question!

5. I don't know .... to answer that!

6. He's very rich. He .... six TV channels!

Now look at the text and check your answers.

Now ask a partner What do you think of the food / the people / the leader / the TV / the weather / in our / your country? Do you agree with your partner's ideas?

4 | Using grammar: comparatives

- We don't say ~~more good~~, we say better.
- We don't say ~~more bad~~, we say worse.
- When we talk about two countries, we often say things in one country are better than or worse than in the other country.

Translate better than and worse than into your language.

Complete the sentences with better or worse.

1. She's .... than our own leader. She's stronger.

2. The weather here is .... than in the north of the country. It's warmer here.

3. The TV here is .... than the TV in my country. There are more interesting programmes here.

4. It's .... living in the capital city than in my home town. The people are more unfriendly.

5. The food in Japan is .... for you than most English food. It's healthier.

6. Thai food is .... than food from my country. It's nice and spicy.

7. The weather in Glasgow is .... than here. It rains a lot more there.

8. It's .... living in the south than the north. The people in the south are nicer and easier to talk to.

Did you notice how we make comparatives with other adjectives? We add -er at the end of short adjectives. We add more before longer adjectives:

strong – stronger   interesting – more interesting

Underline all the comparatives in the sentences above.

> For more information on using comparatives, see G9.

5 | Practice

Think of three places you know well – towns, areas or countries. How are they different from the place you're studying in? Tell a partner. The sentences in Activity 4 will help you.

6 | Pronunciation: weak forms – *of, to, than*

⌒ **We often pronounce these words /əv/, /tə/ and /ðən/. Listen and repeat these expressions.**

better than me   kind of   need to do it   think of him

⌒ **Listen to ten sentences and write them down. Compare what you wrote with the tapescript at the back of the book. Then practise saying the sentences.**

Is there a bank near here? • There's one five minutes' away from here. • There's a nice internet ca
James Street. • I need to change some money. • I need to buy some aspirins. • I need to get m
developed. • Where did you get your shirt? It's really nice. • I'm not very fit. I need to join a gym
couple of friends are going to help me. • I'd like to learn how to play the cello. • I'd like to go to Eth

9 What are you doing now?

Conversation

1 | Using vocabulary: shops and places

Look at the photos. What are the most famous shops in your country? For example:

- Asda is a famous supermarket in my country.

Are there any of these places near your school? For example:

- There's a bookshop near here.
- There's a bank on Oxford Road.

Where do you do these things?

1. send a few e-mails
2. change some money
3. buy a dictionary
4. do some shopping
5. get your film developed
6. get the paper
7. get something to eat
8. buy some aspirins
9. get a coffee

2 | Listening: *What are you doing now?*

🎧 **Listen to three conversations. In each one, two people are talking after a class. Answer these questions.**

1. Which of the things in Activity 1 do the speakers talk about?
2. Which things do the two people decide to do together, and which do they want to do on their own?

Listen again and decide whether these statements are true or false.

1. a. They're going to eat at a pizzeria.   T / F
   b. The cash machine is next to the restaurant.   T / F
2. a. One person needs to go home and do some homework.   T / F
   b. They are going for a coffee together now.   T / F
3. a. They are away from home.   T / F
   b. It's four o'clock now.   T / F

Real English: a couple of

A couple means two.
I saw that film a couple of weeks ago.
A couple of friends came over for dinner last night.

a bank   a newsagent's

a supermarket   a chemist's

3 | Listen again

Listen to Conversation 3 between Rod and Michael again. Complete the conversation with the words in the box.

about	left	see you	somewhere
better	need to	some presents	two hours

R: What are you doing now?

M: I'm going to look for an internet café.
I (1) .... send a few e-mails. The last time I wrote to my family was about two weeks ago. What (2) .... you? What are you doing?

R: Oh, I think I'm going to go shopping. I want to buy (3) .... to take back for my family. I need to get a new film for my camera. I've only got three pictures (4) ....

M: You should get a digital camera.

R: Maybe, but the pictures are (5) .... on my camera.

M: Yes, I know what you mean. Anyway, do you want to meet (6) .... later?

R: Yes, OK. What time?

M: Four o'clock? That gives us (7) ....

R: OK. Fine.

M: Shall we just meet back here?

R: Yes, I'll see you in a couple of hours then.

M: Yes, (8) ....

Practise reading the conversation with a partner.

a restaurant

a photo place

a bookshop

an internet café

4 | Using grammar: *need to*

We use **need to** + verb to show it's very important to do something. We often add a reason why it's important.

Match the sentence beginnings with the endings.

1. I need to go to the photocopying shop ☐
2. I need to go to the chemist's ☐
3. I need to buy a few presents ☐
4. I need to go to the post office ☐
5. I need to call my friend ☐

a. to tell her I'm going to be late.
b. to send a parcel.
c. to take back home for my family.
d. to get something for my cold.
e. to get a copy of my passport and visa.

Now match these sentences with the follow-up sentences.

6. I need to get something to eat. ☐
7. I need to stay at home and study tonight. ☐
8. I need to get some new film for my camera. ☐
9. I need to get some more sun cream. ☐
10. I need to call my mum. ☐

f. It's her birthday today.
g. I haven't got any left.
h. I'm really hungry.
i. I've got an exam tomorrow.
j. I've only got a few pictures left.

Which of the things above do YOU need to do today or this week? Why do you need to do these things? Tell a partner.

▶ For more information on using *need to*, see G10.

5 | Practice

Here are some other things you might need to do. Write the reasons why. Use your dictionary and ask your teacher for help.

1. I need to talk to my teacher ... .
2. I need to work late tomorrow ... .
3. I need to go to the chemist's ... .
4. I need to go to the doctor ... .
5. I need to phone a friend ... .

Is there anything else you need to do? Use these time expressions.

*   I need to ... sometime today.
*   I need to ... sometime this week.

Find other students who need to do the same things.

6 | Role play

You are with someone you have met on holiday. Have a similar conversation to that in Activity 3. Use these ideas. Then try to continue the conversation.

A: What are you doing now?
B: I'm going to ... . I need to ... . What about you? What are you doing?
A: Oh, I'm going to ... . I need to ... . Do you want to meet somewhere later after you've finished?
B: Yes, OK. What time ... ?

7 | Pronunciation: /iː/, /uː/, /ɔː/ and /aː/

∩ **Listen and repeat the sounds /iː/, /uː/, /ɔː/ and /aː/. Look at the pictures on page 144 for help if you need to.**

Say the words in each line. Cross out the one word in each group that does NOT have the vowel sound. Use your dictionary for help if you need to.

/uː/ do, few, new, food, two, group, couple, who's
/ɔː/ call, talk, all, foreign, four, sports, boring, more, born
/aː/ parcel, dance, camera, guitar, half, hard, car
/iː/ we, mean, need, present, meet, leave, see, week, dream

∩ **Listen and check your answers.**

Reading

1 | Using grammar: *I'd like to ...*

When we talk about things we want to do sometime in the future, we often say **I'd like to +** verb (*I'd = I would*).

Match each sentence starter with two possible endings.

1. I'd like to spend ☐ ☐
2. I'd like to buy ☐ ☐
3. I'd like to go ☐ ☐
4. I'd like to learn ☐ ☐

a.   how to play the piano.

b.   swimming more often.

c.   less time working.

d.   a bigger flat.

e.   to China.

f.   more time with my boyfriend.

g.   a new car.

h.   how to ski.

2 | Using grammar: time expressions

When we talk about the future with **I'd like to**, we often use a time expression beginning with **sometime**. For example:

*   I'd like to move house sometime soon.
*   I'd like to have a baby sometime in the next two or three years.

Put the words in order and make time expressions.

1. the / sometime / in / future
2. the / in / sometime / year / next
3. next / years / in / the / sometime / few
4. next / weeks / in / sometime / few / the
5. three / the / months / in / sometime / next / or / four

Use the ideas in Activities 1 and 2 to say something true about you.

▶ For more information on using *I'd like to*, see G11.

3 | Before you read

Look at the photos. What do you think the people would like to do in the future? Compare your ideas with a partner. Begin like this:

*   I think ... would like to spend / buy / go / learn ... .

Karen

Alan

Rick

Charlotte

4 | While you read

🎧 **Now read what the four people in the photos would like to do in the future. Did you guess correctly?**

Things I'd like to do

Karen

I'd really like to go to Japan sometime in the next two or three years. I've always wanted to go there. I love Japanese food, and I find the culture and the language really interesting. I'm learning Japanese at the moment. I go to classes two evenings a week. I have a friend who's from Tokyo, so maybe one day I'll go and visit him.

Alan

I'd like to buy a big red sports car – maybe a Ferrari or a Porsche. I'd also really like to learn how to play the guitar. When I was younger, I always wanted to be a rock star, but then I got a great job working for a big company. I've got quite a lot of money now and have more free time, so it's a good time to make my dreams come true!

Rick

I know it sounds strange, but I'd like to spend less time with my wife and son. My son was born a year and a half ago, and I haven't had a good night's sleep since then! My wife has changed a lot – she spends more time with our son than with me. I don't feel wanted in the house. I'd like to go out and see my old friends more!

Charlotte

I was very ill last year, and I put on a lot of weight and got fat. I'd like to lose weight this year and then I'd really like to go dancing more often. My husband is a good dancer and when we were younger, we went dancing a lot. I'd also like to go swimming more often, but I need to get thinner first! One final thing – I'd like to join a singing group sometime in the next few months. I love singing!

5 | Comprehension

Which of the four people:

1. is quite rich?
2. is a father?
3. wasn't very well?
4. is studying a foreign language?
5. is a successful businessman?
6. wants to get fit?
7. is tired all the time?
8. is interested in travelling?

<u>Underline</u> the words in the text which tell you.

6 | Speaking

What do you think of the four people? Tell a partner. Use these expressions.

- ... sounds really nice / strange / unhappy.
- ... doesn't sound very nice.

Would you like to do any of the things the people talk about?

7 | Pronunciation: /s/ and /z/

🎧 **Listen and repeat the sounds with /s/ and /z/. Look at the pictures on page 145 for help if you need to.**

🎧 **Decide if the underlined sounds in these sentences are /s/ or /z/. Then listen and repeat the sentences.**

1. I need to <u>s</u>pend more time <u>s</u>tudying English.
2. I li<u>s</u>ten to all kind<u>s</u> of mu<u>s</u>ic.
3. <u>C</u>eline Dion'<u>s</u> a great <u>s</u>inger.
4. I love <u>S</u>teven <u>S</u>pielberg'<u>s</u> film<u>s</u>.
5. I find dan<u>c</u>ing embarra<u>ss</u>ing.
6. The weather'<u>s</u> wor<u>s</u>e in the <u>s</u>ummer.
7. I hate <u>s</u>pi<u>c</u>y thing<u>s</u>.
8. Chine<u>s</u>e food'<u>s</u> deliciou<u>s</u>.

Do you agree with the sentences above? Tell a partner. For example:

- Number 1 is true for me.
- Number 2 isn't true for me. I only listen to classical music.
- I'm not sure about number 3. I don't know Celine Dion.

I went to the cathedral yesterday morning. • Have you been there? • We went there a couple of y
ago. • What are you doing today? • The weather was awful. • We got really wet. • You should go to Vier
It's got some beautiful buildings. • Have you read any good books recently? • It was nice meeting y
Good luck. • Enjoy your holiday. • It's a famous old town in the North. • The castle is over a thou
years old. • The scenery is amaz
Where's a good place to go?

10 Have you been to ...?

Conversation

1 | Using vocabulary: past time phrases

Look at the calendar. Today is Friday the 12th of August. Match the time phrases with the dates.

JULY				
M	4	11	18	25
TU	5	12	19	26
W	6	13	20	27
TH	7	14	21	28
F	1	8	15	22	29
SA	2	9	16	23	30
SU	3	10	17	24	31

AUGUST				
M	1	8	15	22	29
TU	2	9	16	23	30
W	3	10	17	24	31
TH	4	11	18	25
F	5	(12)	19	26
SA	6	13	20	27
SU	7	14	21	28

1. last weekend
2. last Friday
3. last week
4. yesterday morning
5. the day before yesterday
6. a couple of weeks ago
7. a few days ago
8. a few weeks ago

a. 10 a.m. on the 11th of August
b. the 10th of August
c. the 7th, 8th or 9th of August
d. Saturday the 6th and Sunday the 7th of August
e. Friday the 5th of August
f. Monday the 1st of August to Friday the 5th of August
g. Monday the 25th of July to Friday the 29th of July
h. anytime between the 7th and the 21st of July

Now work with a partner.
Student A: Say a date.
Student B: With your book closed, say the time phrase.

2 | Practice

Tell a partner some things you did using the time phrases from Activity 1. For example:

*   I went shopping yesterday morning.
*   I didn't do anything last weekend.

3 | Before you listen

Read the short text and answer the questions.

Every year thousands of people buy a special train ticket called an Inter Rail card. For around three hundred pounds you can travel by train anywhere in Europe for a month. Some people plan where they want to go before they leave. Some people just decide each morning where they are going to travel to next. People often take a tent or stay in cheap hotels and hostels. Some just sleep on the trains.

Would you like to get an Inter Rail card? Where would you go? What places would you stay in? Check out Inter Rail on the internet.

4 | Listening: *Have you been there?*

🎧 **Listen to a conversation between Stefan, Edward and Kirsty in a hostel in Florence, Italy. They are all travelling by Inter Rail.**

Which of these places do they talk about?

the cathedral	the hill outside the city	Rome
Germany	Istanbul	the tower
Greece	the museum	Vienna

What did they say about each place? Listen again and check.

5 | Listen again

Listen again and complete the conversation with the words in the box.

cathedral	enjoy	leave	view	went
couple	few	pack	weather	yesterday

S: What are you doing today?

E: We're going to go to the (1) .... Have you been there?

S: Yes, I (2) .... there a few days ago when I arrived. It's lovely.

E: Oh good. It sounds great. Did you go up the tower?

S: No, I didn't want to pay. I walked to the hill outside the city. Have you been there? You get a really good (3) ....

E: Yes, we went there yesterday, but it rained really badly.

S: I know. The (4) .... was awful yesterday. I went there the day before (5) .... when the weather was OK, so I was quite lucky.

E: Yes, you were. We got really wet. So what are you going to do today?

S: Oh, I think I'm going to (6) .... I think I've seen everything I want to see here.

E: So where are you going next?

S: I still haven't decided. Have you been to Vienna? There's a train that goes there this afternoon.

E: Yes, we went there a (7) .... of weeks ago. It's nice, but it's quite expensive.

S: Yes, I've heard that. If I go to Vienna though, I can get a train to Istanbul.

E: Istanbul! Oh yes. It's great there. I went a (8) .... years ago with my girlfriend.

K: I'm sorry?

E: I mean my ex-girlfriend.

K: Thank you. I don't want to hear what you did with your ex-girlfriend.

E: OK, sorry, you're right. But Istanbul IS amazing. You should go there. And it's cheaper than here.

S: Well, maybe I'll do that. I should go and (9) .... my bag.

E: OK. See you.

K: Good luck, if we don't see you again.

S: Thanks. It was nice meeting you and (10) .... the rest of your trip.

Practise reading the conversation in groups of three.

6 | Using grammar: *Have you been to …?*

When we want to know if someone was in a place before now, we usually ask Have you been to … ? Look at these examples.

A: Have you ever been to Glasgow?

B: No, I haven't. Is it nice?

A: Have you been here before?

B: Yes, I came here a couple of weeks ago. What do you think of it?

A: Have you been to Kew Gardens?

B: Yes, I went there last week with some friends.

A: Have you been to the cinema recently?

B: Yes, I went to see that film *No Man's Land* last weekend.

A: Have you ever been to Africa?

B: No, never. Have you?

Which adverbs are used in the questions? Ask your teacher which ones mean:

any time in your life .... and
....

some time near to now ....

Notice we don't use I've been to with past time expressions – *last weekend, a couple of weeks ago*, etc. We use the past simple instead.

Practise reading the conversations with a partner.

Now have conversations using these ideas.

1. A: the castle?
   B: yesterday afternoon

2. A: the restaurant across the road?
   B: last Friday / some friends

3. A: the new sports centre in town?
   B: nice?

4. A: the cinema recently
   B: a few days ago

5. A: ever / the States?
   B: never / you?

Reading

1 | Using vocabulary: describing places

When we want to recommend a place, we often say **You should go to ...** . Complete these sentences with the name of a city, an area or a country you know.

1. You should go to .... It's got some incredible shops.
2. You should go to .... It's got lots of great parks.
3. You should go to .... It's got great nightlife.
4. You should go to .... It's got lots of lovely, sandy beaches.
5. You should go to .... It's got some great restaurants.
6. You should go to .... It's got lots of beautiful old buildings.
7. You should go to .... The scenery is amazing.

Compare your ideas with a partner. Do you agree? If you don't agree, you can say No, ... is (much) better!

2 | While you read

∩ **We asked four different people about good places to go in their countries. Read what they said on the opposite page. As you read, think about your answers to these questions.**

1. Have you been to any of these places before?
2. Would you like to go? Why / why not?

3 | Roleplay

Work in pairs.
Student A: You are at home in your country.
Student B: You are a tourist on holiday in Student A's country.
Have a conversation like that in Activity 5 on page 49. Begin like this:

A: What're you doing today?
B: I'm not sure. Where's a good place to go?
A: Well, have you been to ... ?

You should go to ...

Nacho

If you come to Spain, you should go to Granada. It's a famous old town in the south of the country and it's got lots of really beautiful old buildings. The most famous is called The Alhambra. It's over five hundred years old and thousands of tourists visit it every year. It's not too far from the sea. In about an hour, you can get to lovely sandy beaches, where you can go swimming and sunbathe.

Tony

If you come to England, first of all you should come to my home town, London. It's got everything. It's got great parks, great museums, great nightlife. It's also got the best football team in the world – Arsenal! The weather isn't very nice of course, but no-one goes to London for the sunshine! If you have time, you should also go to the Lake District in the north-west of England. It's a wild and beautiful area. It's very quiet and peaceful, and it's got incredible scenery – mountains and hills and lakes. It's lovely!

Maki

If you visit Japan, I think the best place to go to is Miyajima island. It's a small island near Hiroshima and it's really beautiful. It's very green and it's got amazing scenery. You can go to the top of the mountains there and you can also see lots of strange animals. It's got great food too – they make a special kind of biscuit there. They're really delicious!

Clare

If you visit Scotland, there are lots of different things to do. It depends what you like. If you like cities, you should go to Edinburgh. It's a really old city, so it's got lots of amazing old buildings. It's got a few great parks as well, and some great bars and restaurants. If you prefer the countryside, you should visit some of the small islands to the west of Scotland. They've got incredible scenery and the wildlife there is amazing.

---

4 | Using grammar: the present perfect

Have you been to ... ? is an example of the present perfect. We can use the present perfect to ask about someone's experiences before now.

We make the present perfect using have + past participle. The past participle is the third form of irregular verbs:

eat – ate – eaten	know – knew – known
go – went – gone	meet – met – met
have – had – had	see – saw – seen

For regular verbs the past participle is the -ed form:

decide – decided   play – played   try – tried

Complete these questions with past participles.

1. Have you .... yet? (eat)
2. Have you .... what you're doing tomorrow? (decide)
3. Have you .... around a lot? (travel)
4. How long have you .... each other? (know)
5. Have you .... before? (meet)
6. Have you .... your parents recently? (see)
7. Have you .... of Teen Hope? They're a pop group. (hear)
8. Where's he .... ? (go)

In groups of three, ask and answer the questions. For example:

A: Have you eaten yet?
B: Yes, I had a sandwich earlier. What about you?
C: No, I'm really hungry.

> For more information on using the present perfect, see G12.

5 | Pronunciation: contractions

We often say two words together. For example:

I have → I've	I am → I'm
He has → He's	It is → It's
I have not → I haven't	I would → I'd

These are called contractions. This is the normal way to say these words.

🎧 **Listen and repeat the contractions.**

🎧 **Listen to ten sentences and write them down. Compare what you wrote with the tapescript at the back of the book.**

Practise saying the sentences.

Is there a newsagent's near here? • Is this the right way? • I think we're lost. • There's one opposite her
Turn right at the traffic lights. • Take the number 73. • Get off at the stop in front of the cinema. •
need to change trains at Oxford Circus. • Hurry up! • We're going to miss our train. • I never use pu
transport • Could you draw me a map? • How much will it cost? • We took the wrong turning. • It's
first turning on the righ
I fell asleep on the bus.

11 Is there one near here?

Conversation

1 Using vocabulary: prepositions of place

Here are six answers to the question Is there a bank near here? Match the answers with the pictures.

1. Yes, there's one opposite the station.
2. Yes, there's one next to the station.
3. Yes, there's one round the corner from the station.
4. Yes, there's one on the corner.
5. Yes, there's one up the road, on the left.
6. Yes, there's one up the road, on the right.

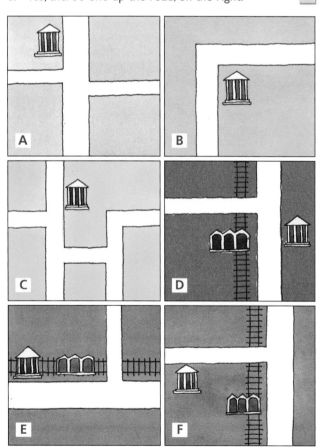

Work with a partner.
Student A: Ask about places you want to go to.
Student B: Give true answers. Use some of the expressions above. For example:

A: Is there a bookshop near here?

B: Yes, there's one next to the supermarket.

A: Is there a chemist's near here?

B: Sorry, I'm not sure. I don't know this area.

2 Understanding directions

Match the sentence beginnings with the endings.

1. Go up
2. Turn left
3. It's the second
4. It's just round
5. Go up this road until

a. you come to the end.
b. turning on the left.
c. at the traffic lights.
d. this road here.
e. the corner from there.

3 Listening: *Is there one near here?*

🎧 **Listen to three conversations. Draw on the map the place each person is going to.**

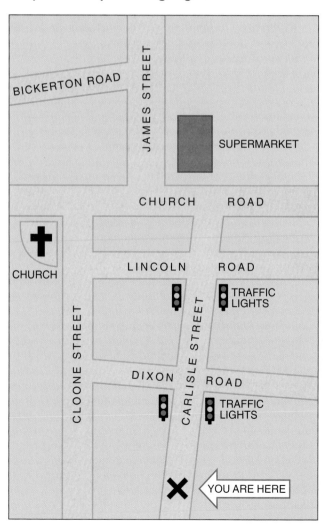

4 | Listen again

Listen to Conversation 3 again. Lenny and Kim are both students at university. They are talking after class. Complete the conversation.

L: What're you doing now?

K: Well, I'm quite hungry. (1) .... get some lunch. Is there a good restaurant near here?

L: Yes, there's one quite near here – (2) .... Lincoln Road.

K: I'm not sure where that is. (3) .... tell me how to get there?

L: Yes, of course. You go up Carlisle Street until you (4) .... the second set of traffic lights. Lincoln Road is there. If you (5) .... at the traffic lights, it's up the road there, (6) ....

K: OK. I think I know where you mean. I'll try to find it.

L: It's easy to find. You'll be OK. Have a good meal.

K: Thanks. I'll see you tomorrow.

L: OK. Bye.

Practise reading the conversation with a partner.

5 | Practice

Work with a partner.
Student A: Look at the map on page 160.
Student B: Look at the map on page 158.
Ask each other Is there a ... near here? to find the places you're looking for. Use the language in Activities 1 and 2 when you give directions.

6 | Using grammar: making requests

When we ask someone to do something for us, we often use could you + verb. For example:

• Could you show me the way, please?

• Could you move this for me, please?

Complete the questions with the verbs in the box.

| draw | help | open | post | show | write down |

1. Could you .... the name of the street, please?
2. Could you .... me a map, please?
3. Could you .... me how to get there on this map, please?
4. Could you .... the window, please?
5. Could you .... this letter for me, please?
6. Could you .... me move this table, please?

Have conversations like this with a partner:

A: Could you open the window, please?

B: Yes, of course.

A: Great. Thank you.

Now write two Could you ...? questions you'd like to ask other students. Have conversations with some other students using your questions.

For more information on making requests, see G13.

7 | Pronunciation: /θ/ and /ð/

∩ Listen and repeat the sounds /θ/ and /ð/. Look at the pictures on page 145 for help if you need to.

∩ Decide if the underlined sounds in these sentences are /θ/ or /ð/. Then listen and repeat the sentences.

1. I went there the day before yesterday.
2. How long've you known each other?
3. Have you been there before?
4. What do you think of the weather?
5. Thank you for everything.

∩ We often use /θ/ when we say dates. Listen to twelve dates and write them down.

Reading

1 | Using vocabulary

Complete the conversations on the right with the words in the boxes.

Work with a partner.
Student A: Act or draw the activities. DON'T use any words.
Student B: With your book closed, say the activities. Can you remember all the activities?

Practise reading the conversations with a partner.

Have similar conversations with your partner. Change the names of the places. Use places in your town / city / region.

2 | Speaking

What's public transport like in the place where you live? Use these sentences to help you.

- Public transport is *good / bad* where I live.
- There isn't an underground in my town.
- There *aren't any / are lots of* buses late at night.
- Taxis are quite *cheap / expensive*.
- The trains are *nice and comfortable / horrible*.
- The trams *never / always* run on time.

What transport do you use each week? To go where?

Tell a partner. For example:

- I usually take the bus to come here.
- I get the train to work every day.

3 | Before you read

Match the expressions with the words which have the opposite meaning.

1. caught the train ☐   a. woke up
2. got lost ☐   b. arrived
3. fell asleep ☐   c. found my way
4. got on the train ☐   d. missed the train
5. left ☐   e. got off the train

All the verbs are in the past tense. What are the present forms?

Conversation 1

get off	go	take

A: Could you help me? I want to .... to Leith.
B: Oh, you can .... an 87 bus from that stop over there.
A: Which stop do I need to .... at?
B: It's difficult to explain. Ask the driver.

Conversation 2

line	station	take

A: Could you help me? How do I get to Mile End from here?
B: Oh, you need to .... the underground. There's a .... down this road.
A: OK. Thanks. Which .... do I need to take?
B: I'm not sure. Sorry. Ask someone at the station.

Conversation 3

cost	driver	taxi

A: Hello. Could you call a .... for me, please?
B: Yes, of course, sir. Where are you going?
A: Kings Heath. How much will it .... ?
B: I'm not sure, probably about £7. I'll ask the ....

Conversation 4

change	leave	the next one	25 past

A: Hello. I want to go to Barnes.
B: Yes, you need to get the train to Cambridge and .... at Fordham.
A: What time does it .... ?
B: .... is at 9.25. Then after that, there's one at .... every hour.
A: OK. Thanks.

Conversation 5

change	explain	problem	take

A: Could you help me? I want to go to Mile End.
B: Oh right. It's a bit difficult to .... Have you got a map?
A: Yes. Here.
B: OK. Well, there's a .... on this line, so you need to .... at Baker Street. Then take this yellow line to Liverpool Street and then take the red line.
A: How long will it .... ?
B: About 40 minutes.

4 | While you read

Read the stories about people getting lost. Before you listen, complete the stories with these last lines.

a. They continued up the motorway all the way to Scotland, 450 kilometres away from London!

b. When I saw a bus going to the city centre, I got on it and went home.

c. She had to show the driver how to get there on the map and it took another two hours!

d. We arrived exactly at the moment my friend and his new wife came out of the church.

⌒ Listen and check your answers. Who had the worst experience?

<u>Underline</u> **the expressions from Activity 3.**

I got lost

▣ There was a story in the paper recently about a woman who had an accident. The doctors told the ambulancemen to take her to a hospital near her home in Shoreham, Sussex. The woman fell asleep on the way. When she woke up, the ambulancemen told her they'd arrived. She looked out of the window, but she didn't recognise the place. They were in the wrong town! They were in Shoreham in KENT, one hundred kilometres from her home. ☐

▣ I was going to a friend's wedding once and we wanted to catch the train. Unfortunately, we went to the wrong station, so we missed our train and had to wait an hour for the next one. When we arrived in Canterbury, where my friend was getting married, we got a taxi. ☐

▣ There was a story in the newspaper recently about a German couple who drove to Britain to visit London. They didn't have a map and they didn't speak English. They started driving along the motorway, but they missed the turning to London. ☐

▣ I had an interview for a job once. I took the bus. I asked the bus driver to tell me which bus stop to get off at and I had a map from the bus stop to the company's offices. Unfortunately, I'm not very good at reading maps. When I got off the bus, I started walking in the wrong direction. I tried to go a different way. I got completely lost. I walked round in circles for about two hours, but I didn't find the office. I missed the interview. ☐

5 | Comprehension

Cover the text. Use the pictures and words below to retell the stories.

accident / take her to hospital / didn't recognise the place / show the driver

wedding / missed our train / had to wait / came out of the church

map / English / the turning / continued

How much of the last story can you remember? Tell a partner. Then look back and check.

6 | Speaking: *Have you ever got lost?*

Have you ever got lost? Tell a partner what happened. Use some of these sentences.

- I got lost on the way (to Oxford) once.
- I took the wrong turning.
- I went to the wrong station.
- I missed my stop.
- I got on the wrong bus.
- I went round in circles for (three hours / forty minutes).
- I had to wait (an hour / half an hour).
- I had to ask someone the way.
- They showed me where to go.

Is it business or pleasure? • How long've you been here? • Is this seat free? • The nightlife is great. • Th
out at the moment. • He's not feeling very well. • I'm here on business. • I'm on the bus. It's coming
Fairfax Road now. • I'm staying in a bed and breakfast. • It's not very clean, but it's cheap. • It's run by a
friendly family. • It's half an hour by bus from the city centre. • I like keeping fit. • We need to put the
up now. • It's g
gym and a sauna.

12 What are you doing here?

Conversation

1 | Meeting people for the first time

Match the questions with the answers.

1. Do you speak English?
2. What are you doing here? Is it business or pleasure?
3. Where are you staying?
4. How long've you been here?
5. Have you been here before?
6. When are you leaving?
7. What do you think of it here?
8. Are you doing anything later?

a. Next Friday.
b. Not long. We arrived here on Monday.
c. It's just pleasure. We're here on holiday.
d. No, it's my first time here.
e. Yes, a little.
f. We're in a small hotel in the centre of town.
g. Yes, we're going out for something to eat.
h. It's great. Everyone's been really friendly.

🎧 **Listen to the questions. Which words are stressed? Then practise the questions and answers with a partner.**

2 | Listening: *What are you doing here?*

🎧 **Listen to two conversations. In each one people who are travelling abroad are talking. Which questions in Activity 1 do the speakers ask?**

Can you remember the answers to any of these questions? Listen again if you need to.

3 | Listen again

Complete the sentences from each conversation with ONE word. Listen again if you need to.

Conversation 1

a. Is this seat .... ?
b. Are you going to .... ?
c. I arrived in London last ....
d. Your English is very ....
e. I work for an export ....

Conversation 2

a. I'm trying to .... the Louvre.
b. I'm going in that .... I'll show you, if you ....
c. I'm just here on .... I'm travelling all round ....
d. It's true what people say. It's very ....
e. Perhaps you would like a guide. See the .... ?
f. I think I'll probably just get something to eat and go to bed quite ....

Real English: I'll probably

When someone asks what we are doing in the future and we haven't decided, we often use I'll probably.

A: *What are you doing later?*
B: *I don't know. I'll probably stay at home.*
or: *I haven't decided. I'll probably go out somewhere.*

---

4 | Speaking

Role play the two conversations in Activity 3 with a partner.

5 | Using grammar: present continuous

We use the present continuous to talk about unfinished temporary activities around now. For example:

PAST	NOW	FUTURE
	I'm travelling all round Europe	

- I'm here on holiday. I'm travelling all round Europe.

Complete the sentences with the words in the box.

doing	getting	studying	trying
feeling	opening	talking	visiting

1. They're out at the moment. They're .... some shopping.
2. I'm here on holiday. I'm .... some friends who live here.
3. He's in bed. He's not .... very well.
4. I'm at university. I'm .... French.
5. We're lost. We're .... to find Vicarage Road.
6. She's in the shower. She's .... ready to go out.
7. He's on the phone. He's .... to his mum.
8. I'm here on business. My company's .... a new office here.

Spend two minutes memorising the pairs of sentences above. Then work with a partner.
Student A: Say the first sentences.
Student B: With your book closed, say the present continuous sentences.

For example:

A: They're out at the moment.

B: They're doing some shopping.

Complete these present continuous sentences with ONE word.

a. I .... not feeling very well.
b. .... you looking for something?
c. He .... getting some drinks from the bar.
d. Who .... she talking to?
e. It .... raining again! I don't believe it!
f. We .... staying at the Holiday Inn.
g. They .... waiting for us outside.

6 | Practice

Write short conversations using the ideas below.

1. **On a mobile phone**
   A: Where / you? / We / wait / for you.
   B: Sorry. / the bus. / It / come along Tyne Street now.
   A: OK. We / wait / outside the cinema.

2. **Meeting friends**
   A: Hi. / on your own? / Where / Carlos?
   B: He / home / bed. / not feel / well.
   A: I / sorry.

3. **At a hotel**
   A: Hi. / Where / Dave?
   B: He / just have / shower.
   A: OK.

4. **In a café**
   A: What / do / here in Brighton?
   B: I / holiday. I / just stay / for a week.
   A: Where / stay?
   B: youth hostel / near the park.
   A: nice?
   B: not clean / cheap!

Now read your conversations with a partner.

> For more information on using the present continuous, see G14.

Reading

1 | Speaking

Which of these answers is true for you? Tell a partner.

When I go to other towns or countries, I usually stay:

a.   with friends.

b.   with relatives.

c.   somewhere cheap.

d.   in a nice hotel.

Make sure that you understand the words in red. Then discuss these questions with a new partner.

Have you ever stayed in a:

•   5-star hotel?

•   bed and breakfast?

•   tent?

•   youth hostel?

•   self-catering apartment?

2 | While you read

Read about five places to stay in Britain. Complete the descriptions with the words in red from Activity 1.

🎧 **Listen and check your answers.**

3 | Comprehension

Which places sound good if you like:

a.   going camping?

b.   going out at night?

c.   going swimming?

d.   going sightseeing?

e.   keeping fit?

f.   playing computer games?

g.   cooking?

Imagine you are going on holiday to Britain. Decide which of the five places you would most like to stay in. Tell a partner. For example:

•   I'd like to go to Hill Farm. I like going camping and it sounds good.

Places to stay

Western House

Western House is a lovely two-hundred-year-old house with a beautiful garden. It's a .... in the south of England. It's run by a very friendly family – and their dog Sheba! It's only five minutes on foot from the historic town of Rye and it's ten minutes by car from the sea. Full English breakfast included – £50 per person per night.

The Go-Go

The Go-Go is a .... for the younger traveller. It's in the centre of Cardiff, very close to all the pubs and clubs. You can buy breakfast or cook for yourself. The cost is £20 per person per night in a large shared room or £30 per person per night in a four-bed family room.

The Home from Home

This is a .... in a nice green area in one of the quieter parts of Birmingham, England's second city. You can do your own cooking here, watch TV, use the computer – just like in your own home. It's half an hour by bus from the city centre. Only £200 a week.

Hill Farm

You can put your .... up in the fields of this lovely old farm in the north of Scotland. It's twenty kilometres from the nearest town, in the middle of some beautiful countryside. The hills and mountains in this area are incredible. There's a shower and a toilet you can use in one of the fields. Only £60 per week.

The Clifford

This .... is in the centre of London, only five minutes from all the shops and close to all the famous sights, like Big Ben and Buckingham Palace. There's a gym, a swimming pool and a sauna downstairs. All are free to guests. The cost is £220 per person per night.

4 | Conversation: booking a room

You are going to listen to a conversation between a receptionist at Western House and Ann, who is booking a room. Before you listen, complete the conversation with the words in the box.

arriving	book	checking	leaving	pay	take

R: Good morning, Western House.

A: Hi, I'd like to (1) .... a single room for two nights, please.

R: Certainly, madam. For which dates?

A: I'm (2) .... on the 14th of April and I'm (3) .... on the 16th.

R: OK. I'm just (4) .... on the computer. OK. That's fine. How are you going to (5) .... ?

A: Is American Express OK?

R: Yes, of course. The full cost is £100. Can I (6) .... your number?

A: Yes, sure. It's 0489–6666–1072–3465.

R: And the expiry date?

A: 04–09.

R: And your name as it appears on the card?

A: Mrs A. Jones.

R: Great. Thank you, Mrs Jones. That's one single room for April the 14th and 15th. We look forward to seeing you then.

A: Great. Thank you. Bye.

∩ **Now listen to the conversation and check your answers. Then practise reading the conversation with a partner.**

5 | Practice

Work with a partner.
Student A: You are a receptionist at The Clifford in the text.
Student B: You want to book a room.
Role play the telephone conversation.

6 | Using vocabulary: *How was your holiday?*

We often use not very + a positive adjective to talk about bad things. For example:

• The owner of the bed and breakfast wasn't very nice.

• The beaches weren't very clean.

Rewrite the sentences using not very + the adjectives in brackets.

1. The weather was really awful. (good)

2. The hotel was really dirty. (clean)

3. The English breakfasts were really disgusting. (nice)

4. The owners of the bed and breakfast were very unfriendly. (friendly)

5. The town was really boring. (interesting)

6. Our hotel room was really cold. (warm)

Have you ever had any problems like this on holiday? Tell a partner. For example:

• Once, I went to Norway and the weather wasn't very good. It was really cold!

• We went to England a few years ago and our hotel room wasn't very clean. They didn't clean it for three days!

7 | Pronunciation: /b/ and /p/

∩ **Listen and repeat the sounds with /b/ and /p/. Look at the pictures on page 145 for help if you need to.**

Now practise saying these sentences.

1. I'm here on business.

2. It's not very clean, but it's cheap.

3. The business is doing badly.

4. I'm reading a book about Peru.

5. It's a bit boring.

6. I forgot to buy the paper this morning.

7. Have you got a pen?

8. Have you got a piece of paper?

∩ **Listen and check your pronunciation.**

Review: Units 7-12

1 | Questions

Match the questions with the answers.

1. Did you have a nice weekend?
2. Really? How often do you do that?
3. Do you like sport?
4. Have you ever been to Mexico?
5. What did you think of the food?

a. Quite often. Maybe once or twice a month.
b. It was OK, but it was quite spicy.
c. Yes, it was great. I went windsurfing. I had a great time.
d. No, not really. I don't really do any exercise.
e. Yes, I went there last year on holiday. It was great.

Now match these questions with the answers.

6. Did you enjoy the party on Friday?
7. Is your hotel far from here?
8. Have you heard the news? Jim's going to get married.
9. Did you buy me the paper?
10. How long have you been here?

f. Oh, sorry, I forgot! I knew I needed to get something else!
g. Not long. We arrived here on Friday, so only three days.
h. Not really. It's ten minutes in a taxi.
i. No, not really. I didn't know anyone, so it was quite boring.
j. No! That's great. I didn't know he had a girlfriend!

2 | Grammar: tense and questions

Write down which questions in Activity 1 use:

1. the present tense
2. the past tense
3. the present perfect tense

3 | Grammar: questions

Read the examples. Then complete the rules about questions.

The present
- How often do you do that?
- Do you like coffee?
- Is it nice?

a. We use .... + a verb.
b. We use .... + an adjective.

Specific times in the past.
- What did you do last night?
- Did you have a nice weekend?
- Was it good?

a. We use .... + a verb.
b. We use .... + an adjective.

General experiences before now
- Have you ever tried Japanese food?
- Where have you been?

We use .... + the past participle of a verb.

Now complete the questions with the words in the box.

did you   do you   have you   was it

1. A: Where .... go for your holiday?
   B: Actually, we didn't go anywhere. We just stayed at home.

2. A: Where .... work? Is it near here?
   B: Not far. It takes me about 20 minutes on foot.

3. A: What was the weather like? .... OK?
   B: No, it wasn't. It was horrible. It rained all day.

4. A: .... bought any good CDs recently?
   B: Yes, I got the Lost Souls new album. It's great.

5. A: What .... think of the film you saw yesterday?
   B: It was OK. Nothing special.

6. A: When .... arrive here?
   B: A couple of days ago.

7. A: .... know anyone at this party?
   B: Only you!

8. A: .... done your homework?
   B: No, I didn't have time.

With a partner, write three questions – one present, one past and one present perfect – to ask your teacher.

4 | Verbs

Complete the collocations with the verbs in the box.

change	get	get off	need	send	spend

1. .... an e-mail / a parcel / me a postcard
2. .... a coffee / something to eat / lost
3. .... some money into euros / trains at Watts Station / a lot
4. .... at the next stop / the bus / at Victoria Station
5. .... to go to the chemist / to call my friend / to get a new film for my camera
6. .... too much money / some time with my family / some time on my own

Discuss these questions with a partner.

1. What do you need to do this week?
2. Do you like to spend time on your own?

5 | What's the forecast for tomorrow?

Match the answers to the question above with the pictures.

1. It's going to rain. ☐
2. It's going to be very hot. ☐
3. It's going to be cold. ☐
4. It's going to be warm. ☐
5. It's going to be sunny. ☐
6. It's going to snow. ☐

6 | Look back and check

Work with a partner and do one of these activities.
a. Do Activity 6 on page 41 again.
b. Make sure that you remember all the vocabulary in Unit 11 Activities 1 and 2 on page 52. Ask your partner or teacher if you don't. Then ask your partner Is there a ... near here? Give true answers and explain how to get there.

7 | What can you remember?

With a partner, write down as much as you can remember about the texts you read in Unit 8 and Unit 10.

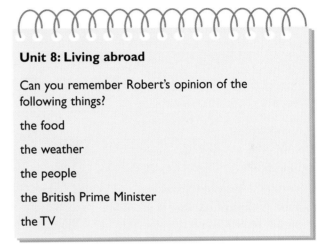

Unit 8: Living abroad

Can you remember Robert's opinion of the following things?

the food

the weather

the people

the British Prime Minister

the TV

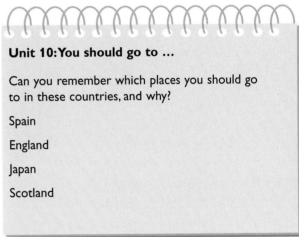

Unit 10: You should go to ...

Can you remember which places you should go to in these countries, and why?

Spain

England

Japan

Scotland

Have you been to any of these places? What did you think of them?

8 | Vocabulary builder: People and clothes

Tell a partner about someone you know who is:

- really tall.
- really short.
- really thin.
- really fat.
- really good-looking.

Label these pictures with the words in the box.

black hair	jeans
blonde hair	leather shoes
glasses	skirt
grey hair	suit
jacket	T-shirt

Work with a partner. Cover the pictures. Try to answer the questions.

1. Who's the guy with the white T-shirt?
2. Who's the blonde woman?
3. Who's the black guy with the leather jacket?
4. Who's the white guy with the suit?
5. Who's the Asian woman?
6. Who's the woman with the curly hair?
7. Who's the woman with glasses?

Now ask questions like those above about people in your class.

Work with a new partner. Have conversations like this:

A: I like your shoes / dress.

B: Thanks.

A: Where did you get them / it?

B: In a shop in Madrid / King Street.

Paul

Sally

curly hair

tie

Patrick

Lita

Sharon

dress

9 | Listening: *My brother's there now*

🎧 **Listen to a conversation between Adrian and Sandra during a coffee break at work. Sandra is reading the paper. Cover the conversation below. What do you find out about Adrian's brother?**

Listen again and complete the conversation. Write ONE word in each space.

A: Is there anything interesting in the paper?

S: No, nothing much. Just more bad news. It's really (1) .... There's quite an interesting story about Uzbekistan, though. I didn't really know anything about the country before.

A: Can I (2) .... it? My brother's there now.

S: Your brother is in Uzbekistan! What's he (3) .... there?

A: Oh, he's living there.

S: He's living there! Er. Why? I mean, what does he (4) .... ?

A: Well, he's an engineer really, but at the (5) .... he's teaching English.

S: OK, but why Uzbekistan?

A: Well, his (6) .... is from there.

S: Ah I see. So why don't they live here in Britain?

A: They (7) .... But her parents are quite old and she wanted to go back there.

S: So how long have they (8) .... there?

A: Not long. About six months.

S: So, what does he (9) .... of it?

A: It's quite hard. It's very different to Britain and he doesn't (10) .... much of their language. That's why he's teaching English. He can't work as an engineer.

S: He must really love her!

A: Yes, I suppose so.

Discuss these questions with a partner.

1. Do you know anyone who lives abroad? Why do they live there?

2. Would you like to live abroad?

10 | Pronunciation: the letter 'o'

The letter 'o' can be pronounced in lots of different ways. For example:

/ə/	second
/ɒ/	not
/ʌ/	come
/ʊ/	good
/uː/	food
/əʊ/	know
/ɔː/	poor

🎧 **Listen and repeat the sounds and words.**

Look at the grid. Try to find a way from START to FINISH which only uses the sound /ɒ/. You can only go → , ← or ↓ .

🎧 **Now listen and check your answer.**

START			
hot	open	woke up	cold
cost	sorry	lost	found
for	took	job	could
move	lose	on	once
come	stop	wrong	road
took	a lot	window	company
second	top	long	golf
good	transport	corner	problems
			FINISH

11 | Collocation

Now find another way from START to FINISH by choosing the correct words to complete the sentences below.

1. It's very .... in here.

2. Could you .... the window?

3. .... , what did you say?

4. Sorry I'm late. I got .... on the way here.

5. I'm not working at the moment. I'm looking for a ....

6. .... you show me how to get there on this map?

7. A: So how often do you do that?
   B: Usually .... a week.

8. A: Is there a bank near here?
   B: Yes, there's one on this .... , on the left.

9. I was late because I got on the .... bus.

10. It's cold in here. Could you close the .... ?

11. A: How .... have you been doing that?
    B: Quite a .... time. Maybe four or five years.

12. A: Is there a photocopying place near here?
    B: Yes, there's one just round the ....

13. There are a lot of .... in my country.

It's half past seven. • It's a quarter to six. • Is that the time? • I should go. I'm late. • It'll probably take [an] hour to get there. • What time do you want to meet? • What time's your flight? • We need to be at [the] station by six. • I'm exhausted. • Let's go out and do something. • What time did you get to bed last nig[ht]? • When was the first time you came here? • I can't remember. • It was a long time ago. • I was re[ally] nervous. • It went very well. • I was really prou[d] [of] myself. • My parents got divorced last year.

13 | What time is it?

Conversation

1 | Using vocabulary: telling the time

Match the times with the clocks.

1. It's five to three. ☐
2. It's five past three. ☐
3. It's a quarter past six. ☐
4. It's a quarter to five. ☐
5. It's ten to five. ☐
6. It's five to ten. ☐
7. It's half past six. ☐
8. It's half past seven. ☐

a

b

c

d

e

f

g

h

Real English: a quarter past / quarter past

You can say either a quarter past / to or quarter past / to. Both are natural and correct. You can also say half past six or six thirty.

---

2 | Listening: *What time?*

🎧 **You are going to listen to four conversations. In each one, people talk about times. As you listen, complete these sentences.**

1. It's .... o'clock now.
2. a. She went to bed at ....
   b. She got up at ....
3. a. His flight's at ....
   b. They should leave the house at ....
4. a. The film starts at ....
   b. They decide to meet at ....

Compare what you heard with a partner. Can you remember anything else you heard?

3 | Listen again

You are going to listen to Conversation 4 between Roger and Jane again. Before you listen, try to complete the conversation. Compare your ideas with a partner.

R: So what time (1) .... you want to meet tonight?

J: I'm not (2) .... What time is it now?

R: 4.30.

J: OK. Well, what time (3) .... the film start?

R: Eight.

J: Right. Well, I (4) .... to go home first and have a shower and (5) .... my clothes. That'll probably (6) .... me an hour.

R: OK. So (7) .... meet at seven. Is that OK?

J: Yes, that's fine. Where do you want to meet?

R: Let's just meet outside the (8) ....

J: OK. See you later.

R: Bye.

🎧 **Listen again and see if you were right. Then practise reading the conversation with your partner.**

Translate these expressions from the conversations.

1. I should go. I'm late for work.
2. I'm exhausted.
3. Some friends came to my house for dinner.
4. How long does it take to get there from here?
5. What time do you want to meet tonight?
6. Let's just meet outside the cinema.

4 | Common questions

Match the questions with the answers.

1. What time does the match start?
2. What time does the film start?
3. What time's your flight?
4. What time's your train?

a. Seven thirty-five, so I need to get to the airport by about five thirty.

b. Three o'clock, so we need to get to the stadium by half past two.

c. Twenty-five past nine, so we need to get to the cinema by ten past.

d. Five to four, so I need to get to the station by a quarter to.

Now match these questions with the answers.

5. What time do you finish work?
6. What time did you go to bed last night?
7. What time do you want to meet?
8. What time are you going to get to the party tonight?

e. Quite late, actually. It was about midnight, I think.

f. Twenty past five, so let's meet outside my office at half past.

g. I'm not sure. I'll probably be there by nine.

h. I don't know. What time's good for you?

Practise asking and answering the questions with a partner.

Work with a new partner. Ask the same questions. Change the times in the answers and have conversations like this:

A: What time does the match start?

B: Eight o'clock.

A: Right, so we need to get to the stadium by a quarter to.

5 | Using grammar: *Let's*

When we're making plans with other people, we often make suggestions using Let's + verb. For example:

A: Let's meet outside my office at half past five.

B: OK.

Complete the conversations with the pairs of words in the box.

do + go   get + take   go + try   meet + say   see + try

1. A: What do you want to .... tonight?
   B: Let's .... and see a film.

2. A: What film do you want to .... ?
   B: Let's .... *Miss Snowblood*. It looks OK.

3. A: Which restaurant do you want to .... to?
   B: Let's .... that new Thai place. It looks good.

4. A: How do you want to .... there?
   B: Let's .... the train. It's quicker.

5. A: What time do you want to .... ?
   B: Let's .... at half past six – in front of the station.

6 | Practice

Work with a partner. Make plans for this evening. Use these questions.

- What do you want to do tonight?
- Where do you want to meet?
- What time do you want to meet?

Make suggestions using Let's + verb.

> For more information on using *Let's*, see G15.

Reading

1 | Using grammar: making questions with the past simple

Complete these questions with the past simple form of the verbs.

1. When was the first time you .... abroad? (travel)
2. When was the first time you .... on a plane? (go)
3. When was the first time you .... someone? (kiss)
4. When was the first time you .... someone from a different country? (meet)
5. When was the first time you .... somewhere without your parents? (stay)
6. What was the first record / CD you .... ? (buy)
7. What was the first film you .... at the cinema? (see)
8. What was the first job you .... ? (have)

Now ask some other students the questions. Try to use some of these expressions when you answer.

- I can't remember.
- I've never done anything like that.
- It was when I was at school / university.
- It was when I was about 15 or 16.

To continue the conversation, ask and answer like this:

A: Did you enjoy it?

B: Yes, it was great.

or: It was OK.

or: It was awful.

or: I don't want to talk about it, if you don't mind.

2 | Before you read

You are going to read about three first-time experiences. First, decide which photos you think these words go with.

awful	it went really well
grades	nervous
I felt really grown-up	not very friendly
I got paid	washing up
I wrote to a pen pal	

A

My first job

B

The first time I went abroad

C

The first time I spoke in public

3 | While you read

🎧 **Now read the text on the opposite page and check your ideas. Did you guess correctly?**

4 | After you read

Discuss these questions with a partner.

1. Did the three people enjoy their experiences? How do you know?
2. Have you ever had any experiences like these? When?

Now cover the text. Use the photos and the expressions in Activity 2 to help you tell as much of the stories as you can remember.

Do you remember the first time?

They say you never forget the first time you do some things. Sometimes the first time is exciting, sometimes it's painful, but one thing is certain – we all remember many of our first-time experiences. We asked three people about experiences that they remember. Here's what they told us.

Hugh (17)

My parents got divorced a few years ago and I live with my dad now. He works really hard, but we don't have much money. I started working part-time a couple of years ago. I've got a job in a restaurant, washing up and chopping vegetables. I get paid £15 a night and I still remember how I felt when I first got paid. It was brilliant. I was really proud of myself. I felt really grown-up. My dad was pleased too – he didn't have to worry so much about giving me money!

Jeremie (22)

I grew up in a small town in the south of France and I was 16 when I went abroad for the first time. I went to stay with an English family in Huddersfield, in the north of England. I studied English at school, and everyone in my class wrote to English pen pals and then went to stay with their families. I thought it was going to be great, but really it was awful! It rained all the time, the family weren't very friendly and I didn't really like my pen pal very much. I love travelling, but I'm afraid I don't want to visit England again!

Ruth (19)

The first time I spoke in public was really frightening. I was about 15 or 16 and in secondary school. I studied business and as part of the course, we all had to give ten-minute presentations. The teacher gave us grades for them – from A+ to E. I spent weeks planning what to say, but the night before, I was really nervous. I didn't sleep very well. I was lucky though, because it went really well. Everybody enjoyed it. I felt great. Now I'm studying economics at university and I have to give presentations all the time.

5 | Speaking

Write two more questions you'd like to ask other students in your class.

1. When was the first time you ... ?
2. What was the first ... you ... ?

Now ask some other students your questions.

6 | Word check

Complete the sentences with these words from the text.

afraid	divorced	frightening	proud
all	exciting	give	spent

1. I had a great time when I went abroad for the first time. It was really ....
2. My parents got .... when I was 13.
3. I felt really .... of myself when I passed my exams.
4. The weather was awful. It rained .... the time.
5. I'm .... I didn't really like England.
6. I thought I was going to die. It was really ....
7. I have to .... a presentation at work next Monday.
8. I .... weeks thinking about what to say to her.

7 | Pronunciation: /ʃ/

⌒ **Listen and repeat the sounds with /ʃ/. Look at the picture on page 145 for help if you need to.**

⌒ **Listen and repeat these words.**

share	short	shut
shower	shirt	English
cash machine	shoes	station
should	shelves	

⌒ **Listen to eight sentences and write them down.**

Compare what you wrote with the tapescript at the back of the book. Then practise saying the sentences.

I can't see the board. • Can you get that magazine from the top shelf? • Thanks. • The sun's re
bright. • I can't think with all this noise. • What have you got in there? It's really heavy. • They pla
really well. • I got hurt really badly. • I broke my arm when I was six. • It's a bit dark in here. • I'll turn
light on if you like. • I'm cold. Could you lend me your jacket? • Can you check on the computer? • I
stupid. I crossed the road without looking.
show you if you like. • I can't cook very we

14 Can you help me?

Conversation

1 Using grammar: *I can't*

Match the sentences with the pictures.

1. I can't lift it.
2. I can't get the top off.
3. I can't reach.
4. I can't do this exercise.
5. I can't hear you.
6. I can't think.
7. I can't see the board.
8. I can't find it on the map.

Translate the sentences into your language.

Work with a partner and test each other.
Student A: Point to the pictures.
Student B: With the sentences covered, say the sentences.

> For more information on using *can* and *can't*, see G16.

2 Practice

Which of these things CAN'T you do?

- drive
- cook very well
- play a musical instrument
- read without glasses
- ride a bicycle
- run very fast

Have conversations like these with a partner.

A: I can't drive.
B: No, me neither.
A: I can't cook very well.
B: Really? I can.

3 | Listening: *Sorry, could you help me, please?*

🎧 **Listen to eight conversations. They are the same situations as in Activity 1. Complete the questions you hear with one or two words.**

1. Sorry, could you .... with this suitcase, please?

2. Can you see if you can .... , please?

3. Excuse me, you're tall. Can you get that magazine from the .... , please?

4. Can you help me with .... , please?

5. Sorry, can you .... , please?

6. I'm sorry. Could you turn the music .... , please?

7. I'm sorry, Bill. Can you .... the curtains, please?

8. OK, sorry. Can you .... on the map, please?

Look at the words in the box. What or who in the conversations was described using these words?

heavy   tight   quiet   loud   bright

Listen again if you need to.

🎧 **Listen and repeat the can / could questions from the conversations.**

Real English: Could you ... ?

We often say could you and not 'can you' because it's more polite – especially if you don't know the person you are speaking to. We also say I'm sorry or Excuse me before the question – and please at the end.

4 | Speaking

Role play the eight conversations you heard in Activity 3. Use the pictures and the language from Activities 1 and 3.

5 | Further practice

Work with a partner. Write conversations like those in Activity 3. Use the ideas below. Look at the tapescript at the back of the book if you want to.

1. A: Excuse / move? / not see the board.
   B: Sorry / see now?
   A: thanks.

2. A: Sorry / turn the stereo up? / not hear it.
   B: Sure / a bit quiet.
   A: thanks.

3. A: sorry / turn the light on / not see the writing very well.
   B: Sure / a bit dark / better?
   A: Yes thanks.

4. A: Sorry / help us? / look for a restaurant called La Mancha.
   B: Yes / in Thames Road.
   A: show us / map?
   B: Of course.

Now read your conversations with your partner.

6 | Using grammar: *well* and *good*

Well is an adverb; good is an adjective. We use well after a verb and good before a noun or with the verb *be*. Look at these examples:

- My mum can sing really well.
- My mum's a really good singer.
- The match was really good (NOT the match was really ~~well~~)

Do you know the opposites of well and good?

Choose the correct form.

1. I can't speak English very well / good.
2. I'm quite a well / good student.
3. My brother's a really badly / bad driver.
4. My team played really well / good in their last match.
5. My dad cooks really bad / badly.
6. I can't see very good / well.
7. The programme I watched last night was really bad / badly.
8. My gran can't hear very well / good.

Which of the sentences above are true for you? Can you change the false sentences to make them true? For example:

- I can speak English quite well.
- My brother's a really good driver.

▶ For more information on using adverbs and adjectives, see G17.

Reading

1 | Before you read

You are going to read two stories about people who were helped by strangers. The sentences below are all in the stories. Check any words you don't know. Put the sentences into two groups of five.

1. A bus hit me.
2. I was hurt quite badly.
3. I got to the airport the night before.
4. He was a nurse.
5. I slept there.
6. They checked the time of the flight on the computer.
7. A woman called an ambulance.
8. The date was wrong.
9. I was really hungry.
10. I broke several bones.

2 | While you read

∩ Read the stories and check your ideas. Did you guess correctly?

3 | Comprehension

Work with a partner. Try to answer the questions without looking at the text.

1. When's Terry's birthday?
2. Why did Terry sleep at the airport?
3. Why did Terry cry?
4. How much did the man give him?
5. What did Terry do with the money?
6. How did Li Ying get hurt?
7. What did Li Ying think of English people before the accident?
8. Why did she stay in hospital for a week?

Look at the text to check your answers.

The kindness of strangers

Terry

When I was 19, I went travelling for three months. I went to Israel and Egypt and a few other places in the Middle East. I had a plane ticket to get home on January 23rd. I remember the date because it's my birthday. I got to the airport the night before. I had to sleep there because my flight was quite early in the morning and I didn't have any money to pay for a hotel. I'd spent it all. At about six o'clock in the morning, I looked to see if my flight was on the TV screens, but it wasn't. I looked again at seven, but no. It was strange because my ticket said the flight was at 9.10. I went to ask someone what the problem was. They looked at my ticket and checked the time of the flight on the computer. 'I'm sorry,' they said 'This flight goes on January 25th!' The date was wrong. I had to wait two more days! I went and sat down on a seat and started to cry. I was really hungry, I had no money and I wanted my mum!

A man came up to me and asked, 'What's the matter?' I told him the story. 'Listen,' he said, 'I've got some money left. I'm not going to change it back to dollars. I was only going to buy some cigarettes with it. Take it. You need it more than me.'

He gave me the money and walked off. When I looked to see how much it was, I found I had more than £50 in shekels. It was enough money to go back into town and find a cheap place to stay and buy food for two days. I don't even know the man's name. It's the kindest thing anyone's ever done for me.

Li Ying

I was in London, studying English. One day, I visited a place called the Old Bailey. I went with some other students. We were in a big group. My friends crossed the road and I followed, but I didn't look. A bus came round the corner and hit me. I was hurt quite badly. Some people got off the bus. I remember one was a tall black man. He told people not to move me and he looked after me because he was a nurse. Another woman called an ambulance on her mobile phone. Someone else brought me some water.

Before that, I'd been in England for two months. I thought English people were quite cold and not very nice. People were quite rude sometimes and didn't help, but these people were very kind.

I broke several bones and I was in hospital for a week. I'm OK now, though.

4 | Speaking

Discuss these questions in groups.

1. Have you ever broken a bone? Do you know anyone who has? Which one? When?

2. Have you ever missed a plane? What happened?

Use some of these sentences.

- No, never.
- Yes, I broke my arm / leg / foot / hand / finger / nose.
- It was five / six / ten years ago.
- I was six / ten / twenty.

5 | Using vocabulary: helping people

Complete the collocations with the verbs in the box.

| lend me   show me   stay   take me |

1. .... to the station / to hospital
2. .... how to do it / where to go
3. .... some money / your jacket
4. .... with you / for a week

Now complete these collocations with the verbs in the box.

| carry   give me   help me   push |

5. .... my bags / the buggy up the stairs
6. .... some money / some food
7. .... the car / the buggy
8. .... move house / look for my keys

What are the past forms of the verbs above?

Tell a partner about someone you have helped or someone who has helped you. For example:

- A friend lent me some money yesterday.
- I showed a tourist how to get to the train station.
- A few days ago, I helped someone carry a buggy up some stairs.

6 | Using grammar: *I'll do it*

Look at these ways of offering to do things:

A: Look at this mess! It's so dirty!

B: It's OK. I'll help you clean up, if you like.

A: I can't do it now.

B: It's OK. I'll do it, if you like.

Write responses to the statements below with I'll ... if you like and verbs from Activity 5.

1. 'I haven't got any money.'
2. 'I can't find my keys.'
3. 'I'm going to miss my train.'
4. 'It's raining again! I'm going to get really wet.'
5. 'I don't know how to get there.'

Practise your conversations with a partner.

> For more information on making offers with *I'll*, see G18.

7 | Pronunciation: /k/ and /g/

🎧 **Listen and repeat the sounds with /k/ and /g/. Look at the pictures on page 145 for help if you need to.**

🎧 **Listen and repeat these words.**

cook	group	get	back	kiss
crossed	close	big	guess	goes
give	broke	keys	buggy	

🎧 **Listen to eight sentences and write them down. Compare what you wrote with the tapescript at the back of the book. Then practise saying the sentences.**

I'm going to see a play at the theatre. • I need to tidy up the flat. • My room's in a mess at the mome
I think I'll probably go shopping. • I haven't really decided. • It depends on the weather. • I might just t
it easy. • It depends how I feel. • I'm going to be really busy. • I'll probably play football on Friday. • L
meet at the entrance to the shopping mall. • Sorry I missed you yesterday. • It's my fault. • I overslep

15 What're you doing this weekend

Conversation

1 | Using vocabulary: weekend activities

Complete the collocations with the verbs in the box.

cook	go	play	see	stay

1. .... dinner for some friends
2. .... a play at the theatre
3. .... shopping for some new clothes
4. .... at home
5. .... computer games

Now complete these collocations with the verbs in the box.

go	meet	study	take	tidy up

6. .... it easy
7. .... to a disco
8. .... the flat
9. .... English
10. .... some friends

Which of these activities do you sometimes / often / usually do at the weekend? Which of these activities are you going to do this weekend?

Tell a partner. Use these sentence starters:

- I sometimes / often / usually ... at the weekend.
- I'm going to ... on Saturday morning / afternoon / night.

2 | Listening: *So what're you doing this weekend?*

∩ **Listen to three conversations. Which things in Activity 1 do the people talk about? Compare what you heard with a partner.**

3 | Listen again

Listen to Conversation 3 between Shona and Mel again. Complete the conversation.

S: So what're you doing this weekend?

M: I'm not really sure yet, actually. I don't have (1) .... What about you?

S: Well, tonight I'm just going to stay at home. I might study some English. It depends (2) .... If I feel lazy, I think I'll probably just (3) .... instead.

M: Oh, OK.

S: Yes, and then tomorrow, I think I'll probably go shopping for some new clothes.

M: Oh really? (4) .... fun.

S: Well, look, why don't you (5) .... ?

M: Really? Is that OK?

S: Yes, of course. I don't really like going shopping on my own.

M: OK, thanks. So where (6) .... to meet?

S: Let's meet at the entrance to the shopping mall.

M: OK. What time?

S: (7) .... or is that too early?

M: No, that's fine. It's great.

S: OK. Well, I'll see you tomorrow.

M: OK. Thanks again.

S: (8) ....

Practise reading the conversation with a partner.

4 | Using grammar: *going to / will*

In the conversations, you heard these sentences:
- I think I'll probably go shopping for some new clothes.
- On Sunday, I'm going to study for my English exam.

We use probably with 'll to show we are not 100% sure about our plans. When we have plans and we are 100% sure, we use going to.

Complete the sentences with I'm going to or I'll.

1. I'm not sure, but I think .... probably go shopping with my mum.
2. .... go shopping for shoes with my wife tomorrow.
3. .... meet my husband and go to the cinema.
4. I'm not really sure yet. I think .... probably just write some e-mails and tidy up my flat.
5. .... go on a trip to Holland for three days.
6. It depends on my husband. If he's busy, I think .... probably stay at home and cook.
7. It depends on the weather. If it's nice, I think .... probably go to the beach.
8. .... study for my Spanish exam next week.
9. It depends how I feel. If I feel OK, I think .... probably go to a disco with some friends.
10. .... stay at home and read tonight.

🎧 **Listen and check your answers. Then repeat the sentences.**

> For more information on using *going to* and *'ll*, see G19.

Real English: I might

If we are only 50% sure of our plans for the future, we say I might. It means 'Maybe I will'. For example:

I'm not really sure about tomorrow. I might just stay at home.

I might cook tonight. I might not. It depends how I feel.

5 | Using vocabulary: *I'm not sure*

Here are six expressions to show your plans are not 100% certain. Put the words in order.

1. know / don't / I
2. really / sure / I'm / not / yet
3. any / have / I / plans / don't
4. decided / really / I / haven't
5. depends / it / I / feel / how
6. weather / on / the / it / depends

Now practise saying the six expressions.

6 | Practice

Ask some other students What're you doing tonight / this weekend? Try to use the grammar and vocabulary from these pages.

Reading

1 | Using vocabulary

You are going to read a story about a man called Rick who has arranged to meet someone. The verbs in this activity are all in the text.

Complete the collocations with the verbs in the box.

> feel   look   order   take   wear

1. .... out of the window / around the room / angry
2. .... nice clothes / a short skirt
3. .... happy / uncomfortable / embarrassed
4. .... some food / a bottle of wine
5. .... a seat / a coffee break together

Now complete these collocations with the verbs in the box.

> forget   pour   serve   sit   taste

6. .... a customer / you in a moment
7. .... some wine into a glass / some water
8. .... to bring my mobile phone / her name
9. .... by the window / down / outside
10. .... really nice / good / horrible

Work with a partner.

Student A: Act the collocations. **DON'T** use any words.

Student B: With your book closed, say the collocations.

What are the past simple forms of the verbs in the collocations?

2 | While you read (1)

🎧 Now read the first part of the story and think about these questions.

1. Who is Rick going to meet?
2. What will probably happen next?

Discuss your answers with a partner.

The meeting

RICK ARRIVED at the café fifteen minutes early. He quickly looked around, but she wasn't there.

'Can I help you?' asked a waiter.

'No, it's OK. I'm waiting for a friend. I'm early.'

'Of course. Well, if you'd like to take a seat, I'll serve you in a moment. Are you going to sit outside?'

It was sunny outside, but it was still only April. It might be a bit cold later. 'I think we'll sit inside, thanks,' he said. 'Can I have the table by the window?'

'Sure,' said the waiter, 'I'll be with you in a minute.'

Rick sat down and looked out of the window. He waited. Outside, an old man was selling seeds to give to the birds. A little boy was chasing the birds. He was shouting and laughing. The old man looked angry.

Rick read the menu. He ordered a bottle of wine and two wine glasses. He waited. He looked out of the window.

'Is this seat taken?' a woman asked.

He turned round, surprised by her voice. 'Sorry?'

'Can I take this seat?' the woman repeated.

'Er ... no, sorry. I'm waiting for a friend.'

The woman looked at him. She looked a bit angry. He felt uncomfortable. Embarrassed. Was Debbie really a friend? He didn't know her very well. They'd only had a few conversations at work. They sometimes took their coffee break together.

3 | While you read (2)

∩ **Read the rest of the story and find out what happens.**

Rick looked at the two empty wine glasses. He waited. He waited for Debbie. He poured himself a glass of wine. He looked out of the window. It was getting dark and it was a bit cold. He thought about Debbie. He thought about the clothes she wore. He smiled. It WAS a good idea to sit inside.

The waiter came. 'Would you like to order something to eat or would you like to wait … for your friend?'

Rick didn't like the way the waiter said 'your friend'. He thought the waiter was laughing at him.

'Yes, could I just have some olives, please?'

He waited. He didn't have his mobile phone with him. Stupid! He forgot to pick it up when he ran out of the house. Maybe she was trying to phone him now. He ate the olives. They tasted very good. The wine was good too.

He ordered steak and chips. He poured some more wine in his glass. He thought about his small flat. It was clean and tidy for the first time in months. 'I think I'll finish this food and go home – the Champions League football is on TV later,' he thought to himself. He felt quite happy.

When he got home, he went into the kitchen and gave the cat some milk. He saw his mobile phone on the table. It had six messages. He listened to them. Then he sat down and turned on the TV.

4 | Comprehension

Discuss these questions with a partner.

1. What do you think happened to Debbie?
2. What do you think the messages on Rick's mobile were?
3. Do you think Rick is a nice man?
4. Do you feel sorry for Rick? Why / why not?

5 | Listening

∩ **Listen to the messages on Rick's phone. Complete the sentences with ONE word.**

1. I'm going to be .... I had a .... at work.
2. a. The ....'s awful.
   b. I hope you get this ....
3. I've lost the piece of .... with the name of the café.
4. I'm really sorry. It's my .... Call me later.
5. a. I'm just .... what time we're going to meet tomorrow.
   b. .... you!
6. I'm home. You've got my ....

Discuss these questions with a partner.

1. Who's phoning Rick in the fifth message?
2. What do you think of Rick?
3. What do you think happens next time Rick and Lucy meet?

6 | Saying sorry for being late

Complete the sentences with the words in the box.

awful	lost	problem
forgot	missed	work
left	overslept	

1. I got .... on the way here.
2. I .... the bus.
3. There was a .... on the train.
4. The traffic was ....
5. I had a problem at ....
6. I was talking to a friend and I .... the time.
7. My mum phoned just before I .... the house.
8. I .... I woke up an hour late.

Which are good reasons for being late? Which are bad?

Have conversations like this with a partner:

A: Sorry I'm late. I got lost on the way here.

B: That's OK. You're here now.

7 | Pronunciation: /l/

∩ **Listen and repeat the sounds with /l/. Look at the picture on page 145 for help if you need to.**

∩ **Look at the words in the box. Listen and tick the words you hear.**

lots / let's / late / light / left / lost /
plans / plays / place / plate / please /
ill / I'll / well / sell / shelf / still /
call / tall / fall / felt / fell / full / pull

∩ **Listen to eight sentences and write them down. Compare what you wrote with the tapescript at the back of the book. Then practise saying the sentences.**

I'm feeling a bit sick. • Do you want something for it? • I think I'll just lie down for a moment. • Do
want me to help you? • Maybe you should just go home. • I'll be all right. • What have you done to y
arm? • I hurt it playing basketball. • I hurt it dancing. • I need a holiday! • I'm so bored I want to di
I wish you were here. • What was the weather like? • It was awful! • We spent all week lying on
beach. • What was the hotel like? • It was great. • The kids
a great time. • See you soon. • Poor you! • I've got a headac

16 Are you OK?

Conversation

1 Using vocabulary: *Are you OK?*

Complete the conversations on the right with the words in the boxes.

Spend five minutes memorising the five conversations. Then work with a partner. Cover the conversations and use the pictures to have the conversations. Start by asking Are you OK?

Conversation 1

| coffee   home   tired |

A: Are you OK?
B: Yes. I'm just a bit ....
A: Oh, right. Do you want to go .... ?
B: No, it's OK. I'll be all right. I just need a ....

Conversation 2

| lie down   OK   sick |

A: Are you OK?
B: No. I'm feeling a bit ....
A: Oh no. Do you want to .... ? You can use my bed.
B: Yes, thanks. I'm sure I'll be .... in a bit.

Conversation 3

| a bit   a headache   an aspirin |

A: Are you OK?
B: No, not really. I've got ....
A: Oh no. Do you want .... ? I think I've got some.
B: No, it's OK. I think I'll just lie down for ....

Conversation 4

| an ambulance   cuts   fine |

A: Are you OK?
B: Yes, I think so. It's just a few small .... Thanks.
A: Are you sure? Do you want me to call .... ?
B: No, no, really. I'll be ....

Conversation 5

| eat   get   hungry |

A: Are you OK?
B: Yes, but I'm quite ....
A: Do you want me to make you something to .... ?
B: No, it's OK. I'll .... something on my way home.

2 | Using grammar: *Do you want ... ?*

Look at these three patterns from Activity 1.

- Do you want an aspirin?
- Do you want to go home?
- Do you want me to call an ambulance?

Match the patterns with the question endings.

1. Do you want ... ?   ☐ ☐ ☐ ☐
2. Do you want to ... ?   ☐ ☐ ☐ ☐
3. Do you want me to ... ?   ☐ ☐ ☐ ☐

a.   make you a sandwich

b.   something for it

c.   have a rest

d.   a glass of water

e.   make you some rice

f.   go outside and get some fresh air

g.   help you

h.   some cake

i.   have something to eat

j.   a plaster

k.   sit down

l.   take you to hospital

> **Real English:** something for it
>
> In this expression, it means any illness or pain. Something for it could be some medicine or a drink or some food which will help you feel better.
>
> *A: I've got a stomach ache.*
> *B: Oh no, do you want something for it?*

What do you take for a cold?

3 | Practice

Have conversations like those in Activity 1. Change the questions. For example:

A: Are you OK?

B: Not really. I'm tired.

A: Oh, right. Do you want to have a rest?

B: No, it's OK. Let's finish this work. Then we can go home sooner.

4 | Listening: *You're very quiet*

🎧 **Listen to a conversation between Tracy, an English teacher, and Yong, a Korean student in her class. As you listen, answer these questions.**

1. What two problems does Yong have?
2. Do you know why he has these problems?

5 | Listen again

Listen to the conversation again. Complete the conversation.

T: Yong. Are you OK? You're very quiet.

Y: No, not (1) .... I'm not feeling very well.

T: You don't look very well. Do you want to go and (2) .... a glass of water?

Y: Yes. I think I need to (3) .... some fresh air.

T: Maybe you should just go home.

Y: No, it's OK. I think if I go out for a (4) .... minutes, I'll be OK. I'll go now. I'll be back in five minutes.

T: Of course, take your time. There's no (5) .... Yong! What have you done to your leg?

Y: I (6) .... it dancing.

T: Dancing?

Y: Yes. It's difficult to explain.

T: OK, I'm sorry. Can someone open the door for Yong? Thanks.

Y: Thanks. I'll be (7) .... in five minutes.

T: Sure. As I say, take your time.

Y: Thanks.

T: Poor Yong!

Practise reading the conversation with a partner.

6 | What have you done to your leg?

Work with a partner. Write five conversations using the ideas below.

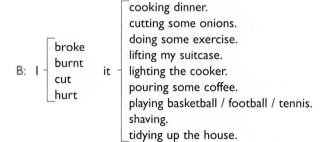

A: What have you done to your ⎧ arm?
                                back?
                                face?
                                finger?
                                foot?
                                head?
                                nose? ⎭

B: I ⎧ broke   ⎫ it ⎧ cooking dinner.
       burnt   cutting some onions.
       cut   doing some exercise.
       hurt ⎭   lifting my suitcase.
                       lighting the cooker.
                       pouring some coffee.
                       playing basketball / football / tennis.
                       shaving.
                       tidying up the house. ⎭

Practise reading your conversations with your partner.

7 | Practice

Tell some other students about a time you hurt yourself. For example:

- Last week I hurt my back doing some gardening.
- I once cut my arm really badly playing with my brother.

Reading

1 | Using vocabulary: holiday activities

Look at the list of activities. Which do you think are boring (B)? Which are fun (F)?

1. going to amusement arcades
2. going to discos
3. going to museums
4. going to cafés or bars
5. going fishing
6. going to theme parks
7. walking in the countryside
8. lying on the beach

Compare your ideas with a partner. Have conversations like these:

A: I think going to amusement arcades is fun.

B: Me too.

A: I think walking in the countryside is boring.

B: Really? I think it's fun.

2 | While you read

⌒ **You are going to read a letter from Linda and Mike to some friends of theirs. Linda and Mike are on holiday with their children. As you read, try to answer these questions.**

1. Where are Linda and Mike staying?
2. Are they having a good time or a bad time?
3. What kind of things do they like doing when they are on holiday?

Real English:
We spent all afternoon there

We can spend time in a place and we can spend time doing something.

We spent all afternoon at the zoo.
I spent the day in bed.
We spent all week lying on the beach.
I spent all weekend studying.

Family Holidays

Dear Ray and Sheila,

Hope you're both well. We're having a lovely time in Dorset. The weather is nice and we're staying near the sea. The countryside here is lovely and we're going to go for a nice long walk later today. It's good to be out in the fresh air, getting some exercise. The kids are having a good time as well. Jenny and Michael are sleeping in the little tent and it's nice to see them having fun together. Jenny complains about things sometimes, but most of the time she's OK. We spent three days on the beach last week and I think she enjoyed that. She went swimming a lot.

Yesterday we took the kids to a local museum and that was very interesting. We spent all afternoon there.

Anyway, we're going to be back home next week. Maybe we can meet for dinner sometime soon.

All the best,

Linda and Mike

3 | Speaking

Discuss these questions with a partner.

1. Did you ever go on holiday with your family when you were a teenager?
2. Where to? Did you usually have a good time?
3. Do you like doing the same kind of things as the rest of your family?

4 | While you read

🎧 **You are going to read an e-mail from Linda and Mike's daughter – Jenny – to a friend of hers. As you read, try to answer these questions.**

1. Is she having a good time or a bad time?
2. What kind of things does she like doing when she is on holiday?
3. Is there anything both Jenny and her parents like doing?

5 | Using grammar: *What was it like?*

We often ask What was your holiday like? when we want someone to tell us about their holiday. We can use similar questions to ask about the food, the weather, the hotel, the people, etc.

Match the questions with the answers.

1. What was your holiday like? ☐
2. What was the town like? ☐
3. What was the hotel like? ☐
4. What was the food like? ☐
5. What was the weather like? ☐
6. What were the people like? ☐

a. It was OK. The rooms were nice and big.
b. It was great. We had a really good time.
c. They were great. They were really nice and friendly.
d. It was awful! It rained nearly every day.
e. It was great. It was really delicious – but I think I ate too much!
f. It was awful! It was too small. There was nothing to do there.

🎧 **Listen and check your answers.**

Kate,

Help! I'm on holiday with my parents in Dorset – and I'm so bored I want to die! We arrived here ten days ago, but it feels like ten years ago. There's nothing to do here – no cafés, no amusement arcades, nothing! My mum and dad made me go to a museum yesterday and it was really, really boring. Why do they think I'm interested in old plates and pictures and rubbish like that?

The only good thing was going to the beach last week. I wore that new swimsuit I bought when I went shopping with you. I met some really nice boys there. They were on holiday too.

Today my parents want us to go for a walk in the hills. My dad is wearing all his walking clothes and he looks really stupid. I don't want people to see me with him. It's embarrassing! Michael is really annoying too. I have to sleep in the same tent as him and he cries every night – and his feet smell! I wish you were here. Four more days to go. I'll phone you when I'm back and we can go out and have some fun.

See you soon,
Jenny

6 | Practice

Think about the last time you went on holiday. Decide how to answer the questions in Activity 5. Ask your teacher for help if you need to. Then ask a partner the questions. Give true answers.

7 | Pronunciation: sounding positive

🎧 **We can say It was OK in two different ways. Listen to two people. Which person sounds more positive?**

🎧 **Now listen and repeat six short sentences. Make sure that you sound positive.**

I don't really like squid. • I hate prawns! • They're a kind of bean. They're round. • It's quite soft. • What you want for the main course? • Do you like spicy food? • That sounds nice. • You should try this. It's re nice. • What would you like to drink? • Have you got anything non-alcoholic? • I'll have a Coke, pleas Do you want still or sparkling? • It was disgusting! • It tastes like fish. • What's this made from? • I'm thank you. • I should go getting late.

17 Are you ready to order?

Conversation

1 | Using vocabulary: food

Put the words in the box into the different groups.

carrots	lamb	oranges	potatoes	squid
cheese	mussels	pasta	prawns	watermelon
chicken	nuts	pork	rice	

meat
beef
....
....
....

seafood
crab
....
....

other kinds of food
beans
fish
....
....
....
....

vegetables
cabbage
....
....

fruit
bananas
....
....

Which of these foods DON'T you like? Tell a partner. Use these sentence starters.

- I don't really like ... .
- I hate .... .

2 | It's a kind of ...

Cover the words in Activity 1. Match the questions and answers.

1. What are prawns? ☐
2. What's cabbage? ☐
3. What's pork? ☐
4. What's watermelon? ☐
5. What are peanuts? ☐
6. What are chickpeas? ☐

a. It's a kind of vegetable. It's green.
b. It's a kind of meat. It's from a pig.
c. They're a kind of nut.
d. They're a kind of seafood. They're pink.
e. They're a kind of bean. They're round.
f. It's a kind of fruit. It's really big. It's red inside, with lots of seeds.

squid
mussel
crab
beans
prawns
watermelon

3 | Practice

Work with a partner.
Student A: Look at page 160.
Student B: Look at page 158.
Ask each other about the food items in the box. Use your pictures to describe the food your partner asks about. Use these expressions.

A: What's ... ?

B: It's a kind of ... .

Do you know the name of any other kinds of fruit / meat / cheese / fish / nut?

4 | Listening: *What would you like?*

🎧 **Listen to a conversation between Kate and Robert. They are in a restaurant in Coimbra, Portugal, where Robert teaches English. How does Robert describe these dishes?**

- requeijão
- crème de camarão
- cabrito asado
- frango no churrasco

What does Kate decide to eat?

5 | Listen again

Listen again and complete the conversation.

K: This is very nice.

R: Yes, it is, isn't it?

K: Do you come here often?

R: (1) .... Especially in the summer. You can sit outside.

K: Mmm.

R: So what would you like?

K: I don't know. What's 'requeijão'?

R: It's (2) .... cheese. It's quite soft and white.

K: OK. I don't really like cheese. What about 'crème de camarão'?

R: Oh, that's a kind of soup. It's made with ... I don't know the name in English. It's a kind of seafood. They're like small mussels.

K: OK. Well, that (3) .... nice. I'll have that for a starter.

R: And what do you want for the main course?

K: I don't know. Can you (4) .... anything?

R: Right, well, the 'cabrito asado' is very nice, if you like goat.

K: Mmm, I don't really like red meat. I (5) .... chicken or fish really.

R: OK. Well, if you like chicken, you should try the 'frango no churrasco'. Do you like spicy food, because it's quite hot?

K: Yes, (6) ....

R: Well, you should try that then. You'll love it.

K: OK.

R: Do you want rice or vegetables with that?

K: Vegetables are fine.

R: OK. What (7) .... to drink?

K: I'll just have water.

R: OK, are you sure? You don't want wine?

K: No thanks. Actually, (8) ....

R: OK – do you want sparkling or still water?

K: Still's fine.

R: OK.

Practise reading the conversation with a partner.

Real English: I'll have

When we order food, we say I'll have.

A: *What would you like as a starter?*

B: *I'll have the pasta, please.*

C: *Yes, and I'll have the tomato salad.*

---

6 | Speaking

Discuss these questions with a partner.

1. Do you like eating food from other countries?

2. Do you like any of these kinds of food?

British	French	Japanese	Mexican	Spanish
Chinese	Italian	Korean	Russian	Thai

3. Have you tried food from any other country? Did you like it?

7 | Restaurant questions

Match the orders with the questions the waiter / waitress asks.

1. I'll just have some water, please. ☐
2. I'll have a Coke, please. ☐
3. I'll have some wine, please. ☐
4. I'll have the fried chicken, please. ☐
5. I'll have a coffee, please. ☐

a. Would you like it with milk or without?

b. Would you like red or white?

c. Would you like that with chips or rice?

d. Would you like ice and lemon?

e. Would you like still or sparkling?

With a partner, have conversations like this:

A: Are you ready to order, Sir / Madam?

B: Yes, I'll have a coffee, please.

A: Do you want it with milk or without?

B: With, please.

8 | Role play

Work with a partner.
Student A: You are having dinner in a restaurant in Italy. Look at the menu on page 160.
Student B: You are from Italy. Look at the menu on page 159 with English translations.
Have a conversation like that in Activity 5.

Reading

1 Speaking

Discuss these questions in groups.

1. Do you like sweet / spicy / bitter things?
2. What was your favourite food when you were growing up?
3. What's your favourite food now?

2 While you read

🎧 **Read the text on the opposite page and decide who has bad food memories and who has good ones.** Underline **the words that tell you.**

Do any of these experiences remind you of people or stories you know? Tell a partner.

3 Word check

The missing words in these sentences are all in the text. Complete the sentences without looking at the text.

1. That .... me of something that happened to me once.
2. A: Mmm. This soup is delicious. What's it .... from?
   B: Carrots, beans, peas and lamb.
3. A: I can't eat this. It's horrible.
   B: I know. It's .... , isn't it?
4. The food she cooked was disgusting. When I got home, I was .... three times!
5. Mmm. This is the best pasta I have .... tasted.
6. The food last night was nice, but not .... good .... in the Turkish restaurant we went to last week.
7. I hated rice when I was young, but my mum .... me eat it.
8. I tried frogs' legs once. They were nice. They tasted .... chicken.

Now look at the text and check your answers.

4 Using vocabulary: having dinner at a friend's house

Decide who says these things. Is it the host (H) – the person who cooked the dinner – or the guest (G)? The first one has been done for you.

1. Wine! How lovely! (G)
2. Let me take your coat.
3. Mmm, that smells delicious. What are you cooking?
4. Would you like something to drink before we eat?
5. Have you got anything non-alcoholic?
6. OK. Dinner's ready.
7. Where would you like me to sit?
8. Mmm, this looks great.
9. Don't wait for me. Just start eating.
10. Mmm, this is delicious. What's in it?
11. Could I have some more?
12. Have you had enough?
13. I'm fine.
14. I'm full, thank you. It was great.
15. Would you like a coffee or tea or something?
16. I should go. It's getting late.
17. Thanks for a lovely meal.
18. Thanks for coming.

Now translate the eight expressions you like best into your language.

Do you say all these things in your country? Is there anything you DON'T say? Why not?

Do you usually take a present for the host? What do you normally take?

5 Writing

Work with a partner. Write the conversation you have when one or two people visit your house for dinner. Use some of the expressions in Activity 4.

Act out your ideas for another pair of students.

Food memories

A recent book by the English chef Nigel Slater, Toast, talks about the food he ate when he was growing up. As he describes the food, it reminds him of people and stories. We thought this was a great idea and so we decided to ask some people to do the same.

Ian: white sausages

I once went on an exchange. I stayed with a foreign family for two weeks. They were very nice and they cooked some lovely food, but one day they cooked me some white sausages. I don't know what they were made from, but they were disgusting. I didn't want to be rude, so I ate them all. That night I was very sick. I was sick in my bed and I was sick in the bathroom. I can't even look at sausages now.

Jackie: apple pie

Eating apple pie always reminds me of my gran. She made the best apple pie I have ever tasted. It was sweet and light and warm – like her! If I'm in a restaurant and apple pie is on the menu, I always eat it – but it's never as good as Gran's.

Lee: meat and vegetables

I never liked vegetables when I was young. My parents made me eat them – carrots, peas, everything. I always ate the vegetables first and left the meat until last. It was better that way. Now I like vegetables, but I still leave the meat until last. It's strange, isn't it?

Mary: snake

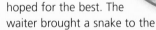

I had snake once when I was travelling in Asia. I went to a restaurant and the menu was all in the local language, which I didn't really understand. I ordered two or three things and hoped for the best. The waiter brought a snake to the table – it was still alive – and killed it in front of me. I was really shocked. He then took it back to the kitchen to cook it. It was actually really nice. It tasted like fish.

6 | Pronunciation: /w/

🎧 **Listen and repeat the sound /w/. Look at the picture on page 145 for help if you need to.**

🎧 **Listen and repeat these words.**

water	waiter	would	week	when	sweet
wine	waitress	want	where	what	Sweden

🎧 **Listen to six sentences and write them down. Compare what you wrote with the tapescript at the back of the book. Then practise saying the sentences.**

7 | Pronunciation: linking

When one word ends in 'o' and the next starts with a vowel – *a*, *e*, *i*, *o* or *u* – we usually link the words together so that they sound like one word.

🎧 **Listen and repeat these expressions.**

1. go on
2. go ahead
3. so early
4. no eggs
5. to India
6. go and get
7. two or three
8. Who are you?

I really like Gap. They sell really nice things there. • Where's the stationery department? • They're on top shelf. • It's in the fourth aisle. • Do you sell batteries? • I'll show you where they are. • Would you any cash back? • Could you sign there, please? • Can I pay by card? • Do you sell socks? • I'm a secu guard in a big department store. • I'm a cashier in a supermarket. • It's quite boring. • The money's very good. • It's quite stressful. • It's not much fun have to wear a uniform to work. I hate it!

18 Do you sell ... ?

Conversation

1 | Speaking

Discuss these questions with a partner. Use the words in red to help you.

A: Do you like shopping?

B: Yes, I love it. / It's OK. / No, I hate it.

A: How often do you go?

B: All the time. / Quite often. / Not very often. / Hardly ever.

A: What's your favourite shop? Why?

B: I really like ... . It's cheap. / It sells everything. / They sell really nice things there.

A: Is there a department store where you live? Do you shop there?

2 | Using vocabulary: parts of a department store

Make sure that you understand the words on the left. Match these things with the parts of a department store where you can find them.

1. sandals   a. Cosmetics
2. lipstick   b. Ladieswear
3. envelopes   c. Menswear
4. toothbrush   d. Toiletries
5. boxer shorts   e. The Shoe Department
6. dress   f. The Sports Department
7. swimsuit   g. The Stationery Department

When was the last time you bought any of these things? Where did you buy them?

3 | Using vocabulary: parts of the shop

Label the pictures below with the words in the box.

the aisle	the first floor	the stairs
the basement	the ground floor	the second floor
the bottom shelf	the lift	the till
the escalator	the main entrance	the top shelf

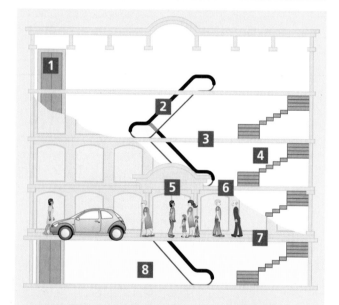

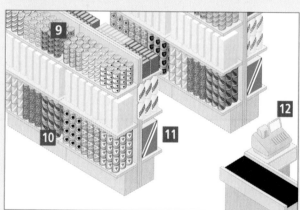

4 | Listening: *Do you sell swimsuits?*

🎧 **Listen to four conversations. Each one is in a different shop. Answer these questions.**

1. What does each customer want to find?
2. Where are the things they want?

Compare your answers with a partner. Listen again if you need to.

5 | Listen again

Listen to the conversations again and complete the sentences with one or two words.

Conversation 1

When you come .... the lift, it's on the left.

Conversation 2

a.   They're just in the .... aisle, on the .... shelf.

b.   Here, I'll .... you.

c.   That was .... of me!

Conversation 3

a.   There's an electronics shop round the ....

b.   You .... right when you come out of .... and then right again.

Conversation 4

a.   Are there any toilets .... ?

b.   There are some on your right when you .... the escalator.

c.   There are .... showing where they are.

d.   You're .... Have a nice day.

Check your answers in the tapescript at the back of the book. Are there any other expressions you don't understand? Ask your teacher.

6 | Speaking

Discuss these questions with a partner.

1.   Are there any things you don't like buying? Why not?

2.   How do you usually pay for clothes – with cash, by cheque or by card?

3.   Can you get cash back in your country? Do you think it's a good idea?

7 | Role play

Work with a partner.
Student A: You are a customer in a shop. Look at the words in the box. Choose three things that you'd like to buy.
Student B: You work in a shop. Decide if you sell these things. If you do, where are they?

CDs	paper	socks
footballs	perfume	toothpaste
guidebooks	shampoo	underwear
newspapers		

Role play the conversation using some of the language you've learnt in this unit.

Real English: cash back

In Britain, you can get money when you buy things by card from some shops – this is called cash back.

A: *Would you like any cash back?*

B: *Yes. £20, please.*

8 | Using vocabulary: things shop assistants say

Put the words in order and make sentences that shop assistants say.

1.   please / next .

2.   28 / that's / altogether / pounds .

3.   cash / any / back / you / would / like ?

4.   sign / could / please / there / you ?

5.   you / would / a / like / bag ?

6.   you / wrap / would / me / to / like / it ?

7.   anything / you / got / smaller / have ?

8.   any / I / have / five-pound / don't / notes .

9.   anything / do / need / you / else ?

10.   a / day / nice / have .

With a partner, write your own conversation between a customer and a shop assistant. Use some of the expressions above.

9 | Pronunciation: /tʃ/ and /dʒ/

♫ **Listen and repeat the sounds /tʃ/ and /dʒ/. Look at the pictures on page 145 for help if you need to.**

Which of these words don't have a /tʃ/ sound?

change / school / children / cheese / stomach / chocolates / cheap / match / headache / choose / chips

♫ **Now listen and check your answers.**

Which of these words don't have a /dʒ/ sound?

change / ages / ago / manager / charge / bigger / just / job / Japanese / lager / large / would you / did you

♫ **Now listen and check your answers.**

Real English: Would you and Did you

When people talk quickly, Would you and Did you are often pronounced /wʊdʒə/ and /dɪdʒə/.

♫ **Listen to six sentences and write them down. Compare what you wrote with the tapescript at the back of the book. Then practise saying the sentences.**

Reading

1 | Using vocabulary: jobs in shops

Match the sentences about jobs with the descriptions.

1. I'm a cashier.
2. I'm a security guard.
3. I'm a cleaner.
4. I'm a shop assistant.
5. I'm the manager of a department.

a. I try to stop people stealing things.
b. I help customers.
c. I'm in charge of ten people.
d. I work on the tills.
e. I do all the cleaning at night.

2 | Speaking

Discuss these questions with a partner. Use the words in red to help you.

1. Which job do you think is the best / worst? Why?
2. Have you ever worked in a shop? What kind of shop was it? What did you do there?
3. Has anybody you know ever worked in a shop?

- I once worked in a ... shop. I was a ... .
- A friend of mine is a ... in a ... shop.

3 | While you read

🎧 **Now read the text. As you read, answer these questions about the four people.**

1. What do they do?
2. What do they like about their job?
3. What don't they like about it?

Who do you think has the best / worst job? Why?

I work in a shop

Kelvin

I'm a security guard in a big department store in central London. It's not a bad job, but sometimes it can be a bit boring. If somebody tries to steal something from the store, an alarm goes off and I have to chase them down the street. I like that part of my job, but the rest of the time, I just have to stand near the door and watch people. That's not much fun.

Lina

I run my own bookshop and employ three people – my son Jake, and two other people. It's quite stressful. I have to make sure I know how much we sell, when we need to buy things and what the best prices are. The shop opens at nine and closes at half past five, but I have to work much longer hours. Sometimes I go to bed after midnight! However, I really like working for myself. It's better than working for somebody else. Nobody tells me what to do!

Janice

I'm a cashier in a big supermarket. It's not a bad job. I like the people I work with and my boss is OK. The money's not very good though, so it's difficult to live on it. Some people think my job sounds boring, but it's not. I'm usually too busy to feel bored. I have to work Saturdays though, which isn't much fun.

Jeremy

I'm a buyer for the Menswear department in a big department store in Manchester. I travel all over the world looking for things to sell. We sell shoes from Spain, shirts from Hong Kong, T-shirts from Japan. I visit the factories where they're all made and decide what to buy and how much to pay. I travel business class when I fly and I always stay in the best hotels, which is great. I earn £45,000 a year. I think I've got the best job in the store. I suppose the only bad thing is I have to work long hours and my partner doesn't like it when I go away for work.

4 | Word check

Complete the sentences with these words from the text.

> boring   fun   employ   go off   earn

1. The money's OK, but I'd like to .... more.
2. I'm the boss. I .... twelve other people.
3. She's a cashier in a shop. It sounds really ....
4. I have to work fourteen hours a day. It's not much .... !
5. Sorry I'm late. My alarm clock didn't .... this morning.

Now complete these sentences with more words from the text.

> steal   rest   run   stressful   bored

6. I work for myself. I .... a restaurant.
7. It's not a great job, but I'm usually too busy to feel ....
8. When people start complaining down the phone, my job can be really ....
9. Sometimes my job is great, but the .... of the time it's not much fun.
10. This boy tried to .... my bag, but luckily a guy stopped him when he shouted.

Real English: not much fun

If we don't enjoy something, we can say It's not much fun. If you enjoy yourself, you have fun. A person you like spending time with can be great fun.

I love Barcelona. It's a fun city.
We went to the beach yesterday. We had great fun.
We had a really fun class last week.

5 | Using grammar: *have to*

We use have to to talk about things we don't want to do, but we have no choice about – because our teacher, boss, or parents tell us to! For example:

- I have to work until nine in the evening.
- I have to clean my dad's car every Saturday.
- We have to do lots of homework.

Complete the sentences with have to and the verbs in the box.

> clean   help   take   travel   wear   work

1. I .... on Saturdays. I hate it!
2. I work in McDonald's. I .... a uniform to work.
3. I .... all the toilets in the building. I hate it!
4. I .... a long way to work. It takes me an hour!
5. I .... my mum with the cleaning in the house. I hate it!
6. I .... my younger brother to school every morning.

6 | Practice

Work with three other students. You should each choose one of the jobs in Activity 1.

Look at the questions about work on pages 16 and 17. Ask each other these questions. Use have to to talk about the things you don't like about your job.

▶ For more information on using *have to*, see G20.

Review: Units 13–18

1 | Questions and answers

Match the questions with the answers.

1. Are you ready to order?
2. What's haddock?
3. Where would you like me to sit?
4. Have you had enough?
5. Do you like chicken?

a. It's a kind of fish. It's nice.
b. Actually, I'm a vegetarian.
c. Anywhere you like.
d. Yes, please. I'll have the prawns.
e. Yes, thanks. I'm fine. It was lovely.

Now match these questions with the answers.

6. What have you done to your leg?
7. You look tired. What time did you go to bed?
8. Do you sell batteries?
9. Do you need anything else?
10. Would you like me to wrap those?

f. Yes please. That'd be great.
g. I cut it shaving!
h. I think it was about three. I was studying.
i. Yes, what size do you need?
j. No. That's everything, thanks.

2 | What was it like?

Complete the conversations with the words in the box.

food   holiday   hotel   town   weather

1. A: What was your .... like?
   B: It was awful. We had a really bad time.

2. A: What was the .... like?
   B: It was great. There were lots of things to do.

3. A: What was the .... like?
   B: Not very nice, actually. The rooms were quite small.

4. A: What was the .... like?
   B: Horrible! I couldn't eat any of it.

5. A: What was the .... like?
   B: It was great. It was really sunny every day.

3 | Grammar: verb patterns

When a verb follows another verb, they can have different patterns. For example:

- I'd like to visit Japan some day.
- I can't do it today. Sorry.
- I love meeting new people.

There is no reason for the difference. That's just the way it is!

Write sentences with the same patterns. Make the sentences true for you.

1. I'd like ... some day.
2. I can't ... .
3. I love ... .

Choose the correct form.

1. A: What time is it?
   B: Eleven. I should to go / go.

2. A: What're you doing tonight?
   B: I'm going visit / to visit a friend.

3. A: I can't to lift / lift this.
   B: I'll help / to help you with it, if you like.

4. A: What happened to your hand?
   B: I hurt it playing / play tennis.

5. A: Where do you want to meet / meet?
   B: Let's say / to say outside the station.

6. A: What was your holiday like?
   B: Great. We spent all week to lie / lying on the beach.

7. A: What're you doing this weekend?
   B: Oh, I have to working / work tomorrow.

8. A: Would you like me wrap / to wrap it?
   B: Yes, please.

9. A: I hate go / going to museums.
   B: Me too.

10. A: What're you doing tomorrow?
    B: I'm not sure. I'll probably just stay / staying at home.

4 | Verbs (1)

Complete the sentences with the verbs in the box.

employ	get off	had	shuts
forgot	got divorced	hurt	turned down

1. The shop opens at nine and it .... at six.
2. I turned the TV up because I couldn't hear it and then he .... it .... because he said it was too loud!
3. The top on this jar is too tight. I can't .... it ....
4. They got married last year and they .... three months later!
5. I reminded him to send his mum a birthday card, but he still ....
6. I felt ill, so I .... a lie-down.
7. I burnt my hand doing the cooking. It really ....
8. I run my own business and I .... nine people.

Now discuss these questions with a partner.

1. Have you ever burnt yourself? How?
2. Have you ever forgotten an important date or meeting? What happened?

5 | Verbs (2)

Complete the collocations with the words in the box.

my leg	nice	you to the station
my wallet	that for me	

1. drive a BMW / ....
2. wrap a present / ....
3. broke a glass / ....
4. stole my bag / ....
5. smells delicious / ....

Now complete these collocations with the words in the box.

it's OK	the taxi driver	you some water
on the weather	your suitcase	

6. carry your bag / ....
7. pour the wine / ....
8. depends what you want / ....
9. pay for it / ....
10. check your answers / ....

6 | Look back and check

Work with a partner and do one of these activities again.

a. **Activity 4 on page 69. Make sure that you remember all the language in Activities 1 and 3 before you start.**

b. **Activity 3 on page 77. Make sure that you remember all the language in Activities 1 and 2 before you start.**

7 | What can you remember?

With a partner, write down as much as you can remember about the texts you read in Unit 14 and Unit 18.

Unit 14: The kindness of strangers

Terry

Li Ying

Unit 18: I work in a shop

Kelvin, the security guard

Lina, the owner

Janice, the cashier

Jeremy, the buyer

8 | Vocabulary builder: useful things

Label these pictures with the words in the box.

bowl	fork
saucepan	chopsticks
hammer	scissors
envelope	stamps
folder	needle and thread

Spend two minutes trying to memorise all the words. Then work with a partner. Cover this page. Who can remember more words?

Now discuss these questions with a new partner.

1. Do you have any of the 20 things in the picture with you now?

2. Which thing do you use most often?

3. Are there any of the 20 things you NEVER use?

4. Can you use chopsticks?

1 ....

2 ....

3 ....

4 glue

5 ....

6 ....

7 paper

8 ....

9 string

10 ....

11 spoon

12 exercise book

13 plate

14 ....

15 ....

16 knife

17 stapler

18 ....

19 paper clip

20 sellotape

9 | Listening: *What are you doing this weekend?*

∩ **Listen to a conversation between Ruby and Jake, English teachers who live in Japan. It's Thursday lunchtime. They are talking about their plans for the weekend. Cover the conversation below. Make notes about their plans for:**

1. the weekend.

2. tonight.

Listen again and complete the conversation.

R: What are you doing this weekend?

J: I'm actually going back to Britain on Saturday for (1) ....

R: Really? You didn't say anything about that before.

J: It's all happened quite quickly. I got a very cheap ticket.

R: Right. So (2) .... your flight?

J: Seven o'clock in the morning, so I (3) .... to the airport by five.

R: Really? Is it going from Tokyo Airport?

J: Yes.

R: Oh no, so what time are you going to (4) .... ?

J: I'm not sure. I'll probably leave about one o'clock.

R: That's terrible. I hate those (5) ....

J: Yes, me too.

R: Are you doing anything tonight?

J: I don't have (6) .... I think I'll probably just start packing.

R: Do you want to go out somewhere? (7) .... to see you for ages.

J: Yes, OK. I'll probably have enough time tomorrow to pack. What do you want to do?

R: (8) .... to The Three Lions pub.

J: Yes, OK. I like it there. Do you want to meet there or somewhere else?

R: Let's meet there at, say, half past nine. I finish work at nine.

J: OK. That sounds great. I might phone a couple of other people, (9) ....

R: Of course. I might ring Yoshiki and see if he can come.

Discuss these questions with a partner.

1. Have you ever had a very early flight? What time did it go?

2. What's your favourite place to go out in the evening? Why?

10 | Pronunciation: the letter 'i'

The letter 'i' can be pronounced in lots of different ways. For example:

/ɪ/	trip
/aɪ/	tight
/iː/	magazine
/ɜː/	first

∩ **Listen and repeat these sounds and words.**

Look at the grid. Try to find a way from START to FINISH which only uses the sound /aɪ/. You can only go →, ← or ↓.

∩ **Now listen and check your answer.**

START			
light	mobile	spicy	horrible
wish	friend	sign	kitchen
minute	trip	flight	olives
skirt	exciting	bicycle	birds
disgusting	lie	delicious	hospital
lift	kind	decided	exercise
magazine	missed	hit	bright
still	dinner	sick	tidy
			FINISH

11 | Collocations

Now find another way from START to FINISH by choosing the correct words to complete the expressions below.

1. Can you turn on the ... ? / Have you got a ... ?

2. I ... you were here. / I ... I could drive.

3. Wait a ... ! / I'll be back in a ... .

4. That's a nice ... ! / I have to wear a ... at work.

5. This food tastes ... ! / I think it's ... .

6. I can't ... it. / Shall we take the ... or the stairs?

7. I don't like that ... of thing. / That's very ... of you. Thanks.

8. I ... the class yesterday. / I ... my train.

9. I ... my head. / The car ... me.

10. I feel a bit ... . / I think I'm going to be ... !

11. His flat's really ... . / I need to ... up this mess.

19 Sorry I can't come

Conversation

1 | Using vocabulary: cancelling your plans

Complete the conversations with the pairs of words in the box.

come + go	drive + visit	play + collect
come + going	help + work	

1. A: Sorry, but I can't .... tennis with you this afternoon.
   B: Oh, OK. Why not?
   A: I have to .... my younger sister from school at three.

2. A: Sorry, but I can't .... to the meeting tomorrow.
   B: Oh, OK. Why not?
   A: I have to .... to the dentist's. I've got really bad toothache.

3. A: Sorry, but I can't .... you move house on Saturday.
   B: Oh, OK. Why not?
   A: I have to .... I'm really sorry.

4. A: Sorry, but I can't .... you home today.
   B: Oh, OK. Why not?
   A: I have to go to the hospital to .... my gran. She's quite ill.

5. A: Sorry, but I can't .... to class next week.
   B: Oh, OK. Why not?
   A: I'm .... on holiday with my mum and dad.

2 | Practice

Spend two minutes trying to memorise the conversations in Activity 1. Then cover the conversations.

With a partner, try to have the conversations. Use the words in the box in Activity 1 to help you.

Do you ever have to do any of the things in Activity 1? What other reasons do you give when you cancel your plans?

Have the conversations in Activity 1 again – but this time, add your own reasons.

3 | Listening: *Sorry, I couldn't come*

Listen to three conversations. In each one, someone apologizes – says sorry – for missing something. As you listen, answer these questions.

1. What couldn't each person do?
2. When was it?
3. Why couldn't they do it?

4 | Listen again

Listen to Conversation 3 between Molly and Karen again. Complete the conversation.

M: Sorry I couldn't come out with you for dinner last night.

K: That's OK. Never mind.

M: I had to work late. I've got an important meeting (1) .... and I had to get ready for it.

K: Yes. Diane told me. (2) .... We can do it some other time.

M: Good. (3) .... Which restaurant did you go to?

K: We went to a new place in Brigham. (4) .... They do traditional English food.

M: Oh really? Well, maybe we can go there again together.

K: OK. Great. Let me know when's (5) .... for you.

M: I will.

5 | Pronunciation: stressed sounds in sentences

When we speak English, we say words in groups. In each group, we stress one or two important sounds – we say them a little louder than the others. Look at these sentences. The sounds we stress are in CAPITAL LETTERS. There are spaces between groups of words.

1. SOrry I couldn't come OUT with you   for DInner LAST NIGHT.

2. THAT'S ok.   NEver MIND.

3. it was GREAT.

4. we can DO it   some Other time.

5. let me KNOW   when's a good TIME   for YOU.

🎧 Listen to the sentences. Then practise saying them in the same way.

Now read Conversation 3 in Activity 4 with a partner.

6 | Using grammar: *Sorry I couldn't come*

• We don't use can't to talk about the past. We use couldn't.
• We don't use have to to talk about the past. We use had to.

Look at how we apologise for missing things in the past.

• Sorry I couldn't play tennis with you yesterday afternoon. I had to collect my younger sister from school at three.

• Sorry I couldn't come to the meeting yesterday. I had to go to the dentist's. I had really bad toothache.

Rewrite these sentences with the past forms.

1. Sorry, but I can't come to your party on Friday. I have to work.

   Sorry I .... last Friday.
   I ....

2. Sorry, but I can't come to class tomorrow. I have to look after my dad. He's ill.

   Sorry I .... last Wednesday.
   I ....
   He ....

3. Sorry, but I can't come shopping with you this afternoon. I have to go to the bank.

   Sorry I .... yesterday afternoon. I ....

4. Sorry, but I can't come to the cinema with you tonight. I have to collect a friend from the station.

   Sorry I .... last night.
   I ....

7 | Practice

Work with a partner. Take turns to cancel future plans and to apologize for missing things in the past. Give a reason each time. For example:

A: Sorry, but I can't come to class tomorrow. I have to take my younger brother to school.

B: That's OK. Thanks for telling me. Sorry I couldn't come to class yesterday. I had to go to the dentist's.

A: It's OK. Never mind. Sorry, but I can't come to .... .

8 | Using vocabulary: more reasons for missing things

Complete the sentences with the words in the box.

accident	bad day	meeting
appointment	headache	problems

1. Sorry I couldn't come last night. I had a few .... at work.

2. Sorry I couldn't come last Friday. I had a doctor's ....

3. Sorry I couldn't come yesterday. I had an important .... with my boss.

4. Sorry I couldn't come out with you last night. I had a really .... at work. I just went home and went to bed!

5. Sorry I couldn't come out with you last Saturday. I felt ill. I had a really bad ....

6. Sorry I couldn't come this morning. I had an .... in my car.

When was the last time you missed something? Why? For example:

• I couldn't go to my brother's wedding. I had a few problems at home.

Reading

1 | Before you read

Match the <u>underlined</u> words with the words which have the opposite meaning.

1. it's <u>late</u>   a. passed
2. <u>left</u> my house   b. stopped
3. <u>failed</u> a test   c. early
4. <u>got nervous</u>   d. calmed down
5. <u>started</u> the car   e. got home

The underlined words are from a text called *Why can't I drive?* What do you think the writer will say with these words?

2 | While you read

🎧 **Read the text and check your ideas. Did you guess correctly? <u>Underline</u> the complete expressions that use the underlined words in Activity 1.**

3 | Speaking

Discuss these questions with a partner.

1. Do you prefer to travel by train or car? Why?
2. Can you drive? Did you pass your test first time?
3. Do you get nervous before tests and exams? What do you do to calm down?

Why can't I drive?

I am waiting for my train. It's half an hour late. There are problems on the line. There are often problems on the line. I know from past experience that when the train company says 'It's half an hour late', the train is actually an hour late – sometimes more! I'll probably arrive in Liverpool at around four o'clock. I left my house at eleven, so it's going to take me five hours to travel less than 200 kilometres. I ask myself, 'Why can't I drive?' Life would be simpler and I would get home to Liverpool a lot quicker. I ask myself this question a lot. In fact, I ask myself the question every time I fail my driving test – and I've failed it five times now.

The first time I took my test I was 18. I did OK, but I couldn't park the car. I tried to park three or four times, but I just did it really badly each time.

The second time, I was quite nervous and I wanted to finish the test quickly. Unfortunately, I wanted to finish so quickly I drove too fast! The speed limit was 60 kilometres an hour, but I drove at 75!

The third time, I was very nervous. I was coming out of the car park and I hit another car! The car wasn't badly damaged, but of course I failed the test.

The fourth time, I was really really nervous. I couldn't sleep the night before the test and I was sick in the morning. I tried to calm down, but I couldn't. It took me five minutes just to start the car and the test was really awful.

I suppose I didn't really fail the fifth time. I didn't sleep for a week because I was worrying about the test. I was really tired the morning of the test and I decided I just couldn't do it, so I didn't go. It cost me £150 because I cancelled it. After that, I decided not to take the test again and to just take the train everywhere. And here I am, waiting for my train. Why can't I drive?

4 | Using grammar: *I couldn't do it*

Match the situations with the things people couldn't do.

1. Sorry I'm late. ☐
2. I looked everywhere for my homework. ☐
3. The film was really scary. There was lots of blood. ☐
4. The last question in the exam was really difficult. ☐
5. I'm exhausted! ☐

a. I couldn't find it anywhere.
b. I couldn't sleep last night.
c. I couldn't watch it.
d. I couldn't find a parking space.
e. I couldn't answer it.

Now match these things people couldn't do with the situations.

6. I couldn't hear what he was saying. ☐
7. Sorry I couldn't come yesterday. ☐
8. I couldn't see the band. ☐
9. I couldn't think what to say to her. ☐
10. I couldn't stop laughing. ☐

f. It was really embarrassing.
g. There was somebody standing in front of me.
h. He was speaking really quietly.
i. It was really funny.
j. I had to go to a meeting.

Practise saying the sentences with couldn't.

5 | Practice

Work with a partner. Think of two possible endings for these sentences.

1. I couldn't come yesterday because ... .
2. I couldn't sleep because ... .
3. I couldn't hear what he was saying because ... .
4. I couldn't think because ... .
5. I couldn't leave the house because ... .

Tell a partner about something you couldn't do in the last few weeks. Explain why.

6 | Pronunciation: /h/

⌒ **Listen and repeat the sounds with /h/.**

⌒ **Listen and decide which of the words you hear.**

1. has / as
2. his / is
3. him / I'm
4. hand / and
5. hope / open
6. hair / air
7. heart / art
8. hold / old
9. hear / ear
10. hate / eight

⌒ **Listen to eight sentences and write them down. Compare what you wrote with the tapescript at the back of the book. Then practise saying the sentences.**

Real English: a second

We often use *a second* to mean a short time. We also say *a minute* and *a moment.*

Can you hold my bag for a second? I'm just going to the toilet.
Can you wait a minute? I just need to make a quick phone call.
Can I talk to you for a moment?

Come on United! • I hardly ever go swimming. • I've never been very good at sport. • We need an e:
player. • I haven't got my trainers with me. • I can lend you a racket. • It was in! • Why don't you co
with us? • There's a pool just round the corner. • What was the score? • They're top of the league. • Th
a foul! • I support Estudiantes basketball team. • It took me more than three hours. • The referee stop
the game. • It gave me a lot of confidenc
I go all the time back home. • Well playe:

20 Do you like sport?

Conversation

1 | Speaking

Are any of these sentences true for you? Tell a partner.

1. I go cycling all the time.
2. I always play tennis on Sunday.
3. I usually play basketball at the weekend.
4. I often play golf.
5. I go to the gym two or three times a week.
6. I sometimes go for a walk in the evenings.
7. I hardly ever go swimming.
8. I never do any exercise.

Write some sentences like those above about yourself. Tell a partner what you have written.

2 | Using vocabulary: sport, places and equipment

Complete the table with the words in the box. Use your dictionary if you need to.

boots	cycling	racket	wetsuit
clubs	pool	trainers	

sport	place	equipment
running	round the park along the river	1. .... shorts
tennis	court	2. .... trainers balls
3.	in the country	bike
swimming	4. .... sea	trunks swimsuit goggles
football	pitch	5. .... ball
windsurfing	lake sea	windsurfer 6. ....
golf	course	7. .... ball

Which sports, places and equipment can you see in the photos?

3 | Listening: *Why don't you come with us?*

🎧 **Listen to three conversations between two people who have met on holiday. In each conversation, one person invites the other to join them in what they are going to do later in the day. Match each conversation with one of the photos.**

Listen again and find out if the people accept the invitation. If not, why not? Compare what you heard with a partner.

A

B

C

D

4 | Listen again

Listen to Conversation 3 between Jess and Dario again. Complete the conversation with one or two words.

J: We're going to play tennis.

D: Really? Where are you going to play?

J: There are (1) .... in the park.

D: Are there?

J: Yes. Do you like (2) .... tennis?

D: Yes, I play all the time back home, but I'm not (3) ....

J: Me neither. Well, why don't you come with us and have a game? We need an extra player.

D: I'd love to, but I haven't got (4) .... with me.

J: That's OK. We can lend you one.

D: OK. What time are you going to play?

J: (5) .... six o'clock. It's not so hot then.

D: OK, sounds great. Where shall I meet you?

J: (6) .... here between six and six fifteen.

D: OK.

Now look at the tapescript at the back of the book and practise reading the conversation with a partner. Remember to say the sounds in CAPITAL LETTERS more strongly. Try to say each group of words together.

5 | Useful expressions

Translate these sentences from Conversation 3 into your language.

1. I play all the time back home.
2. I'm not very good.
3. Me neither.
4. Why don't you come with us?
5. I'd love to, but I haven't got ... with me.
6. We can lend you one.
7. Where shall I meet you?

Look at the tapescript for the three conversations at the back of the book. Underline these and similar expressions.

> **Real English: back home**
>
> When people are abroad, they often talk about their own country as back home. For example:
>
> *I have a lot of friends back home, but I don't know many people here.*

6 | Writing

Work with a partner. Choose one of the ideas below and write a similar conversation to those in Activity 3. Use some of the useful expressions in Activity 5.

1. play football / pitch in the park / haven't got any boots / lend
2. go windsurfing / lake near here / haven't got a windsurfer / hire
3. play golf / course near here / haven't got any clubs / lend

Act out your conversation for another pair of students.

7 | Using grammar: questions about the future

We often use are you going to + verb to ask detailed questions about people's plans for the future.

Put the words in order and make questions about future plans.

1. going / where / are / you / go / to ?
2. you / are / what / to / going / see ?
3. meet / are / going / you / to / where ?
4. to / what / you / are / do / going ?
5. are / where / stay / going / you / to ?
6. are / what / going / time / leave / you / to ?
7. going / who / with / play / are / you / to ?
8. how / going / go / are / long / for / to / you ?

🎧 **Listen and repeat the questions.**

8 | Practice

Student A: Say one of the four sentences below.
Student B: Ask questions with are you going to.
Student A: Try to answer the questions.

- I'm going to go for a walk.
- I'm going to visit Japan in the summer.
- I'm going to play golf later.
- I'm going to the cinema tonight with a friend.

Reading

1 | Using vocabulary: talking about teams

First study the league table and results. Then answer the questions.

1. Who are top of the league?
2. Who are bottom of the league?
3. Who are second?
4. Who are third from bottom?
5. Who lost five–one this week?
6. Who won three–two this week.
7. Who did Charlton beat?
8. Were there any nil–nil draws?
9. What was the score in the Bolton–Fulham game?
10. Did Everton win?

	Played	Won	Drawn	Lost	Points
Arsenal	37	25	12	0	87
Ipswich Town	37	23	7	7	76
Manchester United	37	22	6	9	72
Liverpool	37	15	12	10	57
Newcastle	37	12	17	8	53
Aston Villa	37	14	11	12	53
Charlton	37	13	11	13	50
Bolton	37	13	11	13	50
Fulham	37	13	10	14	49
Birmingham	37	11	14	12	47
Middlesbrough	37	12	9	16	45
Southampton	37	11	11	15	44
Portsmouth	37	11	9	17	42
Blackburn	37	12	6	19	42
Manchester City	37	11	8	18	41
Wolverhampton	37	8	14	15	38
Leeds	37	8	12	17	36
Everton	37	5	15	17	30
Chelsea	37	7	9	21	30
Tottenham	37	6	12	19	30

Arsenal 3 – Ipswich Town 2; Aston Villa 0 – Manchester United 2;
Blackburn 0 – Birmingham 0; Bolton 0 – Fulham 2;
Charlton 2 – Southampton 1; Chelsea 0 – Leeds 1;
Liverpool 1 – Newcastle 1; Manchester City 3 – Everton 3;
Portsmouth 5 – Middlesbrough 1; Wolverhampton 2 – Tottenham 0

Discuss these questions with a partner.

1. Do you support a team? Where are they in the league?
2. Do you know any scores from sports matches last week?

2 | While you read

🎧 **Read the article on the opposite page and decide if the people are talking about a success (S) or a failure (F). Underline the words which tell you.**

Check your ideas with a partner.

3 | Comprehension

Cover the text. With a partner, say how the people in the article use these numbers.

Andrew	78 / ten minutes
Ruben	12,332 / 6 hours 12 minutes
Carmina	five kilometres / three hours
Mikel	two years
Denise	3000-metre
Sue	27
Paco	fourth / 58

Now look at the text and check your ideas.

4 | Vocabulary check

The missing words in these sentences are all in the text. Complete the sentences without looking at the text.

1. My .... sporting success was when I won a 100m race at school. I was eight!
2. I played my brother at tennis and I .... really badly.
3. I'm not very good .... sport.
4. I once cycled 150 kilometres in one day. It .... me over eleven hours.
5. Winning the match gave me a lot of ....
6. The worst sporting moment was when Leeds United .... Arsenal. Arsenal lost the league because of that.
7. I .... my arm playing golf once! Don't ask me how!
8. I will always remember the day I .... a goal for my football team. I never did it again!

Now look at the text and check your answers.

Sporting success, sporting failure

Last week the American Samoan football team lost 31–0 to Australia in their World Cup qualifying match. We asked a few people about their greatest sporting successes and failures.

Andrew (22)

When I was at school, I was the captain of the school rugby team. It was really bad though, because our team were the worst team ever. We hardly ever won, and once we lost 78–0 and the referee stopped the game ten minutes early.

Ruben (39)

I've never been very good at sport, but last year I ran a marathon. I came 12,332nd out of 12,500 people and it took me 6 hours 12 minutes. I was so happy. I didn't think I could do something like that, but I did. It gave me a lot of confidence.

Carmina (43)

I love doing sport and I work as a swimming instructor. Last year I swam about five kilometres in the sea – from Alicante to an island near there. It took me more than three hours. I was really tired near the end, but I did it. I got a boat to come back to Alicante!

Mikel (10)

I beat my brother at table tennis. He's two years older than me.

Denise (26)

I don't really do much sport, but I love walking. I went walking in the mountains in Italy once. I got to the top of a 3000-metre mountain. It's the highest I've ever been. I couldn't see anything because I was in the clouds, but I felt great.

Sue (34)

When I was 27, I broke my leg skiing. I've never been skiing since.

Paco (19)

I support Estudiantes basketball team. I go to all their matches, but they're playing really badly at the moment. They're fourth from bottom in the league. They only scored 58 points in their last game.

5 | Speaking

Discuss these questions with a partner.

1. What's your greatest success and worst failure – in sport / in life?
2. What's the furthest you've ever walked / run / swum / cycled?
3. What are you good at / bad at?

6 | Pronunciation: connected speech

♫ **Listen to ten short things people shout when they play and watch sport. Try and write them down. Compare what you wrote with the tapescript at the back of the book.**

When one word ends in a consonant and the next starts with a vowel, we usually link the words together when we speak. When one word ends in 't' and the next starts with another consonant, you often don't hear the 't'.

Practise saying the things you wrote down.

99

You need to get a number 34. • Single or return? • Returning today? • What's the earliest f
on Monday? • It's the worst place I've ever been to. • It's safer to go by train. • They cause a lo
pollution. • You can fly there for almost nothing! • It's a small world. • He never left his home town. •
got easier over the last few months. • I've got a lot fatter since I came here. • I'd like to check t

21 What day are you travelling?

Conversation

1 Using vocabulary: travelling

Put the sentences in order and make conversations.

Conversation 1: at the bus stop

a. Oh, OK. Thanks.

b. No, you need to get a number 34.

c. Excuse me. Does this bus go to Tufnell Park?

1. ☐   2. ☐   3. ☐

Conversation 2: on the bus

a. Yes, it is.

b. Can you tell me when to get off, please?

c. Is this the right bus for Tufnell Park?

d. Yes, no problem. Take a seat.

1. ☐   2. ☐   3. ☐   4. ☐

Conversation 3: at the ticket office (1)

a. OK. That's £29.

b. Return, please.

c. Single or return?

d. I'd like a ticket to Bath, please.

1. ☐   2. ☐   3. ☐   4. ☐

Conversation 4: at the ticket office (2)

a. Returning today?

b. Then that's £63, please.

c. No, on Tuesday.

d. I'd like a return to Leeds, please.

1. ☐   2. ☐   3. ☐   4. ☐

Conversation 5: at the train information desk

a. 10.24.

b. When's the last train to Ealing?

c. OK, great. Thank you.

d. 11.13.

e. And what time does it get in?

1. ☐   2. ☐   3. ☐   4. ☐

∩ **Listen and check your answers. Then practise reading the conversations with a partner.**

2 Practice

Work with a partner. Rewrite the conversations in Activity 1 using places in your town or country.

3 Listening: *What day are you travelling?*

∩ **Harry is an American visiting his friend Michael in London. They are planning to go to Edinburgh in Scotland for a weekend. Michael phones National Rail Enquiries to check times and prices of trains. Listen to the telephone conversation and complete the table.**

	leaves	arrives	cost
the earliest train from London to Edinburgh	6.15		
the last train from Edinburgh to London		23.50	
the earliest Saver Return from London to Edinburgh			

Compare your notes with a partner.

∩ **Listen to the conversation Michael then has with Harry. Check your notes about times and prices again. What do Michael and Harry decide to do?**

4 Listen again

Complete the sentences from the telephone conversation with ONE word. Listen again if you need to.

1. How can I .... you?

2. I'd like to .... train times to Edinburgh, please.

3. What .... are you travelling from?

4. What time would you like to .... ?

5. What's the earliest .... ?

6. What's the .... train back?

5 Role play

Work with a partner.
Student A: You are on holiday in Britain. Look at the information on page 160.
Student B: You work for the National Travel Enquiries telephone help desk. Look at the information on page 158.
Role play the conversation. Use the sentences in Activity 4. When you finish, change roles and have a similar conversation.

6 | Using grammar: superlatives

When we compare lots of things, we often use superlatives. With one-syllable adjectives, we usually make superlatives by adding **the + -est**. For example:

A: What's the cheapest flight on Monday?

B: The 7 a.m. flight from Heathrow.

With longer adjectives, we add **the most**. The superlatives for *good* and *bad* are irregular. We say **the best** and **the worst**. For example:

A: What's the best way to get to the airport?

B: The underground is probably the most convenient for you.

Complete these conversations with the words in the box.

the best	the cheapest	the earliest
the biggest	the most difficult	the quickest

1. A: What's .... place to eat in town?

    B: Snobs in Bradford Street. You can get a meal for £3 there, but the food's disgusting.

2. A: What's .... city after London?

    B: It's Birmingham. A lot of people think it's Manchester, but Birmingham is actually bigger.

3. A: What's .... airline to travel to London?

    B: I'm not sure. Mod-air is probably the cheapest, but I prefer to go with BA. Their planes are more comfortable.

4. A: What's .... you can get home from work?

    B: Half past five, if the traffic is OK.

5. A: How's the English course you're doing?

    B: Awful. It's .... thing I've ever done.

6. A: What's .... way to get to Cardiff from here?

    B: Take the motorway. It's quicker than taking the small roads.

▶ For more information on using superlatives, see G21.

7 | What's the best ... ?

Did you notice this common pattern in Activity 6?

*   What's the best (bus) to (catch)?

Put the words in order and make questions.

1. the / town / what's / eat / best / to / in / place ?

2. the / best / phone / what's / time / to / you ?

3. best / what's / place / the / to / in / town / stay ?

4. what's / best / time / of / the / to / year / visit ?

5. shopping / the / go / best / place / what's / to ?

6. study / the / university / best / at / to / what's ?

7. way / what's / best / to / get / to / house / your / the ?

8. the / places / what / best / to / while / are / here / visit / I'm ?

Work with a partner.

Student A: You are visiting Student B's country. Ask the questions above.

Student B: Answer your partner's questions about your country.

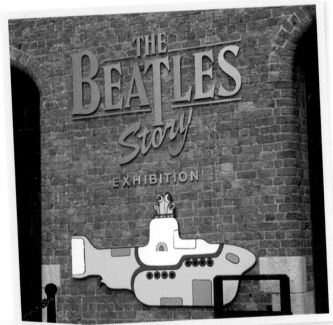

Reading

1 | Speaking

Choose the expression in each sentence that is true for you. Cross out the expression that is NOT true.

1. I've travelled more / less than my grandparents.
2. It's easier / more difficult to travel now than in the past.
3. It's safer / more dangerous to travel now than in the past.
4. It's more / less fun travelling in my own country than going abroad.
5. Getting a visa is easier / more difficult for me now than in the past.
6. Going abroad makes me more / less happy about my own country.

Tell a partner about your choices.

2 | While you read

⌒ **You are going to read an article about travelling. As you read the article on the opposite page, try to answer these questions.**

1. What are lots of people in Britain complaining about? Why?
2. Does the writer agree with them? Why / why not?

3 | Speaking

Discuss these questions with a partner.

1. Do you agree with the writer that air travel is a good thing?
2. Are your grandparents similar to the writer's grandparents?
3. Do you eat much foreign food? Do you watch many foreign films? What kind?
4. Have you heard any other stories like the writer's story about Brazil?

4 | Using grammar: talking about changes

In the article, you read that tickets have got a lot cheaper. We often use the present perfect to describe changes from the past to now. In this sentence, got means 'become'.

Complete the sentences with the words in the box.

better	easier	taller
cheaper	more expensive	thinner

1. Your son has got a lot .... over the last year. I'm sure he's grown twenty centimetres.
2. Air travel has got a lot .... over the last couple of years. The first time I went to Poland, it cost £400. Now it's only £60!
3. When I started my job, it was really difficult, but it's got a lot .... over the last few months.
4. Houses have got a lot .... over the last few years. Even a small flat costs £200 a week to rent.
5. My English has got a lot .... since I came to Ireland.
6. I've got a lot .... since I came here. I've lost about ten kilos. The food's so bad I never eat.

5 | Practice

Complete these sentences so that they are true for you.

1. ... have / has got cheaper over the last few ... .
2. ... have / has got more expensive over the last few ... .
3. ... have / has got a lot easier over the last few ... .
4. ... have / has got better over the last few ... .
5. ... have / has got ... over the last ... .

Tell a partner what you have written. Are your sentences similar?

> For more information on using the present perfect like this, see G22.

6 | Pronunciation: silent 't'

⌒ **Listen to these expressions. You don't hear the /t/ sound in them. Practise saying the expressions.**

1. the worst place
2. the best time
3. the last few years
4. the last train
5. the first coach
6. the most difficult
7. I must go.
8. I can't do it.

⌒ **Listen to eight sentences and write them down.**

Compare what you wrote with the tapescript at the back of the book. Then practise saying the sentences.

It's a small world

The government has recently presented its plans for air travel. It wants to make Heathrow Airport and Stansted Airport bigger. Some people have already started complaining. They say that planes already make too much noise and cause too much pollution. They say that air travel is too cheap and too easy. They say air travel is unhealthy. They say the government should make air travel more expensive and stop people travelling by plane.

I don't usually agree with the government, but this time I do. Of course there are problems with air travel, but there are so many good things about it. My grandparents never went abroad. Never! In their whole lives! In fact, three of my grandparents didn't even have passports. My grandfather once told me that he didn't even leave his home town Reading until he was 15. My grandparents didn't know much about the rest of the world – and didn't want to. They thought the north of England was a foreign country, they didn't like foreign food or foreign people and they weren't interested in learning foreign languages.

My life is very, very different. I work for a German company in London and live with my Argentinian wife. We go to restaurants a lot and eat all kinds of foreign food – Thai, Japanese, Italian, Spanish. We watch movies from all over the world. We both speak three different languages – and we travel as much as we can.

Air travel has changed a lot since my grandparents were young. Back then, it took over 30 hours to fly from America to Europe. Even when my parents were young, air travel was only for rich or famous people. Nowadays, there are lots of small airlines and you can fly abroad for almost nothing! Tickets have got a lot cheaper. We sometimes go to Holland for the weekend – or Germany or Italy or Spain. I feel more European than I feel English.

Last summer we went on holiday to Brazil. It took us 15 hours to get there. When we got to our hotel, we checked in and then we went out for a walk. We stopped for a drink and started talking to some other people. They were very nice and they lived in London too – three minutes from our house. It really is a small world and that really is a good thing!

What's your mum like? • She told me this really funny joke. • My brother's really fit. • She's very quie
I hated my old job. My boss was really horrible. • What're your neighbours like? • They were making a
of noise. • I couldn't sleep. • So how are things? • I've got a new boyfriend. • He works in an art galler
He never tells me anything. • Isn't that Prince Charles? • I don't know. I wasn't looking. • I was standing
the bus stop and he walked past. • He's shorte
real life. • He seemed quite nice. • Work's fine.

22

What's she like?

Conversation

1 | Using vocabulary: describing people

Look at the pictures. Do you know anybody like these people? Tell a partner. For example:

- My friend Rachel is really fit. She goes running a lot.

Complete these sentences with the words from the pictures.

1. My sister's really .... She plays tennis twice a week and she cycles to work every day.

2. My friend Lina's really .... She tells really good jokes.

3. My mum's really .... She plays the violin and she writes great stories.

4. My oldest brother's really .... He never stops talking about work!

5. My younger brother's really .... He's not very good at making friends or talking to people.

6. My dad's really .... He understands maths and computers and things like that.

Now complete these sentences with the words in the box.

easy to talk to	interesting	quiet
horrible	lazy	strange

7. Jane's really .... She doesn't say very much.

8. My brother's really .... He never cleans the house and he never does any work for college either.

9. My mum's really .... I can talk to her about anything.

10. My uncle's really .... He's been all over the world. I love listening to his stories about different countries.

11. My neighbour is really .... She has about 60 cats and she only goes out of her house at night!

12. My old boss was really .... Nobody liked working for him.

Which of the twelve adjectives do you think describe you? Ask a new partner if they agree.

> ### Real English: my old boss
>
> My old boss was my boss in the past, but not anymore. I stopped working for him or her. We can also use my old to talk about past things or places. For example:
>
> *My old flat was bigger than my new one.*
> *I hated my old job. My new one is much better.*
> *My old car was more expensive than my new one.*

really fit

really boring

really shy

really funny

really clever

really creative

2 | Using grammar: *What's she like?*

We ask What's he / she like? when we want to ask about the personality of someone we don't know:

A: I met Lucy's husband last night.

B: Oh really? What's he like?

A: He's great – really nice, really friendly.

Match the questions with the answers.

1. What's your brother like?

2. What's your sister like?

3. What's your mum like?

4. What's your dad like?

5. What're your neighbours like?

6. What's your boss like?

a. She's great. Everyone loves working for her.

b. They're OK. They're better than the old ones. They were really strange!

c. She's great. She's much younger than my dad – and much easier to talk to.

d. He's OK. He's older than me. We're quite different. He's quieter than me. He's really shy.

e. She's great. She's much younger than me, but we're very similar. We're both really creative. We both love art and music.

f. He's OK. He's much older than my mum. He's more difficult to talk to.

Work with a partner. Ask and answer the questions above. Give answers that are true for you.

3 | Listening: *What's she like?*

🎧 **Listen to two conversations. Answer these questions.**

1. Who are Jim and Colin talking about in Conversation 1?

2. Who are Emily and her mum talking about in Conversation 2?

Can you remember which adjectives from Activity 1 the speakers use to describe the people they are talking about? Listen again if you need to.

4 | Listen again

Listen to Conversation 2 again. Complete the conversation.

M: Hello.

E: Hello Mum. (1) .... , Emily.

M: Oh hello, dear. How are you?

E: I'm fine, thanks. And how are you?

M: Very well, very well. So, (2) .... ?

E: Good. Work's fine, everything's fine.

M: Oh, that's good.

E: Yes. Oh, and I saw Jon (3) .... days ago.

M: Oh yes? How was he?

E: Very well. Did you know he's got (4) .... ?

M: No, I didn't, but you know your brother – he never tells me anything. Have you met her?

E: Yes, she was there when I went to his house.

M: And (5) .... ?

E: She's really nice. She's very interesting. She works in an art gallery and she likes painting.

M: Oh, she sounds (6) ....

E: I know. I just don't understand why she wants to be with Jon! He's so boring! He's not interested in art or anything like that.

M: Emily, don't talk about your brother like that!

Now look at the tapescript at the back of the book and practise reading the conversation with a partner. Remember to say the sounds in CAPITAL LETTERS more strongly. Try to say each group of words together.

5 | Practice

Work with a partner. Write a telephone conversation between two friends. You can start in the same way as Conversation 2. Use one of the sentences below to introduce your news. Then ask about the person and describe him or her.

•   Did you know I've got a new neighbour?

•   Did you know I've got a new boss?

•   Did you know I've got a new boyfriend / girlfriend?

•   Did you know I've got a new flatmate?

Read your conversation to some other pairs of students. Would they like to meet this person?

Reading

1 | Speaking

Discuss these questions with a partner. Use the expressions in red to help you.

1. Have you met / seen anyone famous? Who?

    I met / saw ... once.

2. Do you know any of the people in the photos?

    *   That's ... .
    *   He's a famous ... .
    *   Do you know who that is?
    *   I've no idea.
    *   I'm not sure. I think it's ... .

2 | While you read

🎧 **You are going to read an article in which we asked five people, 'Have you ever met anyone famous?' They talked about the people in the photos. As you read, answer these questions.**

1. Who are the people in the photos?

2. How did the people meet them?

Discuss your answers with a partner. Which do you think is the best story?

3 | Vocabulary focus

Make sure that you understand these words.

Michael	shouted out / real life
Andrew	leader / a speech
Shunsuke	a crowd / star
Isobel	an Oscar / bride
Craig	got stuck / the front page

Cover the text. Discuss with a partner how the words were used in the text.

 A  B  C

She's famous!

Michael

I once saw Princess Diana. I was driving along Kensington High Street in London and there was a lot of traffic. We couldn't move. Then I saw a police car and a big black car came past quite slowly. Lady Di was in the back of the black car. I shouted out of my car window, 'Lady Di, I love you.' I don't think she heard me. She looked beautiful. She looked better in real life than in photos. I'll never forget it.

Andrew

I once met Michael Foot. He was quite a famous politician in Britain. He was the leader of the Labour party. When I finished university at Nottingham, he gave a speech and presented our degrees to us. I went up to him and shook his hand, and he said, 'Congratulations.' He seemed quite nice.

Shunsuke

I was walking down Oxford Street in London and I suddenly saw a big crowd of people. There were maybe 150 or 200 people. Some had cameras and they were taking pictures. I waited for ten minutes and then Hidetoshi Nakata came out of a shop. He's the biggest football star in Japan. I don't know why he was there.

Isobel

I once met Ben Kingsley at a wedding. He's quite a famous actor in Britain. I think he's won an Oscar. He was a family friend of the bride (the *woman* who was getting married) and I was a friend of the groom (the *man*). We all danced together until one o'clock in the morning. I didn't actually speak to him, but he seemed quite friendly. He looked different in real life. He was taller.

Craig

I haven't met anyone famous, but I've been famous! I went to live in the Faroe Islands nine or ten years ago. It's a very small country and it has a small population. The first week I was there, I went for a walk. There was a small mountain with rocks and I decided to climb up it and see the view. Before I got to the top of the mountain, my knee got stuck between two rocks and I couldn't move. I started shouting. I shouted for three hours and then someone came to help me. My photo was on the front page of the national newspaper! I was famous in the Faroe Islands!

D   E

4 | Using grammar: past continuous

Look at these examples.

A: I once met Tom Cruise.

B: Really? Where?

A: I was staying in a hotel in Taiwan and he was staying there too.

| PAST | | I met Tom Cruise | NOW |

I was staying in a hotel

A: I phoned you on Sunday, but you weren't there.

B: No, sorry. I was working.

| PAST | you phoned | NOW |

I was working

We use the past continuous to talk about situations that happen around a particular time or action in the past.

Complete the explanations of how you met someone with the correct form of the verbs.

1. We .... a meal at a restaurant in town and he was at the table next to us. (have)

2. I .... at a table outside a café and he walked past. (sit)

3. He .... copies of his new book at a bookshop in town and I went to meet him. (sign)

4. She .... a new shop in town and I went to see her. (open)

5. I was in a queue for the bus and he .... in front of me. (stand)

Now use the correct form of the verb to complete these explanations of why you didn't answer the phone.

6. I .... football. (play)

7. I was out. I .... some shopping. (do)

8. I .... and I didn't want to speak to anyone. (study)

9. I .... a programme on TV and I wanted to see the end. (watch)

10. I was in Matlock. We .... friends who live there. (visit)

> For more information on using the past continuous, see G23.

5 | Practice

Have conversations like those in Activity 4. Use these starter sentences and the explanations in Activity 4.

*   I met / saw ... once / last week.

*   I phoned you ... last night / on Saturday, but you didn't answer.

Now find someone in the class who has met / seen someone famous in real life. Who, where, and how?

6 | Pronunciation: sentence stress and weak forms

In positive expressions, auxiliary verbs aren't usually stressed. In negative expressions, they are stressed.

∩ Listen and repeat these sentences.

1. i was STUdying and i DIdn't want to SPEAK to anyone.

2. i DIdn't HEAR. i WASn't LIStening.

3. i COULdn't SEE. he was STANding in FRONT of me.

4. i can DO it LAter, but i CAN'T do it NOW.

5. he's OK, but he ISn't very EAsy to TALK to.

∩ Listen to eight sentences and write them down. Compare what you wrote with the tapescript at the back of the book. Then practise saying the sentences.

Make yourself at home. • Come in. • How long have you been here now? • Would you like a drink? • I'll just go and put the kettle on. • Could I use your toilet? • I won't be long. • I'll go and get it. • What a r room. It's so big. • I love the view. You can see so far! • How long have you had it? • Where did you it? • We've got a spare room. • It's in the countryside. • It's got a huge living room. • I can't wait. I'm re looking forward to it. • It's not very centr Our house is very convenient for the shop

23 What a great flat!

Conversation

1 Listening: *Come in*

🎧 **Listen to a conversation between two friends, Fiona and Gail. Fiona is visiting Gail's flat for the first time. Answer these questions.**

1. What does Fiona think of the flat?
2. What things does she make comments about?

2 Listen again

Listen to the conversation again. Complete the conversation.

F: Hello!

G: Hi. Great to see you.

F: Come in, come in. Shall I (1) .... ?

G: Yes, thanks.

F: OK. There you are. Well, come through.

G: Thanks. What a (2) .... ! It's quite big, isn't it? How long have you been here now?

F: (3) .... I moved here last August.

G: Gosh, is it that long?

F: Yes, I know. Time goes so quickly, doesn't it? Come and (4) ....

G: Actually, I'd prefer to stand for the moment. I've been in the car for the last two hours. This is a very nice room. It's (5) ....

F: Yes, it's great, isn't it?

G: And (6) .... this painting. Is it new?

F: Yes, a friend gave it to me when I moved in here. It's nice, isn't it?

G: Yes, I really like it.

F: Would you like a drink? Beer? Coke?

G: I'd actually prefer something hot, if that's OK. (7) .... some tea?

F: Of course, no problem. I'll just go and put the kettle on.

G: Hey Fiona. Could I just use your phone a moment? I forgot to recharge my mobile before I left the house this morning.

F: Sure. Go ahead. It's just by the sofa there.

G: Thanks, (8) ....

3 Using grammar: *Could I ... ?*

Complete the conversations with the expressions in the box.

have some milk	leave my bag somewhere
have some tea	use your phone use your toilet

1. A: Could I .... ?
   B: Yes, of course. I'll put the kettle on.
   A: Great. Thanks.

2. A: Could I .... ?
   B: Yes, of course. It's the second door on the right.
   A: OK.

3. A: Could I .... ?
   B: Yes, of course. There's some in the fridge.
   A: OK.

4. A: Could I .... ?
   B: Yes, of course. There's one in the kitchen.
   A: OK, thanks. I won't be long.

5. A: Could I .... ?
   B: Yes, of course. I'll put it in my room.
   A: Thanks.

We often say I'll when we offer or promise to do something. The negative of I'll is I won't.

Underline the three expressions with I'll and I won't in the conversations above. Decide which expressions are offers and which are promises.

4 Practice

Work with a partner. Write conversations like those in Activity 4. Use the ideas below.

1. A: wash / clothes?
   B: Yes. / I / do / if you like!
   A: Really? Thanks.

2. A: raining. / borrow / umbrella?
   B: Yes. / I / go / get it.
   A: Thanks. / I / give it back / you tomorrow.

3. A: I / not / any money. / borrow ten pounds?
   B: Yes.
   A: Thanks. / I / pay you back tomorrow.

Think of two more questions with Could I ... ? Then have conversations like those above with other students.

> For more information on asking for permission, see G24.

108

5 | Speaking

If you compliment someone, you say something nice about them or about something they have.

Discuss these questions with a partner.

1. Do you compliment these people?

men	people you don't know very well
women	the people you work with
your friends	your brother or your sister

2. What things do you compliment them on?

how they look	their hairstyle
their car	the work they do
their clothes	

3. Has anyone complimented you recently? What on?

6 | Complimenting people

Look at these ways of complimenting people.

- I like the / your room. It's really big.
- What a nice room. It's so big.

- These paintings are fantastic. Did you paint them?
- What fantastic paintings. Where did you get them?

Rewrite the first sentence in each pair. Use the words in brackets. Begin each sentence with What.

1. I really like the flat. It's lovely. (great)
2. I love your kitchen. It's so big. (great)
3. I love your shoes. They really suit you. (lovely)
4. This is a great photo. Who took it? (brilliant)
5. I like the shirt. Where did you get it? (fantastic)
6. I love the flowers. They smell wonderful. (lovely)

∩ **Listen and check your answers. Notice the intonation. Then practise saying the sentences with a partner. For example:**

A: What a great flat. It's lovely.

B: Yes, it's nice, isn't it?

7 | Practice

Work with a partner. Have conversations like those in Activity 6 about the things in the photos. Try to continue the conversations. These questions and answers will help.

A: Where did you get it / them?

B: I got it / them in Spain / town / South Street market.

or: A friend gave it / them to me.

A: How long have you had it / them?

B: A long time. / About a year. / Not long. / Since I was a baby.

A: Well, it's / they're really nice.

Reading

1 | Using vocabulary: describing your house

Look at the photos. Which of these sentences can you use to describe them?

1. It's got *one bedroom* / *two bedrooms* / *three bedrooms.*
2. It's got a garden.
3. It's got a balcony.
4. It's got a garage.
5. It's got a huge living room.
6. It's got a tiny kitchen
7. We've got a spare room.
8. It's *an old* / *a modern* building.
9. It's *in* / *near* / *a long way from* the centre of town.
10. It's in the countryside.
11. It's by the seaside.

Choose the words and sentences that describe your house or flat.

Ask some other students these questions.

1. Do you live in a house or a flat?
2. What's it like?

Use the language in this activity to help you.

2 | Before you read

Work with a partner. Think of five reasons why people move house. For example:

- Their children leave home, so they move somewhere smaller.

Compare your ideas with another pair of students.

3 | While you read

⌒ **You are going to read a letter from Luke, who is English, to his French friend, Marcel. As you read the letter on the opposite page, try to answer these questions.**

1. Why is Luke going to move?
2. What's good about his new place?
3. What's not very good about it?

Moving house

Dear Marcel,

Hi, how are you? Are you enjoying your new job? And is everything still fine with Mirelle? I hope so.

Anyway, I'm writing to tell you that we've finally found a new place to live – after months and months of looking! We're going to move in next Saturday. I can't wait. I'm really looking forward to it. Before I forget, our new address is 144, Bowerdean Street, Muswell Hill, London N10 3ZT, and our phone number is 020 9349 3038.

The new house is much nicer than the one we're living in now. It's bigger, so that's good. The kids are growing up now and can't share a room forever. Our new place has got four bedrooms – one for Mary and me, one for each of the kids and a spare one – so you're always welcome to stay with us if you want to visit London again!

The new house has also got a small garden. It'll be nice for the kids to have somewhere to play – and we can sit outside in the summer and have dinner. I know you don't think we have

summers here in England, but we had almost ten hot, sunny days last year! No, I'm only joking, of course – I'm sure we had twelve or thirteen days really!

I don't think you know Muswell Hill. It's not very central, but it's not too bad. It's a nice area, but it's not very convenient for transport. It hasn't got an underground station. You have to take a bus to Highgate and then get the underground from there. It takes about 45 minutes to get into the city centre. It's not too bad for London. Our house is very convenient for the shops, though. There are lots of lovely little shops just round the corner – and a great Turkish shop only three doors down from us.

Anyway, we hope you'll come and see it for yourself sometime soon. We'd love to see you again.

All the best,
Luke (and Mary and Dylan and Jade)

4 | Role play (1)

Work with a partner.

Student A: You are Mary, Luke's wife, and Student B is a friend of yours. Telephone your friend and tell them you are going to move house. Be ready to describe what your new house is like. Use Luke's letter to help you.

Student B: You are a friend of Mary's, Luke's wife. When she phones you, ask her what the new house is like.

5 | Using vocabulary: describing areas.

Complete the sentences with very or not very and the expressions in the box. Use each expression twice.

| central   convenient for transport |
| convenient for the shops |

1. It's .... There's a supermarket just round the corner.

2. It's .... There's a bus stop just round the corner.

3. It's .... The main square is just round the corner.

4. It's .... You have to walk twenty minutes to get to the nearest supermarket.

5. It's .... You have to walk fifteen minutes to get to the nearest tube station.

6. It's .... You have to get a bus and then a tube. It takes nearly an hour to get into the city centre.

Do any of these sentences describe the area you live in? Tell a partner.

6 | Role play (2)

Work with a partner.

Student A: You are going to move to a nicer place in your town or city. Spend three minutes deciding where you're going to move to, what your new house and area are like, and why you're moving. Then telephone your friend, Student B, and tell them your news.

Student B: Your friend, Student A, is going to move house next week. Write down five expressions or questions you want to use when they phone to tell you.

I've passed all my exams. • Congratulations! • It's my birthday on Saturday. • My brother's getting marr
next weekend. • I'm going out for dinner with some friends. • I'll phone you later to tell you when a
where to meet. • We had quite a small wedding. • We h
two hundred guests at the reception. • It was the best c
of my life. • I don't know what
give her. • How about a car?

24 | Are you doing anything to celebrate?

Conversation

1 | Speaking

On a special day, such as a birthday or when we get good news, we often **celebrate** – we do something special with our friends or family. Maybe **we go out for dinner** or **go out for a drink**. Maybe we **have a big party**.

How many reasons for celebrating can you think of?

Discuss these questions with a partner.

1. Where do you usually go when you want to celebrate?

2. When was the last time you celebrated something? What? How?

These sentences will help you.

*   I passed all my exams last summer, so some friends and I went out to celebrate. We went to a nice restaurant in town.

*   My favourite baseball team won the league this year, so some friends and I went out to celebrate. We went bowling and then we went out for a drink. It was great!

2 | Listening: *Are you doing anything to celebrate?*

🎧 **Listen to three conversations. In each one, someone has got some good news. As you listen, try to answer these questions.**

1. What's the good news?

2. Are they doing anything to celebrate? What?

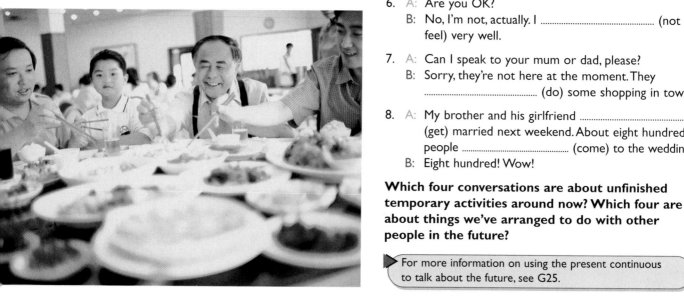

3 | Using grammar: the present continuous for the future

In Unit 12, you saw that we use the present continuous to talk about unfinished temporary activities around now. We can also use it to talk about things we've arranged to do with other people in the future. For example:

*   I'm going out with a couple of friends tonight.

*   My mum and dad are coming to my house for dinner tomorrow.

Complete the conversations with the present continuous form.

1. A: It's my birthday on Saturday.
    B: Oh really? .... you .... (do) anything to celebrate?
    A: Yes, my wife and I .... (go) to Paris for the weekend.

2. A: .... it still .... (rain) outside?
    B: Yes, I'm afraid so.

3. A: Can I help you?
    B: Yes, I .... (look) for some scissors. Have you got any?

4. A: We .... (meet) tonight at eight o'clock. Is that OK?
    B: Yes, that's fine.

5. A: I .... (go) out for dinner with a couple of friends tomorrow. You can come if you want to.
    B: Thanks. I'd love to, but I .... (do) something else tomorrow, actually.

6. A: Are you OK?
    B: No, I'm not, actually. I .... (not / feel) very well.

7. A: Can I speak to your mum or dad, please?
    B: Sorry, they're not here at the moment. They .... (do) some shopping in town.

8. A: My brother and his girlfriend .... (get) married next weekend. About eight hundred people .... (come) to the wedding!
    B: Eight hundred! Wow!

Which four conversations are about unfinished temporary activities around now? Which four are about things we've arranged to do with other people in the future?

> For more information on using the present continuous to talk about the future, see G25.

4 | Role play

Work with a partner.
Student A: You got some good news this morning.
Decide what the good news was – and
what you're going to do to celebrate.
Then tell your partner and invite them
to come and celebrate with you.
Student B: Your partner is going to tell you some
good news. Congratulate them. Ask if
they're doing anything to celebrate.

Now read the tapescript of the three conversations
in Activity 2 at the back of the book. Underline any
expressions you want to use.

Change roles. Role play a similar conversation. Use
the expressions you underlined.

5 | Listening: *I'm just phoning to tell you about tonight*

⋒ **Listen to a telephone conversation between
the two people from Conversation 1 in Activity 2.
As you listen, answer these questions.**

1. Where are they going to meet tonight?

2. What time are they going to meet?

Compare your answers with a partner.

6 | Vocabulary check

**Complete the sentences from the telephone
conversation with ONE word. Listen again if you
need to.**

1. Hi, it's .... I'm just phoning to tell you
.... tonight.

2. So where do you .... to meet?

3. Well, we're thinking .... meeting in The
Social. Do you know .... ?

4. I'm not .... sure. Where is
.... again?

5. Oh, I know the .... you mean.

6. Is seven .... for you?

7. It's a .... early, actually. I
.... to go home and get changed first.

8. Well, let's .... eight o'clock, then.

9. OK, and I'll .... you later.

7 | Pronunciation: sentence stress

Now look at the tapescript of the telephone
conversation at the back of the book and practise
reading the conversation with a partner.
Remember to say the sounds in **CAPITAL
LETTERS** more strongly. Try to say each group of
words together.

Reading

1 | Using vocabulary: relationships

Put these sentences in the order you think they happened: 1 = this happened first, 7 = this happened last.

a. They were married for thirty-five years. ☐
b. They started going out together. ☐
c. They had children. ☐
d. They got married. ☐
e. He died. ☐
f. Their children grew up and left home. ☐
g. She met him at a dance. ☐

Now cover the expressions. Try to complete the story below with words from the expressions.

I first (1) .... my husband over sixty years ago. He worked in a shop near my house. I went in there quite a lot and one day he asked me if I wanted to go to the cinema with him. We saw a film and he was really nice. I really liked him and we started (2) .... out together. We (3) .... married about a year later. It wasn't a very big wedding – just friends and family came. We bought a little house together and decided to start a family. We (4) .... four children – two boys and two girls. The children (5) .... up and (6) .... home and we decided we didn't need such a big place anymore. We sold our house in 1987. My husband and I (7) .... married for fifty-seven years. Sadly, he (8) .... a few years ago. I still think of him every day – I miss him so much!

2 | Practice

Think about the married couples you know. Do you know how they met? Do you know how long they've been married? Have they got any kids?

Spend five minutes planning what you want to say about the couples. Use some of the language in Activity 1 – and ask your teacher for help if you need to.

Now tell some other students as much as you can about the couples.

3 | Before you read

You are going to read an article about two different weddings in Britain. Before you read, discuss these questions with a partner.

1. Have you ever been to a wedding?
2. Who got married?
3. What was the wedding like?

4 | While you read

🎧 **Now read the article on the opposite page. As you read, tick (✔) anything that was the same at weddings you've been to; put a cross (✗) by anything that was different; and put an exclamation mark (!) next to anything that surprises you.**

5 | After you read

Tell a partner about the things you marked in the text. Use these sentences.

• This bit here was the same / different at the weddings I've been to.
• I'm really surprised about this bit here. I can't believe it!

6 | Speaking

Discuss these questions with a partner.

1. Do you usually give presents or money at weddings?
2. Do you usually give anything in these situations?
   • a friend's birthday
   • when you go to a friend's house for dinner
   • at Christmas
   • at New Year
   • when a friend has a baby
3. Are there any other times you give people presents – or get them yourself?

The Big Day

In Britain today, a lot of people get divorced. In fact, around 35% of marriages end in divorce, but people still love to get married – and they spend a lot of money doing it. In Britain, people usually spend around £11,000 on their wedding! However, different people have different weddings. We asked two people to tell us about their big days. Here's what they told us.

David and Elena

We had a very traditional wedding and it was very expensive, but it was worth it. Elena and I only paid half. Her parents paid for everything else. We got married in church. Elena wore a white dress and she looked fantastic. I wore a suit and I think I looked quite good too! We travelled in a big Rolls Royce – for the only time in my life – and we had a big reception. We had 200 guests. The reception was in an old castle, which is now a hotel, and they have some beautiful gardens where we drank champagne and we took all the photos. We had a big party in the evening with a jazz band playing and later we had a disco. It was just a great day – the best day of my life. I remember Elena's dad gave a really long speech after the dinner, which was a bit boring, and at the end of it, he started crying. In the evening, my Auntie Jackie got a bit drunk and started singing very loudly, which was a bit embarrassing. But those things are part of the day. They always happen and we laugh about it now.

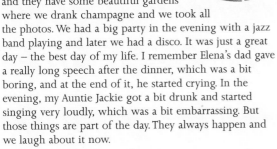

Maria and Colin

I think we only spent £500 on our wedding. We got married in a registry office and then we went for a meal in a local Italian restaurant with just our close families – parents, brothers and sisters. I think there were maybe 25 of us. It was really nice. We didn't have any speeches – just nice food, which my dad paid for. Some friends of ours got married on the same day, so we had a party together in the evening and shared the cost. We hired a big local hall and bought all the drink and got friends to bring food to share. Some other friends played music and DJ-ed for us. We probably invited about 170 people and then there were about 50 kids as well! It was great. I really enjoyed it.

Real English: DJ-ed

A DJ is someone who plays records on the radio or in a club or disco. We also use it as a verb, so when we have a party we need someone to do the DJ-ing or DJ for us.

7 | Using grammar: making suggestions

We often make suggestions by saying Why don't you ... ? **or** How about ... ?

Match the problems with the suggestions.

1. I don't know what to give my mum for her birthday.
2. I don't know what to wear to my friend's wedding next week.
3. My teacher has invited us to a party at his house. I don't know what to take.
4. My friend's just had a baby. I don't know what to give them.
5. My English isn't very good. I don't know what to do about it.

a. How about some clothes for when it's a bit older?
b. Why don't you get a private teacher? That might help.
c. Why don't you wear your grey suit? You look good in that.
d. How about some perfume? Something expensive.
e. Why don't you take some food from your country?

🎧 **Listen and check your answers. In which conversations does the first speaker like the suggestion?**

Work with a partner.
Student A: Read the problems. Listen to your partner's suggestions, then say if you like the suggestions or not.
Student B: Listen to your partner's problems. Make different suggestions for the problems.

> For more information on making suggestions, see G26.

Review: Units 19-24

1 | Grammar: continuous forms

Complete the sentences with the words in the box.

| doing | feeling | looking | meeting | saying | staying |

The present continuous

Positive: I'm .... some friends of mine later.

Negative: I'm not .... anything today.

Question: Are you .... OK?

The past continuous

Positive: We met when we were .... in the same hotel.

Negative: Oh, I'm sorry. I wasn't ....

Question: Sorry, what were you .... ?

Complete the conversations.

1. A: What .... you .... tonight? (do)
   B: I .... some friends for a coffee and a chat. What about you? (meet)
   A: Oh, I .... for dinner with my parents. (go)

2. A: What did he say?
   B: I don't know. I .... (not / listen)

3. A: Where's your wife?
   B: She's gone to the bathroom.
      She .... very well. (not / feel)

4. A: So how did you meet Princess Margaret?
   B: I .... in a shop and she came in one day. (work)

5. A: I phoned you last night, but you didn't answer.
   B: Yes, sorry. I .... a programme on TV. (watch)

6. A: .... it still .... outside? (rain)
   B: No, it's OK. It's stopped.

Now discuss these questions with a partner.

1. What're you doing tonight?
2. Do you ever go out for dinner with your parents? Where to?
3. Have you ever seen or met any famous people? Where?

2 | Describing changes

Complete the sentences with the comparative form of the adjectives in the box.

| cheap | easy | expensive | fat | good | tall |

1. Houses here have got a lot .... over the last few years. They were much cheaper ten years ago.

2. People have got a lot .... over the last fifty years. I'm 1 metre 85, my dad's only 1 metre 60!

3. My English has got a lot .... over the last two or three years.

4. People here have got a lot .... It's a big problem now. Lots of people weigh over 100 kilos!

5. Exams have got a lot .... over the last few years. More people pass them now.

6. Travel has got a lot .... over the last few years. You can fly to another country for about £10 now.

Are any of the sentences true for you or your country? Can you change the false ones to make them true?

3 | I couldn't

Match the problems with the reasons.

1. Sorry I couldn't meet you last night.
2. I couldn't see the actors.
3. I couldn't hear what she was saying.
4. I couldn't understand the film.
5. I couldn't sleep last night.
6. I couldn't think!

a. She was speaking really quietly!
b. I had to work late.
c. I was worried about my exams.
d. I was really really tired!
e. It was all in English!
f. There was a really tall man sitting in front of me.

Work with a partner. Think of one more reason to explain each problem. Compare your ideas with another group.

Have you ever had any of these problems? Why?

116

4 | Questions

Match the questions with the answers.

1. What's the best place to go shopping?
2. What's the best time of year to visit?
3. Are you doing anything to celebrate?
4. What's she like?
5. I like the chair. Where did you get it?
6. What was the score?

a. Spring. It's nice and warm then.
b. She's great. She's really funny and really easy to talk to.
c. Brazil won 3–0.
d. Well, there's a great market in Notting Hill. It's really good.
e. We bought it in Morocco when we went there on holiday.
f. Yes, I'm going out for dinner with a couple of friends.

Put the words in order and make questions.

1. you / sport / like / Do ?
2. you / tennis / like / Do / playing ?
3. your / parents / are / What / like ?
4. the / in / What's / best / eat / to / town / place ?
5. way / to / your / best / get / the / house / What's / to ?
6. you / best / What's / to / phone / the / time ?

Ask a partner the questions and find out their answers.

5 | Verbs

Complete the sentences with the past simple form of the verbs in the box.

| cause | fail | get | lend | spend | take |

1. It .... me two hours to get home last night!
2. It was a very expensive wedding. They .... over £20,000 on it.
3. It was a horrible accident. His hand .... stuck in a machine!
4. I .... him my tennis racket last week and he's still got it!
5. There was an accident in the factory last year. It .... a lot of pollution.
6. A: How was your driving test? Did you pass?
   B: No, I .... !

6 | Look back and check

Work with a partner and do one of these activities again.

a. Use the ideas in Activity 6 on page 97 to have three similar conversations. Read Conversation 3 before you start and make sure that you remember all the vocabulary.

b. Use the ideas in Activity 4 on page 108 to have three similar conversations. Read the conversations in Using grammar before you start and make sure that you remember all the vocabulary.

7 | What can you remember?

With a partner, write down as much as you can remember about the texts you read in Unit 19 and Unit 22.

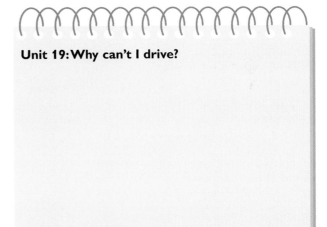

Unit 19: Why can't I drive?

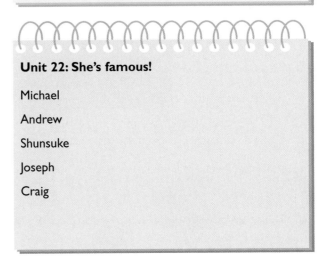

Unit 22: She's famous!

Michael

Andrew

Shunsuke

Joseph

Craig

117

8 | Vocabulary builder: food and cooking

Discuss these questions with a partner.

1. Are you a good cook?
2. What's the best thing you can cook?
3. How do you cook it?

Use the words with these pictures to help you.

Read these questions. Spend five minutes thinking about your answers. Use a dictionary if you need to – or ask your teacher for words.

a. What kind of food do you like boiled?
b. What kind of food do you like steamed?
c. What kind of food do you like grilled?
d. What kind of food do you like fried?
e. What kind of food do you like roasted?
f. What kind of food do you like mashed?

Now discuss the questions with a new partner.

chop

fry

boil

roast

grill

mash

steam

118

9 | Listening: *I like your flat*

🎧 **Listen to a conversation between two friends, Carrie and John. Carrie is visiting John in his new flat for the first time. Cover the conversation below. Make notes on everything you hear about the flat.**

Listen again and complete the conversation.

J: Hi, Carrie. How are you?

C: Fine, thanks. (1) .... to see you.

J: Yes. You too. Come in, come in. Would you like a drink?

C: Oh, yes please. Do you have any fruit juice?

J: Yes, sure. (2) .... ? Orange, apple or pineapple?

C: Orange, please.

J: OK. Just a second. (3) ....

C: Thanks. I like your flat. It's lovely.

J: It's nice, isn't it?

C: Yes, it is. So (4) .... been here?

J: Not long. About three months. Do you want to see the rest of the flat?

C: Yes, great.

J: Well, this is our bedroom.

C: Wow! (5) .... !

J: Yes, I know. And this is the kitchen.

C: Oh, it's great. Wow! What a lovely table. Where (6) .... ?

J: Oh, I got it in a shop in the centre of town. It was on sale.

C: Oh, I love it. (7) .... had it?

J: A long time – about four or five years. I brought it with me when I moved.

C: Well, it's really nice.

J: Thanks. Oh, would you like another juice?

C: Yes please. Could I use your toilet?

J: Yes, of course. It's just there (8) ....

Discuss these questions with a partner.

1. What's the best thing in your house?
2. Where did you get it?
3. How long've you had it?

10 | Pronunciation: the letter 'e'

The letter 'e' can be pronounced in lots of different ways. For example:

/e/   bed

/juː/   new

/iː/   we

/ə/   sister

/ɪ/   racket

🎧 **Listen and repeat these sounds and words.**

Look at the grid. Try to find a way from START to FINISH which only uses the sound /e/. You can only go →, ← or ↓.

🎧 **Now listen and check your answer.**

START			
collect	great	heart	accident
dentist's	children	there	different
get	let	government	prefer
where	tennis	return	interesting
lend	extra	kitchen	open
best	early	ear	really
friendly	celebrate	league	basketball
few	central	wedding	kettle
			FINISH

11 | Collocations

Now find another way from START to FINISH by choosing the correct words to complete the sentences below.

1. I have to .... my daughters from school.
2. What a .... painting! Where did you get it?
3. My uncle died last year. He had a .... attack.
4. The film was really scary. .... was lots of blood.
5. I don't agree with lots of things the .... does.
6. I'd like a .... ticket to Verona, please.
7. It's a great house. The .... is really big!
8. Do you play rugby? We need an .... player.
9. The .... train arrives in Berlin at eight in the morning.
10. Are you doing anything to .... ?
11. Real Madrid are top of the .... now.
12. I'm going to my sister's .... on Saturday.
13. I'll just go and put the .... on.

Tapescript

Unit 1

4 | Listening: *Do you know my sister?* (page 8)

Conversation 1
(P = Peter, Y = Yuka)
P: Hello. Is anyone sitting here?
Y: No. Please. Sit down.
P: Thanks. I'm Peter. What's your name?
Y: Yuka. Hi.
P: So where are you from, Yuka?
Y: Japan. What about you?
P: Switzerland.

Conversation 2
(J = Jane, F = Franco, M = Maria)
J: Hello.
F: Hello! How are you?
J: Fine. And you?
F: Yeah, fine.
J: Do you know my friend, Maria?
F: No, I don't think so.
J: Well, Maria. This is Franco. He's from Italy.
M: Hi. Nice to meet you.
F: Hi. Where are you from, Maria?
M: Brazil.
F: Right. Listen, have you two got time for a coffee?
J: Maria, have we got time?
M: Yes, sure.

Conversation 3
H: Hello!
B: Hi, how are you?
H: Fine. And you?
B: OK. So what are you doing here?
H: I'm doing some shopping.
B: Yes, we are too. Do you know my sister Leanne?
H: No, I don't think so. Hiya, I'm Hiro.
B: Hiro works with me.
L: Oh really. Well, it's nice to meet you. Where are you from, Hiro?
H: Japan. I'm sorry, how do you say your name?
L: Leanne.
H: Oh, OK. Leanne. Right. So Leanne, do you live here?
L: No, I'm just visiting Brenda for the weekend. I live in Hull.

Unit 2

2 | Whereabouts? (page 12)

1. A: Where are you from?
   B: France.
   A: Oh really? Whereabouts?
   B: Paris, the capital.

2. A: Where are you from?
   B: Italy.
   A: Oh really? Whereabouts?
   B: Milan – in the north.

3. A: Where are you from?
   B: Japan.
   A: Oh really? Whereabouts?
   B: Hiroshima – in the south.

4. A: Where are you from?
   B: England.
   A: Oh really? Whereabouts?
   B: Birmingham – the second city.

3 | Listening: *Whereabouts? Is it far?* (page 12)

Conversation 1
(M = Mei, V = Victor)
M: So where are you from, Victor?
V: From Peru, in South America.
M: Oh really? Whereabouts?
V: I'm from Cuzco, the second city.
M: Oh really? Is it far from the capital?
V: Yes. It's about an hour by plane. Anyway, what about you, Mei? Where are you from?
M: I'm from Singapore.
V: Oh really? I know it well. I went there on holiday two years ago. It's really nice.
M: Oh, thanks. I like it too!

Conversation 2
(B = Bart, M = Maria)
B: So where are you from, Maria?
M: Spain.
B: Oh really? Whereabouts?
M: Valencia.
B: OK. I know it. I went there once. It's very nice.
M: Yeah, I like it. So what about you? Where are you from?
B: Belgium.
M: Oh really? Whereabouts? Brussels?
B: No. You probably don't know it. It's called Leuven. It's a small town.
M: Sorry. You're right – I don't know it!
B: That's OK. Not many people do.
M: Is it far from Brussels?
B: No, not really. It's about half an hour by car.

Conversation 3
J: So where are you from, Artur?
A: Poland.
J: Oh really? Whereabouts?
A: I'm from Warsaw, the capital. What about you? Where are you from?
J: I'm from London, actually.
A: Oh really? Whereabouts?
J: Bow. In east London.
A: Oh wow! Is it far from here?

J: No, not really. It's twenty minutes by underground and maybe half an hour by bus.
A: Oh, that's great.

7 | Pronunciation: stressed sounds (page 13)

bra ZIL	MEX i co
ENG land	PO land
I ta ly	south AF ri ca
ja PAN	SWITZ er land
bra ZIL ian	MEX i can
ENG lish	PO lish
i TA lian	south AF ri can
ja pa NESE	SWISS

Unit 3

5 | Listening: *What do you do?* (page 17)

Conversation 1
A: What do you do?
B: I'm a civil servant.
A: Oh right. Where do you work?
B: I work in a government department in the capital city, Zagreb. I work for the Health department.
A: And do you enjoy it?
B: Yes, it's OK. The money's good and the hours are OK. It's a bit boring sometimes, but it's all right.

Conversation 2
A: What do you do?
B: I'm a waiter.
A: Oh right. Where do you work?
B: In a big French restaurant near the station.
A: And do you enjoy it?
B: No, not really. I work really long hours. I start at eleven in the morning and work until twelve o'clock at night. It's horrible!

Conversation 3
A: What do you do?
B: I'm a shop assistant.
A: Oh right. Where do you work?
B: I work in a sports shop near the university.
A: And do you enjoy it?
B: Yes, it's great. I like meeting new people and I like talking to them, so it's good for me. And the money's OK. And what do you do?
A: I'm a lawyer.
B: Oh right. Where do you work?
A: In the centre of the city. I work for a big firm there. We do international law.
B: And do you enjoy it?
A: Yes, I do. It's quite difficult sometimes, but I like it.

Conversation 4
T: What do you do?
L: I'm a doctor.
T: Oh right. Where do you work?
L: In a clinic in a small town in the north of the country.
T: And do you enjoy it?
L: Yes. I work long hours and it's quite difficult sometimes, but I like helping people. The money is good too. What do you do?

T: I'm a teacher.
L: Oh right. Where do you do that?
T: In a primary school in Bournemouth – in the south of England.
L: And do you enjoy it?
T: It's OK. The money isn't very good and I work really long hours. I like working with children, but sometimes I do a lot of paperwork too. That's really boring.

6 | Pronunciation: stressed sounds (page 19)

AW ful	CEN tre
THOU sand	GOV ern ment
a CCOUN tant	COM pany
PA per work	DI ffi cult
de PART ment	un i VER si ty

Unit 4

3 | Listening: *What're you doing tonight?* (page 21)

Conversation 1
A: What are you doing today?
B: Well, this afternoon, I'm going to play tennis with a friend and after that we're going for a coffee. What about you?
A: I don't know. Nothing much.

Conversation 2
A: What are doing after the class?
B: I'm just going to go home. I'm really tired. Why? What are you doing?
A: I'm going to go to the cinema to see the new Tarantino film.
B: Oh yes. I like his films.
A: Do you want to come with me?
B: Thanks, but not tonight. I'm really tired. I'm just going to go to bed early.

Conversation 3
A: What are you doing now?
B: Nothing much. I'm just going to go back to the hotel and have a shower. What about you?
A: I don't know. Nothing really. Do you want to go for a drink?
B: Yes, OK. That'd be nice.
A: There's a nice bar near here.
B: OK. Let's go.

Conversation 4
A: What are you doing at the weekend?
B: Nothing much. I'm going to go shopping on Saturday, but not much else. Why? What are you doing?
A: Well, I'm going to see The Strikes in concert on Saturday. Do you want to come?
B: Yes, OK. That'd be great. How much are the tickets?
A: £20.
B: Oh, right. Thanks, but it's too expensive. I don't have much money. Sorry.
A: That's OK. Maybe some other time.

Conversation 5
K: What are you doing tonight?
N: I'm going to go for a meal in the town.
K: Are there any good restaurants?
N: I don't know. I'm just going to walk round the town and see what there is. What about you?

K: Oh, I don't know. Nothing much. I think I'm just going to stay here and read my book.

N: Do you want to come with me? I'm going on my own.

K: Thanks, but I don't have much money. I'm going to eat here at the hostel.

7 | Pronunciation: /iː/ and /uː/ (page 21)

teach	/tiːtʃ/
do	/duː/
meet	/miːt/
you	/juː/
e-mail	/iːmeɪl/
two	/tuː/
leave	/liːv/
student	/ˈstjuːdənt/
feel	/fiːl/
university	/juːnɪˈvɜːsətɪ/
Greece	/griːs/

Unit 5

3 | Listening: *Did you have a nice weekend?* (page 24)

Conversation 1

A: Did you have a nice weekend?

B: It was OK. Nothing special.

A: Oh right. What did you do?

B: I just went shopping on Saturday and on Sunday I just stayed at home and I read a book, studied a bit. That's all. What about you?

Conversation 2

A: Did you have a nice weekend?

B: Yes, it was OK.

A: What did you do?

B: Nothing much. We went for a walk in the park on Sunday, I did some housework, I read the paper. The usual things.

Conversation 3

A: Did you have a nice weekend?

B: No, not really.

A: Oh dear. What happened?

B: Oh, I was really ill. I stayed in bed all weekend. It was really boring.

A: What a shame. Are you feeling better now?

B: A bit better, thanks, but now I have to go to work!

Conversation 4

J: Did you have a nice weekend?

H: Yes, it was great.

J: Really? What did you do?

H: Well, I went to the cinema on Friday with my friend Jules. We saw a great film. Then on Saturday I went on a trip to York with some people from my class. It was great. We walked all round the old town. We saw the cathedral. It was beautiful. And then we went to the pub together in the evening.

J: It sounds great.

H: Yes, it was. We really enjoyed it.

6 | Pronunciation: /iː/, /e/ and /æ/ (page 25)

read	/riːd/
bed	/bed/
bad	/bæd/
feel	/fiːl/
well	/wel/
that	/ðæt/
meal	/miːl/
went	/went/
had	/hæd/
week	/wiːk/
send	/send/
relax	/rɪˈlæks/
e-mail	/ˈiːmeɪl/
get	/get/
back	/bæk/

7 | Pronunciation: /eɪ/, /aɪ/, /au/ and /əʊ/ (page 27)

1.
round	/raʊnd/
town	/taʊn/
housework	/ˈhaʊswɜːk/
flowers	/ˈflaʊəz/
out	/aʊt/

2.
take	/teɪk/
stay	/steɪ/
paper	/ˈpeɪpə/
great	/greɪt/
rain	/reɪn/
gave	/geɪv/
paid	/peɪd/
came	/keɪm/
late	/leɪt/

3.
open	/ˈəʊpən/
don't	/dəʊnt/
go	/gəʊ/
cold	/kəʊld/
October	/ɒkˈtəʊbə/

4.
write	/raɪt/
nice	/naɪs/
hired	/haɪəd/
bicycle	/ˈbaɪsɪkl/
flight	/flaɪt/
night	/naɪt/
surprised	/səˈpraɪzd/

Unit 6

1 | Using vocabulary: subjects at university (page 28)

business	geography	literature
economics	history	mathematics
engineering	languages	tourism

A: What do you do?

B: I'm a student at university.

A: What are you studying?

B: Geography.

2 | Listening: *I'm a student* (page 28)

Conversation 1

A: What do you do?
B: I'm still at school, actually. I'm in my final year. I'm going to university next September.
A: Oh right. What are you going to study?
B: Business.
A: Oh really? Well, good luck. I hope you enjoy it.

Conversation 2

A: What do you do?
B: I'm a student at university.
A: Oh right. What are you studying?
B: Languages. I'm doing French and Italian.
A: Really? What year are you in?
B: My first.
A: And do you like it?
B: Yes, I do. It's really interesting.

Conversation 3

A: What do you do?
B: I'm a student at university.
A: Oh right. What are you studying?
B: Geography.
A: Really? What year are you in?
B: My second.
A: And do you like it?
B: No, not really. It's quite boring, actually.

Conversation 4

C: What do you do?
M: I'm a student at university.
C: Oh right. What are you studying?
M: Tourism.
C: Really? What year are you in?
M: My third.
C: And do you like it?
M: Yes, it's great. It's quite difficult, but it's really interesting.
C: Well, that's good. What're you going to do after university?
M: I'm going to find a job, I hope. I want to work for a big company and I want to travel more.
C: Well, good luck. I hope you get the job you want.

5 | Pronunciation: *-ed* endings (page 31)

asked	/aːskt/	needed	/'niːdɪd/
called	/kɔːld/	opened	/'əʊpənd/
decided	/dɪ'saɪdɪd/	paid	/peɪd/
enjoyed	/ɪn'dʒɔɪd/	phoned	/fəʊnd/
hated	/'heɪtɪd/	played	/pleɪd/
hired	/haɪəd/	rained	/reɪnd/
learned	/lɜːnd/	stayed	/steɪd/
liked	/laɪkt/	studied	/'stʌdiːd/
listened	/'lɪsənd/	visited	/'vɪzɪtɪd/
lived	/lɪvd/	waited	/'weɪtɪd/
loved	/lʌvd/	walked	/wɔːkt/
moved	/muːvd/	wanted	/'wantɪd/

Review: Units 1–6

10 | Listening: *I'm quite tired* (page 35)

C: Hello. How are you?
M: Hi. I'm fine.
C: Can I sit here?
M: Of course. So how are you?
C: Oh OK. I'm quite tired.
M: Did you go out last night?
C: Yes, I went out with my brother. It was his birthday.
M: Really? How old is he?
C: Twenty-three.
M: Right. What does he do?
C: He's a student.
M: What's he studying?
C: Law.
M: That's the same as you, isn't it?
C: Yes, but he's in his final year.
M: OK. So what year are you in?
C: My second year.
M: Right. I thought you were older.
C: No, I'm only twenty.
M: Right. So what time did you go to bed?
C: Four in the morning.
M: I'm not surprised you're tired.
C: Actually, I'm going out again after the class.
M: Really?
C: Yes, I'm going to see a film with a friend.
M: What film?
C: *Monster*. Are you doing anything later? Do you want to come?
M: I'm sorry. I can't. I've got a French class.
C: Oh well. Maybe some other time.

11 | Pronunciation: the letter 'a' (page 35)

made	/meɪd/
paid	/peɪd/
paper	/'peɪpə/
Monday	/'mʌndeɪ/
take	/teɪk/
game	/geɪm/
say	/seɪ/
wait	/weɪt/
played	/pleɪd/
e-mail	/'iːmeɪl/
great	/greɪt/
late	/leɪt/
April	/'eɪprəl/
came	/keɪm/

Unit 7

2 | Listening: *So what did you do last night?* (page 36)

Conversation 1
A: Hi. How're you?
B: Fine, thanks. And you?
A: Not too bad. So what did you do last night?
B: Oh, I had a driving lesson.
A: Really? How often do you do that?
B: Quite often. It's twice a week at the moment. I've got my test next month.
A: Really? Well, good luck with it! I'm sure you'll be OK.

Conversation 2
A: Hi, Ben.
B: Oh hello. How are you?
A: Fine thanks. And you?
B: I'm fine. So what did you do last night?
A: Nothing special. I just went running for a bit and then I went to bed quite early.
B: Running? How long've you been doing that?
A: About six weeks now. I'm trying to get fit.
B: Right. And how often do you do it?
A: Quite often. Maybe two or three times a week.
B: Really? Well, good luck with it!

Conversation 3
D: Hi, Jan. How're you?
J: Fine, thanks. And you?
D: Oh, not too bad. So what did you do last night?
J: Well, after work, I met a friend and we played golf together for a couple of hours.
D: That sounds good. How often do you do that?
J: Not very often. Once or twice a month, but I'm better than my friend. I beat her last night. Anyway, what about you? What did you do last night?
D: I had a piano lesson.
J: Oh really? You're learning the piano! That's great! How long have you been doing that?
D: Not very long. Yesterday was only my second lesson, actually.
J: Really? Well, good luck with it!

5 | Pronunciation: /f/ and /v/ (page 39)

1. How long've you been doing that?
2. How often do you do that?
3. Not very long.
4. Not very often.
5. I'm a big football fan.
6. It's a really funny film.
7. I laughed a lot.
8. What's your favourite book?
9. I haven't really got a favourite.
10. That's a difficult question.

Unit 8

3 | Listening: free time (page 40)

Conversation 1
A: What did you do yesterday?
B: I went to Wimbledon to watch the tennis.
A: Really? Did you enjoy it?
B: Yes, it was great, but it started raining at about five – so it finished early. Do you like tennis?
A: Yes, it's OK. I usually watch Wimbledon when it's on. Do you like playing?
B: Yes, but I'm not very good.
A: No, me neither, but I quite like playing. We should have a game sometime.
B: Yes, OK. That'd be great.
A: Do you like any other sports?
B: Yes, I really like running.
A: Really? I don't. I find it a bit boring.
B: Really? I love it.
A: How often do you go?
B: Almost every day, if I can.

Conversation 2
A: What's that you're reading?
B: *About a Boy* by Nick Hornby.
A: Oh, I don't know him. Do you like it?
B: It's OK. It's quite funny, but it's not as good as his other books. So do you like reading?
A: Yes. I read a lot.
B: What kind of books do you like?
A: Anything really. I really like Paulo Coelho.
B: Me too. I've read most of his books. What about Dan Jackson? Do you like his books?
A: I don't know him.
B: Really. I think he's my favourite author. You should read his books. They're sad and funny and have really good characters. It's really difficult to stop reading them, you know.
A: Yes. They sound good.

Conversation 3
P: What are you doing tonight?
D: I'm going to my salsa class.
P: Really? How long have you been doing that?
D: Not very long. This is my third lesson. Do you like dancing?
P: No, not really. I'm not very good at it. I always step on other people's feet and I find it really embarrassing.
D: So what do you do in your free time?
P: Well, I love shopping and I go to the cinema a lot.
D: Me too. What kind of films do you like?
P: Action movies and comedies.
D: Me too. Do you like Harry Robbins?
P: Yes. He's great. He's got a new film out.
D: Yes. We should go and see it together.
P: Yes. That'd be great.

6 | Pronunciation: weak forms – *of, to, than* (page 43)

better than me	/ˈbetəðənmi/
kind of	/ˈkaɪndəv/
need to do it	/ˈniːtəduːɪt/
think of him	/ˈθɪŋkəvhɪm/

1. What did you think of it?
2. There's lots of choice.
3. It's better than here.
4. He's worse than me.
5. It's easy to do.
6. He's easy to talk to.
7. I need to go.
8. I'd like to go there some day.
9. What kind of things do you listen to?
10. I like pop music and that kind of thing.

Unit 9

2 | Listening: *What are you doing now?* (page 44)

Conversation 1

A: What are you doing now?
B: Nothing really. Do you want to go and get something to eat?
A: Yes, definitely. I'm really hungry. I just need to go to the bank to get some money first.
B: Me too. I'll come with you.
A: OK. Where do you want to eat?
B: How about the Chinese restaurant in Burke Street?
A: Yes, OK. There's a bank with a cash machine next to the restaurant.
B: Exactly. Shall we go then?
A: Yes.

Conversation 2

A: What are you doing now?
B: I'm just going home. I'm going out later and I need to finish my homework first.
A: Oh right.
B: Why? What are you doing?
A: Oh nothing. Do you want to go for a coffee? Have you got time?
B: Sorry. I really need to go home and do this homework. I have to give it to my teacher tomorrow.
A: Oh well, maybe we could meet tomorrow after the class.
B: Sure.

Conversation 3

R: What are you doing now?
M: I'm going to look for an internet café. I need to send a few e-mails. The last time I wrote to my family was about two weeks ago. What about you? What are you doing?
R: Oh, I think I'm going to go shopping. I want to buy some presents to take back for my family. I need to get a new film for my camera. I've only got three pictures left.
M: You should get a digital camera.
R: Maybe, but the pictures are better on my camera.
M: Yes, I know what you mean. Anyway, do you want to meet somewhere later?
R: Yes, OK. What time?
M: Four o'clock? That gives us two hours.
R: OK. Fine.
M: Shall we just meet back here?
R: Yes, I'll see you in a couple of hours then.
M: Yes, see you.

7 | Pronunciation: /iː/, /uː/, /ɔː/ and /ɑː/ (page 45)

/uː/		/ɑː/	
do	/duː/	parcel	/ˈpɑːsl/
few	/fjuː/	dance	/dɑːns/
new	/njuː/	guitar	/ɡɪˈtɑː/
food	/fuːd/	half	/hɑːf/
two	/tuː/	hard	/hɑːd/
group	/ɡruːp/	car	/kɑː/
who's	/huːz/	camera	/ˈkæm(ə)rə/
couple	/ˈkʌpl/		

/ɔː/		/iː/	
call	/kɔːl/	we	/wiː/
talk	/tɔːk/	mean	/miːn/
all	/ɔːl/	need	/niːd/
four	/fɔː/	meet	/miːt/
sports	/spɔːts/	leave	/liːv/
boring	/ˈbɔːrɪŋ/	see	/siː/
more	/mɔː/	week	/wiːk/
born	/bɔːn/	dream	/driːm/
foreign	/ˈfɒrən/	present	/ˈprezənt/

Unit 10

4 | Listening: *Have you been there?* (page 48)

S: What are you doing today?
E: We're going to go to the cathedral. Have you been there?
S: Yes, I went there a few days ago when I arrived. It's lovely.
E: Oh good. It sounds great. Did you go up the tower?
S: No, I didn't want to pay. I walked to the hill outside the city. Have you been there? You get a really good view.
E: Yes, we went there yesterday, but it rained really badly.
S: I know. The weather was awful yesterday. I went there the day before yesterday, when the weather was OK, so I was quite lucky.
E: Yes, you were. We got really wet. So what are you going to do today?
S: Oh, I think I'm going to leave. I think I've seen everything I want to see here.
E: So where are you going next?
S: I still haven't decided. Have you been to Vienna? There's a train that goes there this afternoon.
E: Yes, we went there a couple of weeks ago. It's nice, but it's quite expensive.
S: Yes, I've heard that. If I go to Vienna though, I can get a train to Istanbul.
E: Istanbul! Oh yes. It's great there. I went a few years ago with my girlfriend.
K: I'm sorry?
E: I mean my ex-girlfriend.
K: Thank you. I don't want to hear what you did with your EX-girlfriend.
E: OK, sorry, you're right. But Istanbul IS amazing. You should go there. And it's cheaper than here.
S: Well, maybe I'll do that. I should go and pack my bag.
E: OK. See you.
K: Good luck, if we don't see you again.
S: Thanks. It was nice meeting you and enjoy the rest of your trip.

Tapescript

5 Pronunciation: contractions (page 51)

1. I've never been there, but I'd like to go.
2. I've heard it's nice.
3. I still haven't decided.
4. I'm going to leave tomorrow.
5. I didn't do anything last weekend.
6. I didn't want to pay to go up the tower.
7. Good luck, if we don't see you again.
8. It's got a lovely sandy beach.
9. It's got great nightlife.
10. It's really wild and beautiful.

Unit 11

3 Listening: *Is there one near here?* (page 52)

Conversation 1

A: What are you doing now?
B: I'm going to look for an internet café. I need to send a few e-mails. Is there one near here?
A: Yes. Well, it's quite near.
B: Great. Could you draw me a map?
A: Yes, of course. OK. We're here on Carlisle Street. You go up this road until you get to the end. You go past two sets of traffic lights and you come to Church Road here. It's just round the corner from there. It's in the first road on the right – James Street. It's just up there, on the left. It's opposite a supermarket. Look – here. OK?
B: Oh, that's great. Thanks for your help.
A: No problem. See you.
B: Bye.

Conversation 2

A: What're you doing now?
B: Nothing much. I'm just going to go home. Why? What're you doing?
A: Oh, I'm going to look for a bookshop. I need to buy a book for my English course. Is there one near here?
B: Yes. There's one about five minutes away. It's quite close.
A: Oh, good. Could you show me how to get there on this map?
B: Yes, OK. One minute. Where are we? Oh, OK. We're here – on Carlisle Street and the bookshop is here – on Cloone Street. It's near the end of the road, next to the church.
A: Oh, great. Thanks.
B: It's quite a big shop. You can't miss it.
A: OK. See you later.
B: Yes, bye.

Conversation 3

L: What're you doing now?
K: Well, I'm quite hungry. I'd like to get some lunch. Is there a good restaurant near here?
L: Yes, there's one quite near here – on Lincoln Road.
K: I'm not sure where that is. Could you tell me how to get there?
L: Yes, of course. You go up Carlisle Street until you come to the second set of traffic lights. Lincoln Road is there. If you turn left at the traffic lights, it's up the road there, on the right.
K: OK. I think I know where you mean. I'll try to find it.
L: It's easy to find. You'll be OK. Have a good meal.
K: Thanks. I'll see you tomorrow.
L: OK. Bye.

7 Pronunciation: /θ/ and /ð/ (page 53)

1. the 4th of January
2. the 5th of February
3. the 6th of March
4. the 7th of April
5. the 8th of May
6. the 9th of June
7. the 10th of July
8. the 11th of August
9. the 12th of September
10. the 21st of October
11. the 2nd of November
12. the 3rd of December

Unit 12

2 Listening: *What are you doing here?* (page 56)

Conversation 1

A: Hello. Is this seat free?
B: Yes. Go ahead. Sit down.
A: Are you going to Glasgow?
B: Yes.
A: Me too.
B: Where are you from?
A: Germany.
B: Oh right. How long have you been here?
A: Not very long. I arrived in London last Thursday.
B: Your English is very good.
A: Thanks.
B: So, what are you doing here? Is it business or pleasure?
A: Business, really. I work for an export company.
B: Oh right. Do you enjoy it?
A: Yes, it's OK. I like travelling, so that's good.
B: Yes. Have you been to Glasgow before?
A: Yes, a few times. We sometimes do business there and I have friends who live there.
B: Oh, OK. That's nice. So it's both business and pleasure.
A: Yes.

Conversation 2

A: Excuse me. Do you speak English?
B: Yes, sure.
A: I'm trying to find the Louvre.
B: Oh right. Actually, I'm going in that direction. I'll show you, if you like.
A: Oh right. Thanks.
B: So where are you from?
A: Colombia.
B: Really! It's a beautiful country.
A: Have you been there?
B: Yes. I visited Bogota two years ago. And what are you doing here in Paris?
A: I'm just here on holiday. I'm travelling all round Europe.
B: Very nice. So have you been here before?
A: No. It's my first time here.
B: Oh really? And what do you think of it here?
A: Oh, it's great. It's true what people say. It's very romantic.
B: Yes. Where are you staying?
A: Near Montmartre.
B: Oh yes. It's wonderful there. I live quite near.
A: Really.
B: Perhaps you would like a guide. See the nightlife?

A: I ... er ...

B: Are you doing anything later?

A: No, I mean, I think I'll probably just get something to eat and go to bed quite early.

B: Yes? I know lots of wonderful restaurants.

A: That's OK. I'll probably eat at my hotel. Are we near the museum?

B: Yes, it's quite near. You're very beautiful.

4 | Conversation: booking a room (page 59)

R: Good morning, Western House.

A: Hi, I'd like to book a single room for two nights, please.

R: Certainly, madam. For which dates?

A: I'm arriving on the 14th of April and I'm leaving on the 16th.

R: OK. I'm just checking on the computer. OK. That's fine. How are you going to pay?

A: Is American Express OK?

R: Yes, of course. The full cost is £100. Can I take your number?

A: Yes, sure. It's 0489–6666–1072–3465.

R: And the expiry date?

A: 04–09.

R: And your name as it appears on the card?

A: Mrs A. Jones.

R: Great. Thank you, Mrs Jones. That's one single room for April the 14th and 15th. We look forward to seeing you then.

J: Great. Thank you. Bye.

Review: Units 7–12

9 | Listening: *My brother's there now* (page 63)

A: Is there anything interesting in the paper?

S: No, nothing much. Just more bad news. It's really awful. There's quite an interesting story about Uzbekistan, though. I didn't really know anything about the country before.

A: Can I read it? My brother's there now.

S: Your brother is in Uzbekistan! What's he doing there?

A: Oh, he's living there.

S: He's living there! Er. Why? I mean, what does he do?

A: Well, he's an engineer really, but at the moment he's teaching English.

S: OK, but why Uzbekistan?

A: Well, his wife is from there.

S: Ah, I see. So why don't they live here in Britain?

A: They did. But her parents are quite old and she wanted to go back there.

S: So how long have they been there?

A: Not long. About six months.

S: So, what does he think of it?

A: It's quite hard. It's very different to Britain and he doesn't speak much of their language. That's why he's teaching English. He can't work as an engineer.

S: He must really love her!

A: Yes, I suppose so.

10 | Pronunciation: the letter 'o' (page 63)

hot	/hɒt/	stop	/stɒp/
cost	/kɒst/	a lot	/ə 'lɒt/
sorry	/'sɒrɪ/	top	/tɒp/
lost	/lɒst/	long	/lɒŋ/
job	/dʒɒb/	golf	/gɒlf/
on	/ɒn/	problems	/'prɒbləmz/
wrong	/rɒŋ/		

Unit 13

2 | Listening: *What time?* (page 64)

Conversation 1

A: Do you want to have a coffee somewhere?

B: Yes, maybe. What time is it now?

A: Eight o'clock.

B: Eight? Really? Oh no! I thought it was earlier. Listen, I should go. I'm late for work.

A: Oh, OK. Bye. See you.

Conversation 2

A: Are you OK? You look really tired.

B: I know. I am. I'm exhausted.

A: Why? What time did you go to bed last night?

B: Quite late, actually. About 2.30.

A: Really? That IS late.

B: I know. Some friends came to my house for dinner and then we started chatting and we had a bottle of wine – or two – and then suddenly I looked at my watch and it was two o'clock.

A: Oh no!

B: Yes, and then I got up this morning at seven, so I don't feel great now.

A: Oh well. It's Saturday tomorrow, so you can sleep more then.

B: Yes, that's true. Thank goodness!

Conversation 3

A: What time's your flight tomorrow?

B: A quarter to ten, I think. In the evening.

A: Oh, OK, so you need to get to the airport by about eight, then.

B: Yes, I guess so. How long does it take to get there from here?

A: About an hour, if the traffic is OK. We should leave the house at around seven.

B: OK.

A: And what time do you land in Berlin?

B: About one, I think. I'm going to get a taxi to my hotel.

A: Yes, that's a good idea.

Conversation 4

R: So what time do you want to meet tonight?

J: I'm not sure. What time is it now?

R: 4.30.

J: OK. Well, what time does the film start?

R: Eight.

J: Right. Well, I need to go home first and have a shower and change my clothes. That'll probably take me an hour.

R: OK. So let's meet at seven. Is that OK?

J: Yes, that's fine. Where do you want to meet?

R: Let's just meet outside the cinema.

J: OK. See you later.

R: Bye.

7 | Pronunciation: /ʃ/ (page 67)

share	/ʃeə/
shower	/ʃaʊə/
cash machine	/'kaʃ məʃiːn/
should	/ʃʌd/
short	/ʃɔːt/
shirt	/ʃɜːt/
shoes	/ʃuːz/
shelves	/ʃelvz/
shut	/ʃʌt/
English	/'ɪŋglɪʃ/
station	/'steɪʃən/

1. She's in the shower.
2. I'll show you where the shop is.
3. She speaks some English.
4. You should go to the new shoe shop.
5. Where did you get that shirt?
6. I like those shoes.
7. Shall we go?
8. I need to use the cash machine.

Unit 14

3 | Listening: *Sorry, could you help me, please?* (page 69)

Conversation 1
A: Sorry, could you help me with this suitcase, please? I can't lift it on my own.
B: Yes, sure. Eughh! It's really heavy! What have you got in there?
A: Oh, just a few things I need for my holiday.
B: How long are you going for – a month?
A: No – I'm just going for a week, but I don't know what the weather's going to be like!

Conversation 2
A: Ugghhhh! Can you see if you can open this, please? I can't get the top off.
B: Ugghhhh! It's really tight. Ugghhhh! Sorry I can't.
A: I thought you were strong!
B: I am! It's just too tight. Here, let me try again. Ugghhhh!

Conversation 3
A: Excuse me, you're tall. Can you get that magazine from the top shelf, please? I can't reach.
B: Sure. This one?
A: No. The one next to it – on the right. That's it.
B: There you go.
A: Thanks.
B: No problem.

Conversation 4
A: Can you help me with this exercise, please? I can't do it.
B: Yes, sure. It IS quite difficult. You need to match these sentences to the pictures.
A: What does 'I can't reach' mean?
B: It means ... well look at this picture. The man's too short. He can't reach the book on the shelf.

Conversation 5
A: So Bijun, have you got the answer to number 1?
B: I can't reach it.
A: Sorry, what was that?

B: I can't reach it.
A: Sorry, can you speak up, please? I can't hear you.
B: Eh?
A: You're very quiet. Maybe you're right – I just didn't hear the answer.
B: I can't reach it.
A: Yes, great. So number 1 is 'I can't reach it'.

Conversation 6
A: I'm sorry. Could you turn the music down, please? I'm trying to study.
B: Yes, sorry, I didn't think it was very loud.
A: Well, it is. I can't think when it's that loud.
B: OK. I'm sorry. Is that quiet enough?
A: Yes, thanks.

Conversation 7
A: I'm sorry, Bill. Can you close the curtains, please? I can't see the whiteboard.
B: Sure. The sun IS very bright.

Conversation 8
A: Excuse me, could you help us, please? We're looking for Mattison Road.
B: Oh right. Yes, it's just down this road. You get to a little shop and then you turn left and go down that road and I think it's the first or second road on the right.
A: OK, sorry. Can you show me on the map, please? I can't see it.
B: Sure. Eh, let me see. We're here and Mattison Road is here.
A: Oh right. Thanks.

1. Sorry, could you help me with this suitcase, please?
2. Can you see if you can open this, please?
3. Can you get that magazine from the top shelf, please?
4. Can you help me with this exercise, please?
5. Sorry, can you speak up, please?
6. I'm sorry. Could you turn the music down, please?
7. Can you close the curtains, please?
8. Can you show me on the map, please?

7 | Pronunciation: /k/ and /g/ (page 71)

cook	/kʊk/
crossed	/krɒst/
give	/gɪv/
group	/gruːp/
close	/kləʊz/
broke	/brəʊk/
get	/get/
big	/bɪg/
keys	/kiːz/
back	/bæk/
guess	/ges/
buggy	/'bʌgɪ/
kiss	/kɪs/
goes	/gəʊz/

1. I can't come to class next week.
2. I'm going to Greece on holiday.
3. I'll give you my jacket, if you like.
4. We don't usually kiss, we just shake hands.
5. I'm going to get back late.
6. Could you give me your keys?
7. I can't close the curtains. They're broken.
8. Could you carry the buggy?

Unit 15

2 Listening: *So what're you doing this weekend?* (page 72)

Conversation 1

A: So what're you doing this weekend?
B: I'm going to be really busy, actually. I'm going to meet some friends from my old job tonight and we're going to see a play at the Soho Theatre. Then tomorrow night, I'm going to cook dinner for some other friends.
A: Oh really? What're you going to cook?
B: I'm going to try making some Indian food. I'm going to do a chicken curry. I need to buy some things in town tomorrow morning first, though.
A: Right. Well, good luck with it.
B: Thanks. Have a good weekend.
A: Yes, you too. Bye.
B: Bye. See you Monday.

Conversation 2

A: So what're you doing this weekend?
B: I'm not really sure yet. I haven't really decided. I might just stay at home tomorrow and take it easy. I need a rest after this week.
A: Yes, I know how you feel. I'm exhausted as well!
B: But then on Sunday, I'm going to go running in the morning for an hour or two and in the afternoon, I think I'll probably go to the park. Anyway, what about you? What're you doing this weekend?
A: Well, tomorrow, I'm going to sleep until lunchtime! I really need a good, long sleep. Then I think I'll probably just stay at home and tidy up the flat. It's in a mess at the moment. On Sunday, I'm going to study for my English exam next week.
B: Oh no! I forgot about that.
A: Well, maybe you should spend some time studying as well, then.
B: Yes, I might. It depends how I feel. Anyway, look, I'll see you on Monday.
A: Yes, OK. Bye.

Conversation 3

S: So what're you doing this weekend?
M: I'm not really sure yet, actually. I don't have any plans. What about you?
S: Well, tonight I'm just going to stay at home. I might study some English. It depends how I feel. If I feel lazy, I think I'll probably just watch TV instead.
M: Oh, OK.
S: Yes, and then tomorrow, I think I'll probably go shopping for some new clothes.
M: Oh really? That sounds fun.
S: Well, look, why don't you come with me?
M: Really? Is that OK?
S: Yes, of course. I don't really like going shopping on my own.
M: OK, thanks. So where do you want to meet?
S: Let's meet at the entrance to the shopping mall.
M: OK. What time?
S: Is eleven OK or is that too early?
M: No, that's fine. It's great.
S: OK. Well, I'll see you tomorrow.
M: OK. Thanks again.
S: No problem.

5 Listening (page 75)

Message 1
Hi Rick. It's Debbie. Sorry, but I'm going to be late. I had a problem at work. I'll see you about seven o'clock.

Message 2
Hi Rick. It's Debbie. I'm really sorry, but the traffic's awful. I'm on the bus and we're just coming down Fanshaw Lane. I hope I'll be at the café by a quarter past seven. I hope you get this message.

Message 3
Hi Rick. It's Debbie. I'm outside the café. I mean, I think I am, but you're not here. I've lost the piece of paper with the name of the café you said.

Message 4
Hi Rick. It's Debbie. I guess you don't have your mobile. Listen, I'm going home. I'm a bit cold. I'm really sorry. It's my fault. Call me later, if you get this message.

Message 5
Hi Rick. It's Lucy. I'm just checking what time we're going to meet tomorrow. You said seven o'clock, right? Call me back. Love you!

Message 6
Hi Rick. It's Debbie. I'm home. You've got my number.

7 Pronunciation /l/ (page 75)

let's	/lets/
light	/laɪt/
left	/left/
plans	/plænz/
plate	/pleɪt/
ill	/ɪl/
shelf	/ʃelf/
call	/kɔːl/
felt	/felt/
pull	/pʊl/

1. Let's leave now.
2. The place was full of people.
3. I'll probably see them later.
4. Don't call me, I'll call you.
5. I'll turn the light on, if you like.
6. We need to go right not left.
7. I'll probably play football on Friday.
8. I don't feel very well. I need to lie down

Unit 16

4 Listening: *You're very quiet* (page 77)

T: Yong. Are you OK? You're very quiet.
Y: No, not really. I'm not feeling very well.
T: You don't look very well. Do you want to go and get a glass of water?
Y: Yes. I think I need to get some fresh air.
T: Maybe you should just go home.
Y: No, it's OK. I think if I go out for a few minutes, I'll be OK. I'll go now. I'll be back in five minutes.
T: Of course, take your time. There's no hurry. Yong! What have you done to your leg?
Y: I hurt it dancing.

T: Dancing?
Y: Yes. It's difficult to explain.
T: OK, I'm sorry. Can someone open the door for Yong? Thanks.
Y: Thanks. I'll be back in five minutes.
T: Sure. As I say, take your time.
Y: Thanks.
T: Poor Yong!

7 | Pronunciation: sounding positive (page 79)

1. Oh really?
2. That's nice.
3. It was all right.
4. Oh yes?
5. Oh right.
6. Wow! That's great!

Unit 17

4 | Listening: *What would you like?* (page 80)

K: This is very nice.
R: Yes, it is, isn't it?
K: Do you come here often?
R: Quite a lot. Especially in the summer. You can sit outside.
K: Mmm.
R: So what would you like?
K: I don't know. What's 'requeijão'?
R: It's a kind of cheese. It's quite soft and white.
K: OK. I don't really like cheese. What about 'crème de camarão'?
R: Oh, that's a kind of soup. It's made with … I don't know the name in English. It's a kind of seafood. They're like small mussels.
K: OK. Well, that sounds nice. I'll have that for a starter.
R: And what do you want for the main course?
K: I don't know. Can you recommend anything?
R: Right, well, the 'cabrito asado' is very nice, if you like goat.
K: Mmm, I don't really like red meat. I prefer chicken or fish really.
R: OK. Well, if you like chicken, you should try the 'frango no churrasco'. Do you like spicy food, because it's quite hot?
K: Yes, I love it.
R: Well, you should try that then. You'll love it.
K: OK.
R: Do you want rice or vegetables with that?
K: Vegetables are fine.
R: OK. What would you like to drink?
K: I'll just have water.
R: OK, are you sure? You don't want wine?
K: No thanks. Actually, I don't drink.
R: OK – do you want sparkling or still water?
K: Still's fine.
R: OK.

6 | Pronunciation: /w/ (page 83)

water	/ˈwɔːtə/
wine	/waɪn/
waiter	/ˈweɪtə/
waitress	/ˈweɪtrəs/
would	/wʌd/
want	/wɑnt/
week	/wiːk/
where	/weə/
when	/wen/
what	/wɑt/
sweet	/swiːt/
Sweden	/ˈswiːdən/

1. Would you like some water?
2. Would you like some white wine?
3. With milk or without?
4. What do you want?
5. We went to Italy for two weeks.
6. Where did the waitress go?

Unit 18

4 | Listening: *Do you sell swimsuits?* (page 84)

Conversation 1
A: Excuse me, do you speak English?
B: Sure.
A: Oh good. Do you sell swimsuits?
B: Yes, of course. You need to go to the sports department. It's on the fourth floor. You can take the lift over there.
A: OK.
B: When you come out of the lift, it's on the left.
A: Left. OK. Thanks.
B: No problem. Have a nice day.

Conversation 2
A: Excuse me. I'm looking for the toothbrushes. I can't see them anywhere.
B: They're just in the next aisle, on the bottom shelf.
A: Really? I couldn't see them.
B: Here, I'll show you. There.
A: Oh, yes. I'm sorry. That was stupid of me!
B: That's OK. Do you need anything else?
A: No, that's fine, thanks.

Conversation 3
A: Excuse me, do you sell batteries?
B: Yes sure. What kind do you need?
A: Umm, not like these. I need smaller ones. Like this. They're for my camera.
B: Oh right. I'm sorry. These are the only ones we've got. We don't sell that kind.
A: Oh right. Do you know where I can get them?
B: There's an electronics shop round the corner. You turn right when you come out of the shop and then right again. It's along that road on your right. It's maybe 100 metres. Maplins, it's called. I think it's next to the bank. Anyway, they'll probably have them.
A: OK, right, thanks. So right, right, and it's on the right.
B: Yes, that's right.
A: OK, great. Could I have a bottle of water, please?
B: That's 85 pence, please.
A: OK.
B: That's 15 change. Thank you.
A: OK, thanks. Bye

Conversation 4

A: That'll be £157.97 altogether, thank you.
B: OK. There you are.
A: Would you like any cash back?
B: No thanks. That's fine.
A: Could you just sign there, please?
B: OK.
A: Would you like me to wrap everything for you?
B: Yes, please.
A: There you are.
B: Thanks.
A: No problem.
B: By the way, are there any toilets in here?
A: Yes, if you go to the second floor, there are some on your right when you come off the escalator. There are signs showing where they are.
B: OK, thanks.
A: You're welcome. Have a nice day.

9 Pronunciation: /tʃ/ and /dʒ/ (page 85)

change	/tʃeɪndʒ/	change	/tʃeɪndʒ/
school	/skuːl/	ages	/ˈeɪdʒɪz/
children	/ˈtʃɪldrən/	ago	/əgəʊ/
cheese	/tʃiːz/	manager	/ˈmænɪdʒə/
stomach	/ˈstʌmək/	charge	/tʃɑːdʒ/
chocolates	/ˈtʃɒkləts/	bigger	/ˈbɪgə/
cheap	/tʃiːp/	just	/dʒʌst/
match	/mætʃ/	job	/dʒɒb/
headache	/ˈhedeɪk/	Japanese	/dʒæpəˈniːz/
choose	/tʃuːz/	lager	/ˈlɑːgə/
chips	/tʃɪps/	large	/lɑːdʒ/
		would you	/ˈwʊdʒə/
		did you	/ˈdɪdʒə/

1. Would you like some cheese?
2. Did you go to church yesterday?
3. Would you like me to show you?
4. Did you find the jeans you wanted?
5. He's just finished a job in Germany.
6. I've just joined a gym to get fit.

Review: Units 13–18

9 Listening: *What are you doing this weekend?* (page 91)

R: What are you doing this weekend?
J: I'm actually going back to Britain on Saturday for a few weeks.
R: Really? You didn't say anything about that before.
J: It's all happened quite quickly. I got a very cheap ticket.
R: Right. So what time's your flight?
J: Seven o'clock in the morning, so I need to get to the airport by five.
R: Really? Is it going from Tokyo Airport?
J: Yes.
R: Oh no, so what time are you going to leave your house?
J: I'm not sure. I'll probably leave about one o'clock.
R: That's terrible. I hate those early morning flights.
J: Yes, me too.
R: Are you doing anything tonight?
J: I don't have any plans. I think I'll probably just start packing.
R: Do you want to go out somewhere? I'm not going to see you for ages.

J: Yes, OK. I'll probably have enough time tomorrow to pack. What do you want to do?
R: Let's go to The Three Lions pub.
J: Yes, OK. I like it there. Do you want to meet there or somewhere else?
R: Let's meet there at, say, half past nine. I finish work at nine.
J: OK. That sounds great. I might phone a couple of other people, if that's OK.
R: Of course. I might ring Yoshiki and see if he can come.

10 Pronunciation: the letter 'i' (page 91)

light	/laɪt/	lie	/laɪ/
mobile	/ˈməʊbaɪl/	kind	/kaɪnd/
spicy	/ˈspaɪsɪ/	decided	/dɪˈsaɪdɪd/
sign	/saɪn/	exercise	/ˈeksɜːsaɪz/
flight	/flaɪt/	bright	/braɪt/
bicycle	/ˈbaɪsɪkəl/	tidy	/ˈtaɪdɪ/
exciting	/ɪkˈsaɪtɪŋ/		

Unit 19

3 Listening: *Sorry I couldn't come* (page 92)

Conversation 1

A: I'm so sorry I couldn't come to the airport to collect you this morning. Did you wait for me there?
B: Well, yes, I waited a while – maybe half an hour, but then I realized you weren't coming.
A: Oh no. I'm really sorry.
B: It's OK. I took the train in the end. It was fine. I'm here now.
A: I know. I'm glad you didn't have any other problems.
B: No, really. I was fine. So what happened to you, anyway?
A: Oh, I had to go to the hospital.
B: Oh no. Really? Why?
A: It's my grandfather – he's quite ill. He went into hospital a couple of days ago and this is the first time I could go and see him.
B: And how is he?
A: Not TOO bad. The doctors told him he should be out of hospital and home again in about a week, but he can't do very much at the moment.
B: Oh well, I'm glad he's OK, anyway.
A: Thanks … well, let's get something to eat. I'm really hungry.
B: Me too.

Conversation 2

A: Hi. Good morning.
B: Oh hello. How are you? What happened to you last Friday?
A: Yes, sorry I couldn't come to the class. I was ill.
B: That's OK. Are you feeling better now?
A: Yes, much better, thanks. Can you give me the papers from last week?
B: Yes, of course. Here you are.
A: Great. Thanks. I'll look at them tonight.
B: OK. No problem.

Conversation 3

M: Sorry I couldn't come out with you for dinner last night.
K: That's OK. Never mind.
M: I had to work late. I've got an important meeting on Friday and I had to get ready for it.
K: Yes. Diane told me. Never mind. We can do it some other time.

M: Good. I'd like that. Which restaurant did you go to?
K: We went to a new place in Brigham. It was great. They do traditional English food.
M: Oh really? Well, maybe we can go there again together.
K: OK. Great. Let me know when's a good time for you.
M: I will.

6 | Pronunciation: /h/ (page 95)

1. has   /hæz/
2. his   /hɪz/
3. I'm   /aɪm/
4. hand   /hænd/
5. open   /ˈəʊpən/
6. air   /eə/
7. heart   /hɑːt/
8. old   /əʊld/
9. ear   /ɪə/
10. hate   /heɪt/

1. It's half past eight.
2. I had to go to hospital.
3. I said hello, but he didn't hear me.
4. I can't help you move house.
5. I hope he has my book.
6. Her husband had a heart attack.
7. I'm late for my art class, so I have to go.
8. Can you hold my bag a second?

Unit 20

3 | Listening: *Why don't you come with us?* (page 96)

Conversation 1
A: I'm going for a run later.
B: Really? Where are you going to go?
A: I think I'll probably just go round the park.
B: Oh right.
A: Do you like running?
B: Yes. I go quite a lot back home.
A: Why don't you come with me this afternoon then?
B: I'd like to, but I haven't got any trainers with me.
A: Oh right. Never mind.
B: Yes, maybe some other time.

Conversation 2
A: I'm going for a swim.
B: Really? Where are you going to go?
A: There's a swimming pool in one of the hotels in the centre of town.
B: Is there?
A: Yes. Do you like swimming?
B: Yes, I love it. I go all the time back home.
A: Well, why don't you come with me then?
B: I'd like to, but I haven't got any trunks with me.
A: Well, maybe you can buy some cheap ones. There's a sports shop just round the corner.
B: Yes, maybe. What time are you going to go?
A: Probably around three o'clock.

Conversation 3
J: we're GOing to play TEnnis.
D: REAlly? WHERE are you GOing to PLAY?
J: there are some TENnis courts   in the PARK.
D: ARE there?

J: YES.   do YOU like playing tennis?
D: YES, i PLAY all the TIME   back HOME,   but i'm NOT very GOOD.
J: ME NEIther.   WELL,   WHY don't you COME with US and HAVE a GAME?   we NEED an EXtra PLAYer.
D: i'd LOVE to,   but i HAven't got a RAcket with me.
J: THAT'S ok.   WE can LEND you one.
D: OK.   what TIME are you GOing to PLAY?
J: PRObably around SIX o'CLOCK.   it's NOT so HOT THEN.
D: OK,   sounds GREAT.   WHERE shall i MEET you?
J: LET'S say HERE   between SIX   and six fifTEEN.
D: OK.

7 | Using grammar: questions about the future (page 97)

1. Where are you going to go?
2. What are you going to see?
3. Where are you going to meet?
4. What are you going to do?
5. Where are you going to stay?
6. What time are you going to leave?
7. Who are you going to play with?
8. How long are you going to go for?

6 | Pronunciation: connected speech (page 99)

1. Come on United!   /ˈkʌmɒnuːnaɪtɪd/
2. Pass it!   /ˈpɑːsɪt/
3. Watch out!   /ˈwɒtʃaʊt/
4. That's a foul!   /ðætsəˈfaʊl/
5. Send him off!   /ˈsendɪmɒf/
6. It was out!   /ɪwəzˈaʊt/
7. It was in!   /ɪwəzˈɪn/
8. Give it to me!   /ˈgɪvɪtəmi/
9. Great shot!   /ˈgreɪʃɒt/
10. Great save!   /ˈgreɪseɪv/

Unit 21

1 | Using vocabulary: travelling (page 100)

Conversation 1: at the bus stop
A: Excuse me. Does this bus go to Tufnell Park?
B: No, you need to get a number 34.
A: Oh, OK. Thanks.

Conversation 2: on the bus
A: Is this the right bus for Tufnell Park?
B: Yes, it is.
A: Can you tell me when to get off, please?
B: Yes, no problem. Take a seat.

Conversation 3: at the ticket office (1)
A: I'd like a ticket to Bath, please.
B: Single or return?
A: Return, please.
B: OK. That's £29.

Conversation 4: at the ticket office (2)

A: I'd like a return to Leeds, please.
B: Returning today?
A: No, on Tuesday.
B: Then that's £63, please.

Conversation 5: at the train information desk

A: When's the last train to Ealing?
B: 10.24.
A: And what time does it get in?
B: 11.13.
A: OK, great. Thank you.

| 3 | Listening: *What day are you travelling?* (page 100) |

Conversation 1

(A = Assistant, M = Michael)

A: Hello. National Rail Enquiries. How can I help you?
M: Yes, I'd like to check train times to Edinburgh, please.
A: Certainly, what station are you travelling from?
M: London. I'm not sure which station the train goes from.
A: Yes, that's London Kings Cross. And what day are you travelling?
M: We're going up there on Friday and coming back on Sunday.
A: OK, and what time would you like to travel?
M: Early morning. What's the earliest train?
A: The first train from Kings Cross leaves at 6.15 and arrives at 11.10.
M: OK, and on the return journey, what's the last train back from Edinburgh.
A: That's at 19.00 and that train arrives in Kings Cross at 23.50.
M: That sounds fine. So how much are the tickets?
A: £94.50
M: Really? That's quite expensive. Is that the cheapest ticket you have?
A: You can get a saver return and that costs £83.20, but you can't travel on any trains before ten o'clock. The earliest train you can get with that ticket is the 10.15 and that arrives in Edinburgh at 15.05.
M: Oh right, that's quite late. OK, well thank you. I'll ring you back.

Conversation 2

(H = Harry, M = Michael)

H: So what did they say?
M: Well, it depends how much you want to pay.
H: OK.
M: If we go after ten – there's one at 10.15 – it's £83.20 and if we get the earliest train, it's £94.50.
H: OK. What time does the 10.15 arrive in Edinburgh?
M: Five past three.
H: Oh right, it takes quite a long time then. We're going to lose half of the day.
M: Yes. The early train arrives at 11.10.
H: That's better really. I guess it's only £10 more expensive. I'd prefer to get there a bit earlier – we've only got three days there. What about coming back?
M: It leaves Edinburgh at seven in the evening and arrives at Kings Cross at ten to twelve.
H: OK, well that's all right. Did you check the prices of flights, by the way?
M: Yes. I looked on the internet earlier, but it's a bit more expensive and you have to get the train to the airport which costs £20.
H: Right.

M: I think if you book in advance, it's cheaper, but that's no good for you.
H: No. OK then, do you want to get the early train?
M: Yes, OK.
H: What time does it leave?
M: 6.15.
H: That is very early.
M: Yes. So we need to get up at around five.
H: OK. I guess we can sleep on the train.

| 6 | Pronunciation: silent 't' (page 102) |

1. I can't drive.
2. What time does the first coach leave?
3. It's got bigger over the last few years.
4. What's the best time to phone you?
5. It's the most difficult thing I've ever done.
6. I can't talk now. I must go.
7. That's the worst place I've ever been to.
8. We missed the last train.

Unit 22

| 3 | Listening: *What's she like?* (page 105) |

Conversation 1

J: Hello.
C: Oh hi, Jim. It's me, Colin.
J: Oh hiya. How are you?
C: Not too good, actually. That's why I'm phoning.
J: Oh no. What's the problem?
C: We've got some new neighbours. They moved into the house next door – and they're horrible, really horrible!
J: Why? What do they do?
C: They're really noisy – they've had four big parties this week. They play loud music. They don't stop until three or four in the morning. It's awful. I can't sleep at night.
J: It sounds terrible. Maybe you should talk to them about it.
C: I tried – but they're not very easy to talk to. The father got angry when I told him the music was too loud. He said he was going to kill me!
J: That's awful!
C: I know. My old neighbours were strange, but at least they were quiet.
J: Yes. Well, if they don't stop having loud parties, you should call the police.
C: Yes, maybe. I don't know if they can do anything about it.
J: Oh well, sorry to hear about your problems, but it's good to talk to you anyway.
C: Yes, OK. Well, see you.
J: Bye. See you soon.

Conversation 2

M: helLO.
E: hello, MUM. it's ME, EMily.
M: oh hello, DEAR. how are YOU?
E: i'm FINE, thanks. and how are YOU?
M: very WELL, very WELL. so, how are THINGS?
E: GOOD. WORK'S FINE, EVerything's FINE.
M: oh, THAT'S good.
E: YES. oh, and i SAW JON a COUple of DAYS ago.
M: oh YES? how was HE?
E: very WELL. did you KNOW he's got a NEW GIRLfriend?

M: NO, i DIdn't, but you KNOW your BROther – he NEver tells ME ANYthing. have you MET her?
E: YES, she was THERE when i WENT to his HOUSE.
M: and WHAT'S she LIKE?
E: she's REAlly NICE. she's very INteresting. she WORKS in an ART GALlery and she likes PAINting.
M: OH, she sounds very creAtive.
E: i KNOW. i just DON'T underSTAND why she WANTS to be with JON! he's SO BOring! he's NOT INterested in ART or ANYthing like that.
M: EMily, DON'T TALK about your BROther like that!

6 Pronunciation: sentence stress and weak forms (page 107)

1. i WASn't LOOking where i was GOing.
2. i DIdn't SEE. i WASn't WAtching.
3. i COULdn't DO it. i was TOO BUsy.
4. i CAN'T COME. i HAVEn't got TIME.
5. he ISn't HERE. he's GONE HOME.
6. WHAT'S her HUSband LIKE?
7. he's very RICH, but he ISn't very FRIENDly.
8. i'm NOT SURE what i'm DOing LAter.

Unit 23

1 Listening: Come in (page 108)

F: Hello!
G: Hi. Great to see you.
F: Come in, come in. Shall I take your coat?
G: Yes, thanks.
F: OK. There you are. Well, come through.
G: Thanks. What a great flat! It's quite big, isn't it? How long have you been here now?
F: Almost a year. I moved here last August.
G: Gosh, is it that long?
F: Yes, I know. Time goes so quickly, doesn't it? Come and sit down.
G: Actually, I'd prefer to stand for the moment. I've been in the car for the last two hours. This is a very nice room. It's very light.
F: Yes, it's great, isn't it?
G: And I love this painting. Is it new?
F: Yes, a friend gave it to me when I moved in here. It's nice, isn't it?
G: Yes, I really like it.
F: Would you like a drink? Beer? Coke?
G: I'd actually prefer something hot, if that's OK. Could I have some tea?
F: Of course, no problem. I'll just go and put the kettle on.
G: Hey Fiona. Could I just use your phone a moment? I forgot to recharge my mobile before I left the house this morning.
F: Sure. Go ahead. It's just by the sofa there.
G: Thanks, I won't be long.

7 Complimenting people (page 109)

1. A: What a great flat! It's lovely.
   B: Yes, it's nice, isn't it?
2. A: What a great kitchen! It's so big.
   B: Yes, it's nice, isn't it?
3. A: What lovely shoes! They really suit you.
   B: Yes, they're nice, aren't they?
4. A: What a brilliant photo! Who took it?
   B: Yes, it's nice, isn't it? My brother took it.
5. A: What a fantastic shirt. Where did you get it?
   B: Yes, it's nice, isn't it? I got it in Berlin.
6. A: What lovely flowers. They smell wonderful.
   B: Yes, they're nice, aren't they?

Unit 24

2 Listening: Are you doing anything to celebrate? (page 112)

Conversation 1
A: I've got a new job. It's in a really great school in Gateshead.
B: Oh really? Congratulations! That's great!
A: Thanks.
B: Are you doing anything to celebrate?
A: Yes, I'm going out for a drink tonight with some friends. We're going to a bar in the town centre. You can come if you want to.
B: Really? Great! I'd love to.
A: OK. Well, I'll phone you later and tell you where and when to meet.
B: OK. Brilliant! I'm really looking forward to it.

Conversation 2
A: It's my birthday today.
B: Oh really? Congratulations! Happy birthday!
A: Thanks.
B: So how old are you?
A: Twenty-one – again. No, I'm only joking. I'm twenty-nine. I'm getting old.
B: Yes. So are you doing anything to celebrate?
A: Yes, I'm going out for dinner with a couple of friends. We're going to a seafood place in Chinatown. You can come if you want to.
B: Really? Great! I'd love to.
A: OK. Well, I'll phone you later and tell you where and when to meet.
B: OK. Great. See you later, then.
A: Yes, OK. Bye.

Conversation 3
A: I got my exam results this morning.
B: Oh yes? How did you do?
A: Very well, actually. I passed them all. I can't believe it.
B: Oh, that's great. Congratulations. Are you doing anything to celebrate?
A: Yes, my dad's going to lend me his car tonight, so I'm going to meet some friends and we're going to go up to the beach and get something to eat.
B: Oh, that sounds nice. I hope you have a good time.
A: Oh, listen. Are you doing anything tonight? You can come if you want to.
B: Oh, really? Thanks. I'd love to.
A: We might go to a disco after dinner – if everyone wants to.
B: That sounds good as well. I don't have to work tomorrow, so that's OK.
A: OK. Well, I'll phone you later and tell you where and when to meet.
B: Right. Great. I'll speak to you then.
A: Yes, all right. Bye.
B: Bye.

5 Listening: *I'm just phoning to tell you about tonight* (page 113)

A: heLLO.
B: HI, it's ME. i'm just PHONing to TELL you about toNIGHT.
A: oh, OK. GREAT. so WHERE do you WANT to MEET?
B: well, we're THINking of MEEting in the SOcial. do you KNOW it?
A: um … i'm NOT really SURE. MAYbe. WHERE is it again?
B: in BLACK PRINCE ROAD, JUST near the PARK.
A: oh, i KNOW the PLACE you MEAN. it's got TWO floors. an UPstairs and a DOWNstairs.
B: THAT'S it. WE'RE going to be in the UPstairs bit.
A: OK. GREAT. what TIME are you MEEting?
B: i'm not SURE yet. is SEven OK for YOU?
A: it's a bit EARly, ACtually. i NEED to go HOME and get CHANGED first.
B: OK. WELL, let's say EIGHT o'clock, then. is THAT OK?
A: yes, that's GREAT.
B: OK. i'll PHONE around and TELL everyone else.
A: OK, and i'll SEE you LAter.
B: OK. BYE.
A: BYE.

7 Using grammar: making suggestions (page 115)

1. A: I don't know what to give my mum for her birthday.
   B: How about some perfume? Something expensive.
   A: No, she doesn't really like perfume. She never wears it.
2. A: I don't know what to wear to my friend's wedding next week.
   B: Why don't you wear your grey suit? You look good in that.
   A: Yes, OK. Maybe I'll do that.
3. A: My teacher has invited us to a party at his house. I don't know what to take.
   B: Why don't you take some food from your country?
   A: I don't really want to. I'm not a very good cook.
4. A: My friend's just had a baby. I don't know what to give them.
   B: How about some clothes for when it's a bit older?
   A: Yes, that's a good idea. Thanks. I'll do that.
5. A: My English isn't very good. I don't know what to do about it.
   B: Why don't you get a private teacher? That might help.
   A: I'd like to, but it's too expensive. I don't want to spend that much money.

Review: Units 19–24

9 Listening: *I like your flat* (page 119)

J: Hi, Carrie. How are you?
C: Fine, thanks. It's really nice to see you.
J: Yes. You too. Come in, come in. Would you like a drink?
C: Oh, yes please. Do you have any fruit juice?
J: Yes, sure. What would you like? Orange, apple or pineapple?
C: Orange, please.
J: OK. Just a second. There you are.

C: Thanks. I like your flat. It's lovely.
J: It's nice, isn't it?
C: Yes, it is. So how long've you been here?
J: Not long. About three months. Do you want to see the rest of the flat?
C: Yes, great.
J: Well, this is our bedroom.
C: Wow! It's huge!
J: Yes, I know. And this is the kitchen.
C: Oh, it's great. Wow! What a lovely table. Where did you get it?
J: Oh, I got it in a shop in the centre of town. It was on sale.
C: Oh, I love it. How long've you had it?
J: A long time – about four or five years. I brought it with me when I moved.
C: Well, it's really nice.
J: Thanks. Oh, would you like another juice?
C: Yes please. Could I use your toilet?
J: Yes, of course. It's just there on the left.

10 Pronunciation: the letter 'e' (page 119)

collect	/kəˈlekt/
dentist's	/ˈdentɪsts/
get	/get/
let	/let/
tennis	/ˈtenɪs/
extra	/ˈekstrə/
lend	/lend/
best	/best/
friendly	/ˈfrendlɪ/
celebrate	/ˈseləbreɪt/
central	/ˈsentrəl/
wedding	/ˈwedɪŋ/
kettle	/ˈketəl/

Grammar commentary

Introduction

This part of the book is NOT a complete grammar of English. It is impossible to learn all the grammar of English from one coursebook. Learning to use grammar well takes a long time. In this book you will learn to use the most useful grammar of English well in everyday contexts. The following grammar notes tell you what is important at your level.

Seeing good examples of how grammar is used in real life is more important than just learning about rules. These notes give you lots of useful natural examples. The best way to improve is to notice and write down more examples of good everyday grammar. There are ideas about how to do this in the Grammar Organiser at the back of the Workbook.

Unit by unit grammar notes

G1 | Possessive *s* (*'s*) (page 9)

1. We use the possessive s to show relationships:

   Mike's sister
   Carol's boyfriend
   my friends' car

   Notice that the apostrophe (') comes after the s in *friends* because it is plural.

   Can you see the difference between these expressions?

   my friend's parents (the parents of one friend)
   my friends' parents (the parents of all my friends)

2. We use the possessive s to show who owns something:

   Jake's car
   Janet's dogs

3. When we talk about two things, we can show the relationship in different ways:

   the hotel garden (NOT the hotel's garden)
   the city centre (NOT the city's centre)

   the end of the class (NOT the class's end)
   the cost of the ticket (NOT the ticket's cost)

G2 | Adverbs of frequency (page 10)

We use adverbs of frequency to talk about how often we do things. They usually come before the main verb. Here are some examples:

I never call my father 'Dad'.
I hardly ever eat beef.
I sometimes call my wife 'Baby'.
I often take the bus to school.
I usually go to bed before midnight.
I always get up at 7.30.

Adverbs of frequency usually come <u>after</u> the verb *be*. For example:

He's often late for work.
I'm never at home before six o'clock.

G3 | *Be* (page 10)

In the present simple, the verb *be* is irregular. You just have to learn the parts of this verb!

I'm tired.	(= I am tired.)
You're late!	(= You are late.)
He's a lawyer.	(= He is a lawyer.)
She's fine.	(= She is fine.)
It's in the south.	(= It is in the south.)
We're both from Leeds.	(= We are both from Leeds.)
You're all in Class 1.	(= You are all in Class 1.)
They're at university.	(= They are at university.)

In spoken English, the contracted forms on the left are normal. In formal writing, we use the full forms on the right.

To make negative sentences, we put *not* after the verb *be*. In spoken English, we use the forms *aren't* and *isn't*. Here are some examples:

I'm not hungry.
You're not in this class. (OR You aren't in this class.)
She's not French. She's Swiss. (OR She isn't French.)
He's not a student, he's the teacher! (OR He isn't a student.)

G4 | Questions with *is* and *are* (page 15)

To make questions with *be*, we put the correct form of the verb <u>before</u> *you, he, she*, etc:

A: Are you hungry?
B: Yes, very.

A: Where are you from?
B: Malaga, in Spain.

A: What's your brother's name?
B: Barnaby.

A: Is your grandmother OK now?
B: Yes, thanks. She's fine.

A: Are they married?
B: I'm not sure. I don't think so.

G5 | More questions (page 17)

To make questions in the present simple, we usually put *do* or *does* <u>before</u> *you*, *he*, *she*, etc:

A: Do you like rap music?
B: It's OK.

A: Do you drive to work?
B: Yes, usually, but in the summer I sometimes cycle.

A: Does your brother still live at home with your parents?
B: Yes, he does.

When we use question words, they come at the beginning of the question:

A: What kind of movies do you like?
B: Lots of things, really.

A: Why does she want to move?
B: I'm not sure.

A: What do your parents do?
B: My dad's a businessman and my mum's a teacher.

G6 | Going to (page 21)

We use *(not) going to* + *verb* to talk about things we've already decided to do – or not to do – in the future. For example:

I'm just going to stay at home tonight and relax.
I'm going to go to the gym later.
I'm going to do some shopping in town.
I feel awful! I'm never going to drink again!
The food was terrible there. I'm not going to eat there again.

Remember that with the verb *go*, you can use either *going to* + *go* or just the present continuous. Both are natural and correct:

I'm going to go to the theatre tonight. OR
I'm going to the theatre tonight.

G7 | The past simple (page 24)

We use the past simple to talk about things which are now finished. Here are some examples:

I saw Jim yesterday. (This is something short.)
I worked there for six years. (This took a long time.)
I went swimming every Saturday morning when I was a kid. (This is something regular in the past.)

The most important thing about all these actions is that they are finished.

To make negative sentences, we put *didn't* before the verb:

I didn't do anything!
You didn't try!
They didn't get my letter.

To make questions in the past simple, we put *did* <u>before</u> *you*, *he*, *she*, etc:

A: Did you enjoy the meal?
B: Yes, thanks. It was lovely.

A: Did your wife call you?
B: Yes, she did, thanks. She's fine.

Notice how *be* changes in the past simple:

I was really tired when I got home.
You were late every day last week.
He was a lawyer, but he lost his job.
She wasn't very well.
It wasn't very good.
We were both really happy about it.
You were great today!
My parents were both over 40 when I was born!

In spoken English, we often use the contractions *wasn't* (*was not*) and *weren't* (*were not*). To make questions in the past simple using *be*, we put *was* or *were* <u>before</u> *you*, *he*, *she*, etc:

A: Were you angry with him?
B: Yes, very!

A: Was *Titanic* popular in your country?
B: Yes, very. Everybody went to see it.

G8 | How often / How long (page 37)

We use the present simple to ask about how often. Notice the typical ways we answer these questions:

A: I'm going to my art class tonight.
B: Oh really? How often do you do that?
A: Quite often – twice a week.

A: I'm playing rugby tonight with my brother.
B: Oh really? How often do you do that?
A: Not very often – only once or twice a year.

A: How often do you go out for dinner?
B: Not very often – only once or twice a month.

Notice how the question changes when we talk about someone else:

A: My brother is going ice-skating tonight.
B: Oh really? How often does he do that?
A: Quite often – two or three times a month.

We use the present perfect continuous – *have / has been -ing* – to ask about *how long* – from the past to now. Notice the typical ways we answer these questions:

A: I'm going to my French class tonight.
B: Oh really? How long've (= long have) you been doing that?
A: Not very long – I started last month.

A: I've got a driving lesson tonight.
B: Oh really? How long've you been doing that?
A: Quite a long time – about six or seven months.

A: How long've you been learning English?
B: Not very long – only three or four weeks.

Notice how the question changes when we talk about someone else:

A: My sister plays the guitar.
B: Oh really? How long has she been doing that?
A: Quite a long time – she started when she was fifteen, so about eight years now.

G9 Comparatives (page 43)

We use comparative adjectives to compare two things or people. Two of the most useful comparative adjectives are irregular: *better* (*good* – *better*) and *worse* (*bad* – *worse*). Here are some examples:

> Don't come in December. The weather is worse then.
> I prefer this restaurant. The food's better than in the other place.

We usually make comparatives of longer adjectives – with two or more syllables – by putting *more* before them:

> This book is more interesting than the last one I read.
> It's more difficult to find a flat here than in my hometown.
> It's nice, but it's more expensive than the place I usually go to.

With shorter adjectives – of one syllable – we add *-er*. If they end in *-y*, we remove the *-y* and add *-ier*:

> I'm shorter than my sister, but taller than my brother.
> My brother is three years older than me.

> I'm healthier than I was when I smoked.
> You look happier than the last time I saw you.

If the adjective ends in a vowel and then a consonant, we double the consonant.

> It's hotter in here than in the other room.
> The other room is bigger than this one.

A small number of two-syllable adjectives have comparative forms with *-er*:

> It's quieter here than in my home town.
> You're cleverer than I am!

G10 Need to (page 45)

We use *need to + verb* to show it's important that we do something. We often add a reason explaining why:

> I need to call my bank and order a new cash card.
> You need to get a haircut! It's too long!
> My dad needs to go to Hull tomorrow to collect some tables.
> She needs to go out more! She spends too much time studying!

We make questions like this:

> A: Do I need to pay now or can I pay later?
> B: Later will be fine.

> A: Do you need to get any money out of the cash machine?
> B: Yes, I do. Thanks for reminding me.

> A: Does your brother need to get a visa for China?
> B: No, he just needs to take his passport.

We can also say we *need something*:

> I need a drink. I'm really thirsty.
> I need a holiday! I'm really tired.
> The dog needs a wash! He's really dirty!

G11 I'd like to ... (page 46)

We use *I'd like to + verb* to talk about things we want to do in the future. We often add a time expression to show when. For example:

> I'd like to see more of my wife and kids next year.
> I'd like to go to South Africa sometime next year.
> I'd like to learn to fly sometime in the future.

We can also say we'*d like something*. It's a more polite way of saying we want something:

> I'd like a cappuccino, please.
> I'd like two of the blue ones, please.

To invite people to do things with you, you can use *Would you like to ...*? We often answer invitations by saying *I'd love to*. Look at these examples:

> A: Would you like to go out for dinner with me sometime?
> B: Yes, I'd love to.

> A: Would you like to come to our party this weekend?
> B: Oh yes, I'd love to.

We can offer people things using *Would you like + noun*? For example:

> A: Would you like something to eat?
> B: Yes, please. I'd love a sandwich.

G12 The present perfect (page 51)

We make the present perfect by using *have / has* + the past participle. We use the present perfect to talk about experiences before now. We <u>never</u> use the present perfect with a past time expression like *yesterday*, *last week*, *three years ago* or *in 1999*. If we want to say <u>when</u> things happened, we use the past simple. Look at these examples:

> A: Have you ever been to Colombia?
> B: Yes, I have. I went to Bogota about six years ago.

> A: Have you travelled around a lot?
> B: Yes, quite a lot. I've been to Syria, Iran, Turkey and Egypt.

> A: Have you two met before?
> B: Yes, we met last year at a party.

We also use the present perfect to talk about something that started in the past and is still true now. Here are some examples showing the expressions we use to talk about periods of time:

> A: How long have you known each other?
> B: For about ten years now. We met in 1997.
> or: Since 1997.

> I've lived here for about twenty years.
> I've lived here since 1985.

We use *for + a period of time* and *since + one particular time*.

> For more information on irregular past participles, see page 142.

138

G13 | Making requests (page 53)

To ask someone to do something for you, you can use *Could you + verb?* or *Can you + verb?* Requests with *Could you* sound more polite and are better if you don't know the person very well. It's a good idea to add *please* at the end of the requests. Notice how we answer requests:

A: Can you post this letter for me, please?
B: Yes, sure. No problem.

A: I'm sorry, but could you close the door, please?
B: Yes, of course. No problem.

If we want to say *No* to a *Could you … ?* request, we often say *Sorry, I can't* and then explain why. Look at these examples:

A: Could you lend me £10, please? Just until tomorrow.
B: Sorry, I can't. I don't have any money on me today.

A: Could you help me move house this weekend?
B: Sorry, I can't. I'm busy.

> For more information on using questions with *could*, see G24.

G14 | The present continuous (page 57)

We form the present continuous using the correct form of *be + verb + -ing*. We use the present continuous to talk about things that started before now and haven't finished yet. In positive sentences, we often use the time expression *at the moment*:

I'm looking for a new flat at the moment.
You're looking in the wrong place!
My sister's working in the Czech Republic at the moment.
We're staying in the Hilton. It's great.

To make negative sentences, we put *not* after the verb *be*. In spoken English, we can use the contracted forms *aren't* and *isn't*. Here are some examples:

I'm not feeling very well.

He's not studying any more. He's working in a bank now.
(OR He isn't studying any more)

They're not living in Leeds any more. They moved last year.
(OR They aren't living in Leeds any more)

To make questions, we put the correct form of the verb *be* <u>before</u> *you, he, she*, etc:

A: Are you feeling OK?
B: No, not really. I need to go home.

A: Is your dad still working for IBM?
B: No, he left a few years ago.

G15 | Let's (page 65)

We use *Let's + verb* to suggest things we want to do with other people in the future. These suggestions are often answers to questions about the future. Look at these examples:

A: What time do you want to meet tomorrow?
B: Let's say about eight o'clock.
A: OK. Fine.

A: What're you doing this weekend?
B: I don't know. Let's do something together.
A: OK. Great. What would you like to do?
B: Let's go to Torquay for the day on Saturday.

> For more information on other ways of making suggestions, see G26.

G16 | *Can* and *can't* (page 68)

We use *can + verb* to talk about things we're able to do. We use *can't + verb* to talk about things we're not able to do. Here are some examples:

I can play the violin.
I can speak a bit of Swedish.

I can't drive.
I can't lift this. It's too heavy.

To ask about ability, we put *can* <u>before</u> *you, he, she*, etc:

A: Can you hear the tape? Is it loud enough?
B: Yes, thanks. It's fine.

A: Can you reach that book on the top shelf for me?
B: Yes, sure. There you are.
A: Oh thank you.

To talk about ability in the past, we use *could* and *couldn't*. For example:

Sorry about yesterday. My husband couldn't get home until late and I couldn't leave the kids on their own in the house.

The exam was really difficult. I answered the first question, but I couldn't do anything else.

> For more information on other ways of using *can* and *could*, see G13.

G17 | *Well* and *good* (page 69)

Good is an adjective. *Well* is the adverb.
Most adverbs are formed by adding *-ly* to the adjective:

bad – badly
quiet – quietly

A few adverbs and adjectives have the same form:

He speaks too fast.
You tried hard.

Notice where adverbs come in the sentence – usually after the verb:

You play very well.
He plays the guitar very well.
He speaks too fast.
I tried hard, but I couldn't do it.

Adjectives come before a noun or after the verb *be*. Adjectives don't change before plural nouns. For example, we say *a bad film* and *bad films*.

Look at these examples:

He's a really good cook.
He makes really bad films.
It's a slow song.

The exam was really hard / difficult.
These shoes are too expensive.
That was really funny.

G18 | I'll (page 71)

We often offer to do things for people by saying *I'll … (for you), if you like / want*. For example:

A: I'll help you with that, if you like.
B: Would you mind?
A: No, not at all.

A: I can't see properly. The sun's in my eyes.
B: I'll close the curtains for you, if you want.
A: Oh great. Thank you.

Notice in all these examples that *I'll* is an immediate reaction NOW to something. If the phone rings, you say *I'll answer it*. Or if the doorbell rings, you say *I'll get it* or *I'll see who it is*.

In spoken English, *I'll* is the normal contracted form of *I will*.

G19 | *Going to, 'll probably* and *might* (page 73)

Here are three different ways of talking about the future:

I'm going to (get up early) tomorrow.
I'll probably (get up early) tomorrow.
I might (get up early) tomorrow.

I'm going to + verb means 'I've already decided to do something'. It's 100% sure:

I've decided I'm going to stop smoking.
I'm going to buy the new Airheads CD at lunchtime.

I'll probably + verb means 'I've thought about it, but haven't definitely decided'. It's less sure than *I'm going to*. We often add *I think* to show this:

I think I'll probably get a pizza tonight. I'm too tired to cook.

A: What're you doing tonight?
B: I'm not sure, but I think I'll probably go and see a film.

We also use *I'll* to talk about something we decide to do at the moment we speak:

A: There's someone at the door.
B: OK. I'll get it.

In restaurants, we often order by saying *I'll have … :*

I'll have the plaice, please.
I'll have a glass of white wine, please.

I might + verb means 'maybe I will do it, but maybe I won't'. It's less sure than *I'll probably*. We often add an expression with *It depends* to show this:

I might go surfing this weekend. I'm not really sure. It depends on the weather.

I might come to class tomorrow. I might not. It depends how I feel.

> For more information on how to use *going to*, see G6. For more information on other ways of using *will*, see G18.

G20 | Have to (page 87)

We use *have to / has to* to talk about things we don't want to do, but we have no choice about:

I have to get a visa if I want to go to Niger.
Sorry, but I can't come. I have to work late tonight.
My sister has to look after her mother-in-law. She hates it!
My husband has to travel a lot in his work. He hates it!

We use *don't have to / doesn't have to* to talk about things we have a choice about:

It's great in my office. We don't have to wear suits! We can wear jeans if we want to!

My brother's so lucky! He doesn't have to get up until ten every day. He usually starts work at eleven.

To talk about things we didn't want to do in the past, but we had no choice about, we use *had to*:

Sorry I'm late. I had to help my mum with the cleaning.
When I was at school, I had to do five hours of homework a night!

G21 | Superlatives (page 101)

We use superlative adjectives to compare lots of things or people. Two of the most useful superlative adjectives are irregular: *the best* (*good – better – best*) and *the worst* (*bad – worse – worst*). Here are some examples:

That's the best film I've seen for a long time.
That's the worst meal I've ever had!
What's the best way to contact you? Phone or e-mail?

We usually make superlatives for longer adjectives – with two or more syllables – by putting *the most* before them:

This book is the most interesting one she's written.
It was the most difficult exam I've ever done in my life!
It's the most expensive shop in town.

With short adjectives – usually of one syllable – we add *the + -est* to them. If they end in *-y*, we remove the *-y* and add *the + -iest*:

I'm the shortest person in my family.
My brother's the tallest person I know. He's nearly two metres tall!
My gran is the oldest person I know. She's 99 this year!

She's the healthiest person I know. She doesn't drink or smoke and she eats lots of fruit and vegetables.
This is the happiest I've been for a long time.

If the adjective ends in a vowel and then a consonant, we double the consonant.

Yemen was the hottest place I've ever been to.
This is the biggest bedroom.

A small number of two-syllable adjectives have superlative forms with *the + -est*:

Is your baby OK? It's the quietest I've ever heard him.
She's the cleverest person I know.

G22 | The present perfect for talking about changes (page 102)

We use the present perfect to describe a change from the past to now. We usually add a time expression to show when this change happened. Here are some examples:

You've got taller since the last time I saw you.
Petrol has got a lot more expensive since the war started.
Computers have got a lot cheaper since I bought this one.

Prices have gone up a lot this year.
My home town has changed a lot since I left.

> For more information on other ways of using the present perfect, see G12.

G23 | The past continuous (page 107)

We use the past continuous to talk about situations that happen around a particular time or action in the past. We form the past continuous using *was / were + verb + -ing*. We usually talk about the time or action in the past using the past simple. For example:

I was sleeping when you called. Sorry.
You were looking for a new job the last time I saw you. Did you find one?
Your sister was working in Holland the last time I saw you. Is she still there?
I met the Prime Minister last year. We were staying in the Hilton and so was he.

To make negative sentences, we put *not* after the verb *was / were*. In spoken English, we use the contracted forms *weren't* and *wasn't*:

I wasn't feeling very well, so I decided to go home.

A: Why did your brother leave his job?
B: He wasn't enjoying the work any more.

The band weren't making any money, so they decided to split up.

To make questions, we put the correct form of the verb *was / were* <u>before</u> *you, he, she*, etc:

A: Were you living in Spain when you met your wife?
B: Yes, I was. I was working in Valencia.

A: I saw Wayne Rooney yesterday in the street!
B: Really? What was he doing?
A: Nothing special. He was just shopping with his girlfriend.

G24 | Asking for permission (page 108)

In G13, you saw that if you want to ask someone to do something for you, you can use *Could you + verb?* or *Can you + verb?* If you want to ask if it's OK to do something, you can say *Could I + verb?* Look at these examples:

A: Could I use your toilet?
B: Yes, of course. It's the first door on the left.

A: Could I borrow your dictionary?
B: Yes, of course. Here you are.

A: Could I make some coffee?
B: Oh, sorry. You can't. We don't have any.

With friends, we also say *Can I + verb?*

G25 | The present continuous for talking about the future (page 112)

In G14, you saw that we use the present continuous to talk about unfinished temporary activities around now. We also use the present continuous to talk about things we've arranged to do with other people in the future.

A: What're you doing tonight?
B: I'm going out with my girlfriend. We're going to a concert in Hammersmith.

My parents-in-law are coming to our house for dinner next Saturday.
I'm having dinner with my sister tomorrow night.

G26 | Making suggestions (page 115)

In G15, you saw that we use *Let's + verb* to suggest things we want to do with other people in the future.

We make suggestions for other people in other ways. When we want to suggest things we think other people should do or try, we often say *Why don't you + verb … ?* or *How about + noun / -ing … ?* Here are some examples:

A: I'm not sure what to buy my mum for Christmas.
B: *Why don't you get* her some clothes?
A: That's a good idea. I might do that.

A: I'm not sure what to cook for my parents-in-law next weekend?
B: *How about fish?* That's always nice.
A: I'd love to, but I'm not very good at cooking fish.
B: Well, *why don't you try* chicken? That's easy.
A: Yes, maybe.

A: I'm worried about my English. It's still not very good.
B: *How about getting* a private teacher?
A: I'd like to, but I don't have enough money.

Irregular verbs

Infinitive	Past simple	Past participle
be	was / were	been
beat	beat	beaten
become	became	become
begin	began	begun
break	broke	broken
bring	brought	brought
buy	bought	bought
catch	caught	caught
come	came	come
cost	cost	cost
cut	cut	cut
do	did	done
drink	drank	drunk
drive	drove	driven
eat	ate	eaten
fall	fell	fallen
feel	felt	felt
get	got	got
give	gave	given
go	went	gone
grow	grew	grown
have	had	had
hear	heard	heard
hide	hid	hidden
hit	hit	hit
hold	held	held
hurt	hurt	hurt
keep	kept	kept
know	knew	known
learn	learnt (learned)	learnt (learned)
leave	left	left
lend	lent	lent
let	let	let
lie	lied	lied
lose	lost	lost
make	made	made
mean	meant	meant
meet	met	met
pay	paid	paid
put	put	put
read	read /red/	read /red/
run	ran	run
say	said	said
see	saw	seen
sell	sold	sold
send	sent	sent
sleep	slept	slept
speak	spoke	spoken
spend	spent	spent
spill	spilt (spilled)	spilt (spilled)
steal	stole	stolen
stick	stuck	stuck
swim	swam	swum
take	took	taken
teach	taught	taught
tear	tore	torn
think	thought	thought
throw	threw	thrown
understand	understood	understood
wake up	woke up	woken up
wear	wore	worn
win	won	won
write	wrote	written

Pronunciation

Introduction

Saying words well is very important! Often you can learn the meaning of lots of words, but when you speak, no-one understands what you are saying! Below is some advice to help you improve your pronunciation. There is a list of phonetic symbols and words with examples of these sounds. On the next two pages, there are some photos and drawings to show you how we make the different sounds.

Some advice

- When you learn a new word or expression, ask your teacher to say the word and copy how they say it.
- Listen to spoken English on cassettes and CDs, and try to copy the speakers. Make sure what you copy is useful language that you want to say.
- Use a dictionary with phonetic script to find out how to say a word.
- Say the word to yourself three or four times as you read it.
- Mark where the stress is on the word.
- Underline the stressed words in expressions.
- Cover the word / expression and say it again. Write it down on another piece of paper. Check that the spelling is correct and say it again.
- Practise some of the individual sounds and use the photos on these pages to help you.
- Use a mirror and your fingers to see and feel your mouth as you say the sounds.
- Practise the individual sounds in whole words and expressions. You could repeat some of the exercises in the coursebook.

Phonetic symbols and words

Vowels

/iː/	meet, seat, leave, we, me
/ɪ/	bit, written, trip, wanted, decided
/ʊ/	put, good, would
/uː/	food, rude, true
/e/	bed, went, said
/ə/	teacher, about, instructor
/ɜː/	first, bird, purse, worse
/ɔː/	course, more, law, poor
/æ/	bad, mad, back, gran, hand
/ʌ/	cut, come, some, funny
/aː/	car, bar, last
/ɒ/	hot, lots, cost
/ɪə/	near, here
/eɪ/	made, fail, stay, came
/ɔɪ/	boy, toy, annoyed
/əʊ/	window, low, note, wrote
/eə/	air, hair, where, there
/aɪ/	write, light, time, fine
/aʊ/	now, town, pound, out
/uə/	sure, tourism

Consonants

/p/	pet, top, open
/b/	bit, rob, about
/t/	sit, situation, top
/d/	dog, odd, lady
/tʃ/	church, chat, catching
/dʒ/	join, manager, age
/k/	could, kick, actor
/g/	game, bag, figure
/f/	fat, laugh, safety
/v/	van, save, never
/θ/	thin, seventh
/ð/	there, leather
/s/	sell, less, castle
/z/	zoo, pens
/ʃ/	shot, wash, station
/ʒ/	Asian, television
/m/	mum, same, famous
/n/	nine, fun, handle
/ŋ/	singer, finger, driving
/l/	love, small, travelling
/r/	red, relative, river
/w/	we, word, once
/j/	yellow, yes, lawyer, staying
/h/	happy, heart, him

1 | Single vowel sounds

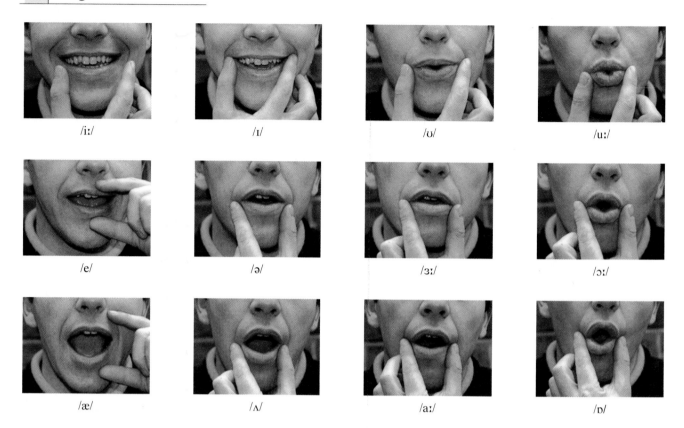

/iː/ /ɪ/ /ʊ/ /uː/

/e/ /ə/ /ɜː/ /ɔː/

/æ/ /ʌ/ /ɑː/ /ɒ/

Look at the twelve photos above and try saying the sounds in each row. Start with the sound on the left and notice that the tongue moves further back in the mouth as you say each of the other three sounds in the row. The photos below show the position of the tongue for the middle row of sounds. Try touching the tip of your tongue as you say the other two rows of vowel sounds above. Can you feel your tongue move back each time?

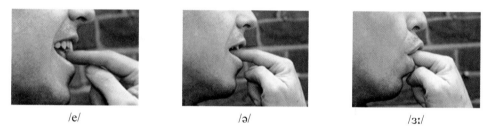

/e/ /ə/ /ɜː/ /ɔː/

Look at the twelve photos again and try saying the sounds in each column. Start with the sound at the top and notice that the tongue moves further down in the mouth as you say each of the other two sounds in the column. This means that the tongue is higher for /iː/ than for /e/, and higher for /e/ than for /æ/. Try touching the tip of your tongue as you say the other three columns of vowel sounds. Can you feel your tongue move down each time?

Look at the diagram on the right. This shows the relative positions of the tongue for the twelve sounds. Remember that when you make the sounds with /ː/, you should make them a little longer.

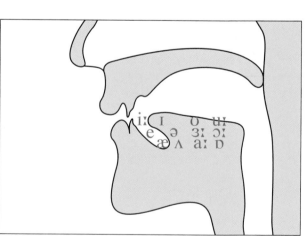

2 | Double vowel sounds

When we say double-vowel sounds like /eɪ/, /aɪ/ and /ɔɪ/, we more or less combine two of the single vowel sounds above. Your mouth and tongue should move slightly as you say the sounds.

Note that /aɪ/ mixes /æ/ and /ɪ/, and /ɔɪ/ mixes /ɒ/ and /ɪ/.

3 | Consonant sounds

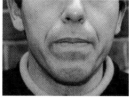
/p/ /b/

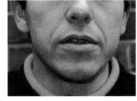
/t/ /d/

/t ʃ/ /dʒ/

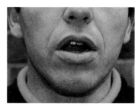
/k/ /g/

As you say each sound, the tongue moves further back along the top of the mouth. Look at the diagrams.

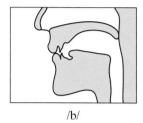
/b/

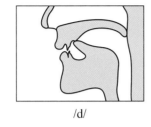
/d/

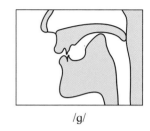
/dʒ/

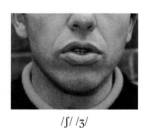
/g/

To say /b/, /d/, /dʒ/ and /g/, we use our voice. If you touch your throat, you can feel it.

To say /p/, /t/, /t ʃ/ and /k/ we use more air. It may sound a little higher.

/θ/ /ð/

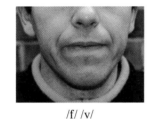
/f/ /v/

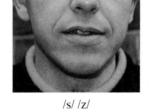
/s/ /z/

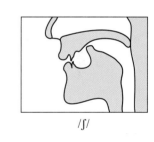
/ʃ/ /ʒ/

As you say each sound, the tongue moves further back in the mouth.

To say /ð/, /v/, /z/ and /ʒ/, we use our voice.

To say /θ/, /f/, /s/ and /ʃ/, we use more air.

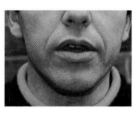
/s/

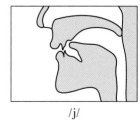
/ʃ/

With /l/ and /r/ the difference is in the shape of the lips and the fact that the tongue doesn't touch the top of the mouth for /r/.

With /w/ and /j/ the difference is the shape of the lips and the fact that the tongue doesn't touch anything.

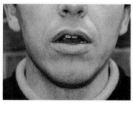

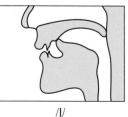
/l/

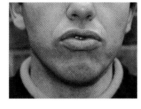

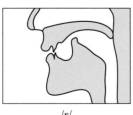
/r/

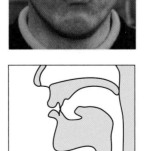
/w/

/j/

We make /m/, /n/ and /ŋ/ by forcing air through the nose. The lips and tongue for /m/ are the same as for /p/. The sound /n/ looks like /d/ and /ŋ/ looks like /k/.

/h/ is an unusual consonant. It changes with the vowel that follows it. Just force air out lightly as you say it.

Expression Organiser

This section helps you to record and translate some of the most important expressions from each unit. It is better to record expressions than single words. Sometimes you can translate very easily. Sometimes you will need to think of an expression in your language with a similar meaning. In each section, there is space for you to add any other expressions you want to remember.

Unit 1

Hi. I'm Hugh. What's your name?

Where are you from?

Is that your surname or your first name?

Nice to meet you.

Do you know my friend Damien?

Let me introduce you.

I'm sorry. How do you say your name?

I usually walk to work.

I hardly ever go there.

I live with my mum and dad.

I live on my own.

What's your sister's name?

Have you got any kids?

Where were you born?

Unit 2

Whereabouts in England?

You probably don't know it.

Is that the capital?

No, it's the second city.

It's in the west.

Is it far from the city centre?

It's about an hour by train.

It's about twenty minutes by bus.

It's a lovely place to live.

It's got good public transport.

It's got great nightlife.

It's very quiet.

It's very crowded.

It's very polluted.

Unit 3

What do you do?	....
I'm a civil servant.	....
I work in a bookshop.	....
I work part-time in a supermarket.	....
I'm a housewife.	....
I work for myself.	....
My dad's a teacher.	....
Where do you work?	....
Do you enjoy it?	....
The money's good.	....
My boss is awful!	....
I work really long hours.	....
He earns about £40,000 a year.	....
Is it far from your house to where you work?	....

....
....
....
....
....

Unit 4

What're you doing tonight?	....
What're you doing this weekend?	....
I'm going to go shopping.	....
I'm going to go swimming.	....
on my own	....
with a friend from work	....
I'm going to the cinema.	....
Do you want to come with me?	....
Yes, OK. That'd be nice.	....
Maybe some other time.	....
I don't really like that kind of thing.	....
It sounds really interesting.	....
It sounds really boring.	....
Entrance is free.	....

....
....
....
....
....

Unit 5

Did you have a nice weekend? ....

We went on a trip. ....

I stayed at home and watched TV. ....

I read the paper. ....

I did some cleaning in the afternoon. ....

I played tennis on Sunday morning. ....

I really enjoyed it. ....

What did you do last night? ....

I went to bed at eight. ....

I was really tired. ....

I was really angry. ....

I was really surprised. ....

We hired a car for a week. ....

We got married last year. ....

....

....

....

....

....

Unit 6

What're you studying? ....

I'm studying economics at Hull University. ....

My brother studied engineering in Berlin. ....

He's unemployed. ....

What year are you in? ....

What're you going to do after university? ....

I hope you get the job you want. ....

I'm going to do a Master's. ....

I left school twelve years ago. ....

Have you got a piece of paper? ....

Can I go to the toilet? ....

I'm sorry I'm late. ....

What does this word mean? ....

Underline it. ....

....

....

....

....

....

Unit 7

I went to my English class last night.

That sounds good.

I had a driving lesson.

My son had a piano lesson yesterday afternoon.

I went to my first yoga class.

It was great.

How often do you do that?

Not very often – once or twice a month.

Quite often – two or three times a week.

How long've you been doing that?

Not very long – only two or three months.

Quite a long time – about eight or nine years.

I went to a concert.

I'm a big fan of theirs.

Unit 8

So what do you do in your free time?

What kind of music do you like?

What kind of films do you watch?

He's my favourite actor.

They're OK. I quite like them.

I really enjoy doing it.

Me too.

I'm not very good at it.

Me neither.

I find it really boring.

It was really embarrassing.

It's delicious.

There's not much choice.

That's a really difficult question.

Unit 9

What're you doing now?

I need to change some money.

I need to get my film developed.

I need to send some e-mails.

I need to get something to eat.

Is there a cash machine near here?

I'll see you in a couple of hours.

I'm not very fit.

I need to join a gym.

I'd like to learn how to play the guitar.

I'd like to spend more time with my kids.

I'd like to spend less time working.

sometime in the future

sometime in the next two or three years

Unit 10

I went to the cathedral yesterday.

Have you been there?

Yes, we went there a couple of days ago.

the day before yesterday

The weather was awful.

We got really wet.

You should go to Vienna.

It's got some beautiful buildings.

It's a famous old town in the east.

It's over five hundred years old.

It was nice meeting you.

Good luck.

Enjoy your holiday.

Have you been to the cinema recently?

Unit 11

Is there a chemist's near here?

There's one opposite here.

There's one up the road, on the left.

It's just round the corner from the station.

Turn right at the traffic lights.

Is this the right way?

I think we're lost.

We took the wrong turning.

Could you draw me a map?

Take the number 73.

Which stop do I need to get off at?

You need to change trains at Oxford Circus.

Hurry up!

We missed our train.

Unit 12

What're you doing here?

Is it business or pleasure?

My company's opening a new office here.

We're here on holiday.

Where are you staying?

We're staying in a nice little hotel.

How long've you been here?

Not long. We arrived here last Friday.

I'm not feeling very well.

What're you doing later?

I'm not sure. I'll probably go out somewhere.

I'd like to book a double room for three nights.

What's the expiry date?

The food wasn't very nice.

Unit 13

What time is it? ....

It's quarter to seven. ....

It's half past eight. ....

What time do you want to meet tonight? ....

What time's good for you? ....

What time's your flight? ....

What time does the film start? ....

We need to be at the station by five. ....

It'll probably take about an hour to get there. ....

I'm exhausted! ....

I should go. I'm late for work. ....

Let's go and see a film tonight. ....

Let's take the train. It's quicker. ....

I don't want to talk about it. ....

....

....

....

....

....

Unit 14

I can't lift it. ....

I can't reach it. ....

I can't hear you. ....

I can't get the top off. ....

Could you turn the music down, please? ....

Could you take me to the station? ....

Can you close the curtains? ....

Could you help me look for my keys? ....

You speak English very well. ....

It was a really good film. ....

I was hurt quite badly. ....

I broke my leg a few years ago. ....

I'll help you, if you like. ....

I'll lend you some money, if you like. ....

....

....

....

....

....

Unit 15

I'm going to be really busy.

I'm going to sleep until lunchtime.

I'm just going to take it easy.

I'm going to see a play at the theatre.

My room's in a mess at the moment.

I haven't really decided.

I think I'll probably go to the beach.

It depends on the weather.

It depends how I feel.

I might go. I might not. I'm not sure.

It was my fault.

I overslept this morning.

Have a good weekend.

I'll see you on Monday.

Unit 16

Are you OK?

I've got a headache.

I'm feeling a bit sick.

I hurt my arm playing basketball.

I burnt it lighting the cooker.

Oh no! Poor you!

Do you want a glass of water?

Do you want something for it?

Maybe you should just go home.

Take your time. There's no hurry.

What was the weather like?

What was the hotel like?

It was great.

It was awful.

Unit 17

Do you like spicy food? ....

Are you ready to order? ....

I don't really like seafood. ....

I hate squid! ....

They're a kind of bean. ....

That sounds nice. ....

What do you want for your main course? ....

What would you like to drink? ....

Do you want still or sparkling? ....

You should try this. It's delicious. ....

It tastes like chicken. ....

It was disgusting! ....

What's this made from? ....

I'm full. Thank you. ....

....

....

....

....

....

Unit 18

Are there any toilets in here? ....

Where's the stationery department? ....

It's on the third floor. ....

They're in the seventh aisle. ....

It's on the top shelf. ....

I'll show you where they are. ....

Can I pay by card? ....

Would you like any cash back? ....

Could you sign there, please? ....

I'm in charge of twelve people. ....

It's quite stressful. ....

I have to work Saturdays. I hate it! ....

I have to travel a long way to work. ....

It's not much fun. ....

....

....

....

....

....

Unit 19

Sorry, but I can't come to the meeting tomorrow.

I have to go to the dentist's.

I have to collect my sister from school.

Sorry I couldn't come out last night.

I had a doctor's appointment.

I had to work late last night.

I had to go to the hospital.

That's OK. Never mind.

I was very nervous.

I tried to calm down, but I couldn't.

There were problems on the line.

I had an accident in my car.

I couldn't find a parking space.

I couldn't sleep last night.

Unit 20

Do you like sport?

I always play golf on Sunday.

I hardly ever go to the gym.

Where are you going to play?

There's a pool just round the corner.

Why don't you come with us?

I'm not very good at tennis.

I haven't got my racket.

I can lend you some goggles.

What was the score?

It was a nil–nil draw.

Who do you support?

They're top of the league.

That was a foul!

Unit 21

Can you tell me when to get off, please? ....

Single or return? ....

How can I help you? ....

I'd like a return ticket to Prague, please. ....

When's the last train? ....

The train arrives at eleven. ....

What's the best way to get there? ....

Is that the cheapest ticket you have? ....

What's the best time to phone you? ....

What're the best places to visit while I'm here? ....

It's cheaper if you book in advance. ....

It's got a lot cheaper over the last few years. ....

You've got taller since the last time I saw you. ....

....

....

....

....

....

Unit 22

What're your parents like? ....

She's really fit. She goes running a lot. ....

He's very creative. ....

He's really shy. ....

She's really quiet. ....

She's really easy to talk to. ....

He's really strange. ....

My old boss was really horrible! ....

He told me a really funny joke. ....

He never tells me anything. ....

I was standing at the bus stop and he walked past. ....

I've got a new boyfriend. ....

Isn't that Prince Rasha? ....

She seemed quite nice. ....

....

....

....

....

....

Unit 23

Come in.

What a great house!

How long've you been here now?

Would you like a drink?

Could I use your toilet?

What a nice room! It's so big.

I love the view!

I like the table. Where did you get it?

We've got a spare room.

It's got a balcony.

It's very light.

It's not very central.

It's very convenient for the shops.

I'm really looking forward to it.

Unit 24

My brother's getting married next weekend.

I've passed all my exams.

Congratulations!

Are you doing anything to celebrate?

I'm going out for dinner with some friends.

We're going to Paris for the weekend.

I'll phone you later to tell you when and where to meet.

It was the best day of my life.

Why don't you buy her a hat?

That's a good idea. Maybe I'll do that.

She doesn't really like perfume.

I don't want to spend that much money.

They got divorced a few years ago.

I can't believe it!

Student B: Unit 17, page 80, activity 3

aubergine	pineapple	sweet potato
ham	sweetcorn	trout

plaice

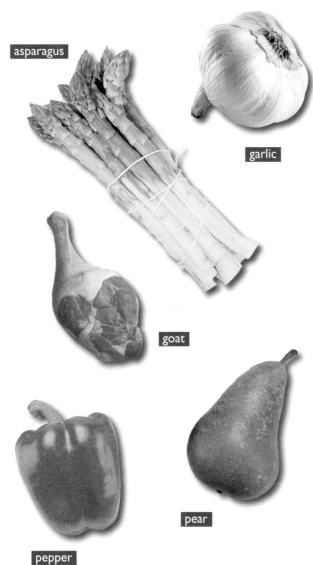

asparagus

garlic

goat

pear

pepper

Student B: Unit 11, page 53, activity 5

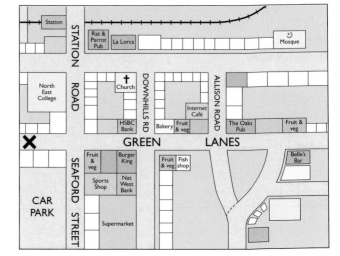

You're looking for: a sports shop, an **HSBC** bank, an internet café, a supermarket, **Belle's Bar** and **La Lorca** Restaurant. You are at ✗.

Student B: Unit 21, page 100, activity 5

- Coaches go from Bath and Bristol to Liverpool every hour.
- The first coach leaves Bath at 5.30 and Bristol at 6.00 in the morning and arrives in Liverpool at 9.30.
- The last coach leaves Liverpool at 11.00 in the evening. It arrives in Bristol at 2.30 in the morning and Bath at 2.55.
- Return tickets from both places on the coach cost £25 on Fridays and £16 on Saturdays.

- Trains go from Bath and Bristol to Liverpool every hour.
- The first train leaves Bath at 6.22 and Bristol at 6.40 in the morning and arrives at 8.45.
- The last train leaves Liverpool at 9.00 in the evening and arrives in Bristol at 11.05 and Bath at 11.27.
- Return tickets from Bristol cost £45 on Fridays and £27 on Saturdays.
- Return tickets from Bath cost £49 on Fridays and £30 on Saturdays.

Student B: Unit 17, page 81, activity 7

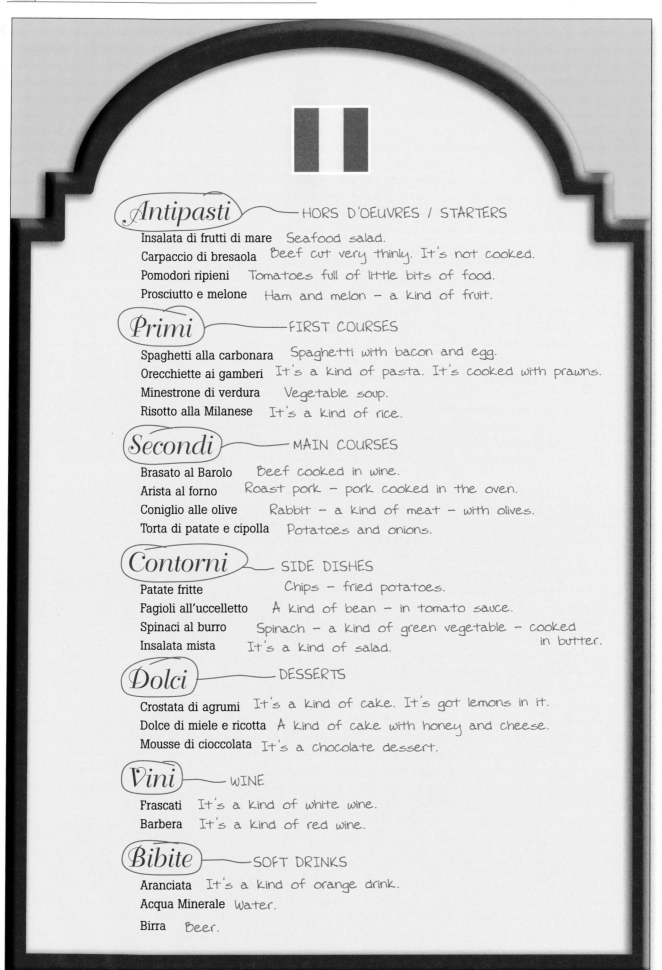

Antipasti — HORS D'OEUVRES / STARTERS

Insalata di frutti di mare   Seafood salad.
Carpaccio di bresaola   Beef cut very thinly. It's not cooked.
Pomodori ripieni   Tomatoes full of little bits of food.
Prosciutto e melone   Ham and melon – a kind of fruit.

Primi — FIRST COURSES

Spaghetti alla carbonara   Spaghetti with bacon and egg.
Orecchiette ai gamberi   It's a kind of pasta. It's cooked with prawns.
Minestrone di verdura   Vegetable soup.
Risotto alla Milanese   It's a kind of rice.

Secondi — MAIN COURSES

Brasato al Barolo   Beef cooked in wine.
Arista al forno   Roast pork – pork cooked in the oven.
Coniglio alle olive   Rabbit – a kind of meat – with olives.
Torta di patate e cipolla   Potatoes and onions.

Contorni — SIDE DISHES

Patate fritte   Chips – fried potatoes.
Fagioli all'uccelletto   A kind of bean – in tomato sauce.
Spinaci al burro   Spinach – a kind of green vegetable – cooked in butter.
Insalata mista   It's a kind of salad.

Dolci — DESSERTS

Crostata di agrumi   It's a kind of cake. It's got lemons in it.
Dolce di miele e ricotta   A kind of cake with honey and cheese.
Mousse di cioccolata   It's a chocolate dessert.

Vini — WINE

Frascati   It's a kind of white wine.
Barbera   It's a kind of red wine.

Bibite — SOFT DRINKS

Aranciata   It's a kind of orange drink.
Acqua Minerale   Water.
Birra   Beer.

Pairwork

Student A: Unit 11, page 53, activity 5

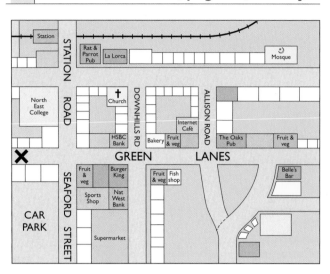

You're looking for: a chemist's, a post office, a photo place, a language school, a newsagent's and Marco's Café. You are at ✕.

Student A: Unit 17, page 80, activity 3

asparagus garlic goat pear pepper plaice

trout

ham

pineapple

sweet potato

aubergine

sweetcorn

Student A: Unit 17, page 81, activity 7

Antipasti
Insalata di frutti di mare
Carpaccio di bresaola
Pomodori ripieni
Prosciutto e melone

Primi
Spaghetti alla carbonara
Orecchiette ai gamberi
Minestrone di verdura
Risotto alla Milanese

Secondi
Brasato al Barolo
Arista al forno
Coniglio alle olive
Torta di patate e cipolla

Contorni
Patate fritte
Fagioli all'uccelletto
Spinaci al burro
Insalata mista

Dolci
Crostata di agrumi
Dolce di miele e ricotta
Mousse di cioccolata

Vini
Frascati
Barbera

Bibite
Aranciata
Acqua Minerale
Birra

Student A: Unit 21, page 100, activity 5

You are on holiday in either Bristol or Bath – you decide. You want to visit Liverpool tomorrow – Friday – or the day after tomorrow – Saturday. You want to arrive in Liverpool at about ten o'clock in the morning. You want to come back to Bristol or Bath the same day. Think about the questions you want to ask. Then phone National Travel Enquiries for information.

160